TRANSFER OF ARMS, LEVERAGE, AND PEACE IN THE MIDDLE EAST

Recent Titles in
Contributions in Military Studies
Series Advisor: Colin Gray

The Last Gaiter Button: A Study of the Mobilization and Concentration of the French
Army in the War of 1870
Thomas J. Adriance

NATO Strategy and Nuclear Defense
Carl H. Amme

A Nuclear-Weapon-Free Zone in the Middle East: Problems and Prospects
Mahmoud Karem

Gentlemen of the Blade: A Social and Literary History of the British Army Since 1660
G. W. Stephen Brodsky

China's Military Modernization: International Implications
Larry M. Wortzel

The Painful Field: The Psychiatric Dimension of Modern War
Richard A. Gabriel

The Spit-Shine Syndrome: Organizational Irrationality in the American Field Army
Christopher Bassford

Behind a Curtain of Silence: Japanese in Soviet Custody, 1945–1956
William F. Nimmo

Armed Forces on a Northern Frontier: The Military in Alaska's History, 1867–1987
Jonathan M. Nielson

The Aegean Mission: Allied Operations in the Dodecanese, 1943
Jeffrey Holland

The World Turned Upside Down: The American Victory in the War of Independence
John Ferling, editor

U.S. Unilateral Arms Control Initiatives: When Do They Work?
William Rose

Transfer of Arms, Leverage, and Peace in the Middle East

NITZA NACHMIAS

CONTRIBUTIONS IN MILITARY STUDIES,
NUMBER 83

GREENWOOD PRESS
New York • Westport, Connecticut • London

Library of Congress Cataloging-in-Publication Data

Nachmias, Nitza, 1935–

    Transfer of arms, leverage, and peace in the Middle East / Nitza
Nachmias.

      p. cm. — (Contributions in military studies, ISSN 0883–6884
; no. 83)

   Bibliography: p.

   Includes index.

   ISBN 0–313–26300–0 (lib. bdg. : alk. paper)

   1. Israel—History, Military. 2. Israel–Arab conflicts.
3. Military assistance, American—Israel. 4. United States—Military
relations—Israel. 5. Israel—Military relations—United States.
I. Title. II. Series.
DS119.2.N33   1988
956′.04—dc19   88–17777

British Library Cataloguing in Publication Data is available.

Library of Congress Catalog Card Number: 88–17777
ISBN: 0–313–26300–0
ISSN: 0883–6884

First published in 1988

Greenwood Press, Inc.
88 Post Road West, Westport, Connecticut 06881

Printed in the United States of America

The paper used in this book complies with the
Permanent Paper Standard issued by the National
Information Standards Organization (Z39.48–1984).

10 9 8 7 6 5 4 3 2 1

Copyright Acknowledgments

Grateful acknowledgment is hereby made to Dr. Henry A. Kissinger for the use of quotations
from his book entitled *White House Years*, © copyright 1979, Dr. Henry A. Kissinger.

IN MEMORY OF MY PARENTS

Contents

Preface

Unresolved arguments among my friends, colleagues, and students on the issue of peace in the Middle East intensified after the Palestinian uprising that began in December 1987. These discussions centered on the ambiguity of the role and interests of the United States in the Israeli-Arab conflict. Whereas the forty-year-old Arab war with the Jewish state has gone through many stages, its end seemed no closer in 1988 than it was in 1948. New parties, tactics, and interests added complexity. The United States, which claims to have a strong interest in peace in the region, has exercised too little leverage to make it happen. A review of the complex issues shows that the continuing conflict defies the traditional theories of international relations. To explain why after four decades of hostilities, five major wars, and intensive diplomatic activity peace has not been attained, innovative approaches are needed. The question of American leverage, or its lack, is the crux of the issue.

The intricate and complex relationships between the United States, the patron state, and Israel, its client state, intrigued me especially in the context of the vast American military aid provided to Israel. Why the United States could not use its client's dependence to influence Israel's foreign policy is both a theoretical and a practical question. During most of the American peace campaigns, including the Shultz initiative of March 1988, the two traditional allies expressed major differences of opinion. Each has been trying to prevail in the controversy. Existing literature fails to provide an adequate explanation as to why the United States has been unable to influence Israel's policies and why the patron-client relationship seems to be reversed with the client enjoying leverage over its patron.

Unlike the concept of power, leverage has received relatively little attention. Writing on leverage is scarce. In conventional theories of international relations, leverage is neither independently defined nor distinguished from power. Indeed, it is rarely considered a cause or an effect of international interactions.

Yet the two superpowers pursue leverage as much as they pursue power. If properly employed, it can be a major vehicle to attain foreign policy goals without the use of force. As the use of force by the United States is all but excluded in the Middle East, influence over events can only be achieved through leverage. However, as the research in this work shows, leverage is as elusive as a desert mirage. This book does not seek to provide the answers to all of the difficult questions it treats. More time and research are needed to study the question of leverage and how it should be applied in the efforts to settle the Israeli-Arab conflict. This work proposes an alternative definition of "leverage" and suggests why transfers of arms do not yield leverage. What alternatives, then, does the United States have to influence Israel's foreign policy if it can not use transfers of arms as leverage? Judging from the only agreements achieved—the disengagement agreements and the Israeli-Egyptian peace treaty—it is apparent that innovative diplomacy, better understanding of the nature of the conflict, non-conventional approaches to the various actors, endless patience, and perseverance could yield some results. Whereas it is impossible to predict when and how the Israeli-Arab conflict, which began a hundred years ago with the first Jewish settlements in Palestine, will be resolved, we must hope that all the parties involved will find the courage to end their animosity and move toward peace.

In my research and writing I have received valuable advice, suggestions, and disputation from friends, colleagues, and former professors at the Graduate School of the City University of New York. I am especially thankful to Ambassador Seymour M. Finger, Professor Emeritus, City University, who guided and advised me, and reviewed the manuscript with dedication and much patience. My friends in Israel provided me with vital information that helped me develop the insight needed to understand the complexities of the issue of peace in the Middle East. The numerous interviews in the United States and Israel were a source of constructive information. I owe special thanks to the director of the Center for Strategic Studies, Tel Aviv University, Aharon Yariv, for his suggestions, advice, and friendship. I also acknowledge useful assistance from Professor Leon Gordenker, with whom I enjoyed many differences of opinion that helped me clarify my ideas. Special thanks are also due to Dan Benderly, my computer consultant and friend, whose professional help played a vital role in the production of this manuscript.

To my son Yaron and my daughter Limor, I am forever in debt. Their moral support, belief in me, and endless love made this difficult project possible.

TRANSFER OF ARMS, LEVERAGE, AND PEACE IN THE MIDDLE EAST

1

Introduction

Since the end of World War II, the transfer of arms has become a crucial dimension of U.S. foreign policy and a major instrument for achieving its goals. In a letter to Congress, Secretary of State George Shultz described the foreign assistance requests for fiscal year 1985 in this way: "The programs presented here constitute the predominant portion of what is, in effect, the foreign policy budget of the United States."[1] Arms transfers have been relied upon to promote peace and stability and to enhance the power and position of the United States in the world. Arms transfers "are much more than an economic occurrence, a military relationship or an arms control challenge; arms sales are foreign policy writ large."[2] The foreign assistance bills for fiscal years 1985 to 1987 amounted to about $15 billion each. They served mainly as means to achieve foreign policy goals. In Schultz's words: "It is that portion of the total Federal budget which directly protects and furthers U.S. national interests abroad [and by which] we contribute to the military capabilities of a friendly or allied country against a common threat."[3]

The United States has been one of the most prominent arms suppliers in the world, accounting for about one-third of total sales worldwide. Since World War II, all administrations have perceived military assistance to be crucial to America's national interest. According to one agency: "Arms sales are the hard currency of foreign affairs. They replace the security pacts of the 50's."[4] Arms transfers are expected primarily to yield leverage and influence and the United States has been prepared to pay the high price that is required to preserve its powerful position in the world. Indeed, the United States manipulates arms transfers in order to achieve political leverage, which is perceived as vital in its competition for power with the U.S.S.R. Once political leverage is gained, the United States expects its client states to comply with U.S. foreign policy. This is particularly true of the situation in the Middle East, where "the most important political benefit of arms transfers may be leverage over other countries' foreign policy decisions. In the Arab-Israeli conflict, the offer of arms has been used to make difficult political and territorial decisions more acceptable."[5]

The increased use of arms transfers as a foreign policy instrument resulted in a sharp increase in the scale of these transactions. In all, between 1971 and 1985, the United States sold more than $130 billion worth of arms under the Foreign Military Sales (FMS) program, more than eight times the amount for the preceding twenty-five years.[6] Military aid programs began with the enactment of Public Law 75, providing military aid to Greece and Turkey after World War II.[7] Whereas in the late 1950s, U.S. arms transfers averaged less than $1 billion per year, they reached $12 billion in the late seventies, and exceeded $21 billion in the eighties. Until the mid-sixties, arms transfers were noncontroversial components of U.S. national security policy. Providing weapons and strengthening allies were seen as important components in America's containment policy. However, since the late sixties the situation began to change and growing doubts as to the purpose and efficacy of transfers of arms have persisted "among members of Congress, government officials, and some segments of the general public."[8]

In the politics and process of arms sales, the President has always played the major role. The Foreign Assistance Act of 1961 replaced previous assistance programs and gave the President vast powers over the sale and grant of military aid. According to Public Law 87–196 of 1961, the President is authorized to furnish military assistance on such terms and conditions as the President may determine, to any friendly country or international organization, the assisting of which the President finds will strengthen the security of the United States and promote world peace.[9]

Until 1970 most of the arms supplied through the FMS program were sold to the NATO powers and to industrialized nations such as Australia and Japan. Since then, however, the bulk of the FMS has been to non-NATO countries, with three-fifths of the total delivered to the Middle East. Moreover, the United States was no longer depleting its surplus stockpiles of World War II weapons; the weapons now being delivered were modern and sophisticated. Indeed, arms transfers became an important business: "Another important trend in foreign assistance is the shift from grants aid to loans. Under the Marshall Plan almost 90 percent of aid to Europe was in the form of grants . . . [later] loans became the principal form of assistance."[10] In fiscal year 1961 military assistance programs were twice as large as military sales. By 1966 the military sales figures doubled those for military aid (not including Vietnam). As a result, as Senator Hubert Humphrey said in 1975, "America has become a kind of arms supermarket into which any customer can walk and pick up whatever he wants."[11]

The increase in quantity and quality of arms transfers and the fact that Washington was manipulating military aid to third world countries as a means of achieving strategic and political goals had many people in Congress and the general public worried. The doubts concerned mainly the existing ritualized assumptions about the purpose and practice of military aid and its efficacy in terms of leverage yielded. Critical questions were raised as to the validity of the argument that high levels of aid are justified for the defense of the free world, regional balance or stability, and important diplomatic efforts.[12]

The view that the executive branch had allowed the arms transfers to develop a momentum of their own and to almost get out of hand resulted in congressional action to put checks on the President's power to transfer arms. With the enactment in 1968 of the Foreign Military Sales Act, the 1961 act was amended to require the administration to state clearly its foreign policy considerations in its arms sales policies. The act limited the President's power to sell arms to countries engaged in human rights violations or impeding social programs.[13] The most important of these measures was the Arms Export Control Act approved by Congress in June 30, 1976. However, none of these measures affected the transfer of arms to the Middle East, which continues to be the number-one recipient of American military aid. In the case of Israel, in 1967 the United States replaced France and England and has since become Israel's sole supplier of arms. In the transfer of arms to Israel, the role of Congress and American public opinion has been limited. The executive branch initiates all withholding and delivery of arms to Israel, and since the late 1960s all administrations have used tactics of coercion and inducement in order to establish leverage over Israel and influence its foreign policy.[14]

The merit of these tactics is, however, questionable. In the patron-client relationships that have developed between the United States and Israel, the donor state has many times been the captive of the recipient state and not vice versa. Arms transfers to Israel between 1968 and 1986 demonstrate that the United States has gained very little, if any, leverage over Israel's policies and politics, thus undermining the argument that Israel's complete dependence on U.S. military aid provides the United States with leverage. In fact, when the United States sought leverage—mainly when it tried to promote the peace process—it encountered frustrating disappointments. Leverage proved to be more a myth than a reality.

In order to understand and explain the paradox of this high level of military aid and low level of political leverage, it is necessary to examine leverage in terms of patron-client relationships and to identify the efforts made by the patron (the United States) to influence and control the policies and politics of its client (Israel). The level of leverage attained is usually determined by international and regional factors, often ignored or underestimated in the formulation of foreign policy, which emphasizes domestic factors, namely, Congress and public opinion. Ignoring the regional and international factors is often detrimental to U.S. foreign policy. The sale of U.S. arms to Iran in 1985–86 is a case in point. The success of U.S. foreign policy in the Middle East is highly dependent on the understanding of the regional and international environments.

The Israeli-Arab conflict, which has dominated the region for over forty years, requires the United States to seek leverage and influence over Israel and the friendly Arab states. Leverage is vital on both global and regional levels. First, it reinforces containment and enhances the U.S. position vis-à-vis the Soviet Union. On the regional level, it enables the United States to enjoy the friendship of both Israel and the Arab states. This is essential for the peace process and the uninterrupted flow of oil from the Middle East to the West.[15]

The best way to achieve leverage seemed to be the manipulation of transfers of arms, that is to use coercion (withholding) or inducement (deliveries). Since the first major U.S.-Israeli arms deal of 1968, this has been a common practice by all U.S. administrations. "Interested in encouraging a settlement in the Middle East, the U.S. has used its control over aircraft supplies as leverage in pressing the Israeli government to make concessions."[16] However, the results were disappointing.

Another common misperception concerns the role of Congress and public opinion.[17] Whereas the role of the executive branch is underestimated, the role of Congress is exaggerated. With some rare exceptions, acts of withholding (coercion) or delivery (inducement) of arms are initiated and implemented by the executive branch, and Congress follows the President's leadership. Congress is instrumental in the appropriation process, not in the formulation and implementation of foreign policy. Hence, domestic factors have but limited influence over policies of arms transfers.

Using an alternative approach, this study assumes that the existence or absence of leverage is a consequence of the international system; namely, the international setting in the Middle East has created two regional and two global built-in systemic dilemmas, which severely limit U.S. leverage.

THE UNITED STATES AND ISRAEL:
THE TROUBLED ALLIANCE

Despite a long tradition of cooperation, the United States and Israel have experienced major conflicts of interests resulting from differences in the two nations' definition of their respective national interest. The United States needed leverage during times of conflict, especially when it initiated peace plans, to bring Israel to accept its principles and strategies. The schism between the two allies has been explained in two ways. The first assumes that ideological-conceptual differences divide them. The second assumes mainly strategic-tactical differences.

The advocates of the first approach argue that Washington and Jerusalem adhere to conflicting political doctrines because their vital interests are in conflict.[18] Peace is an American vital interest because it secures the flow of oil, whereas war threatens it. Moreover, peace would help the United States to maintain friendly relations with both Israel and the Arab states. War imposes the need for America to "choose" between the support of one side or the other. Last but not least, peace helps to curb Soviet influence. For three decades the

U.S.S.R. has been exploiting the Israeli-Arab conflict by playing the "Arabs against the Jews" and has gained influence through the transfer of arms and defense technology. Peace would terminate this practice and Soviet influence could be contained.

From an Israeli perspective, however, the picture looks different. Israel's most vital interest is to protect its security by controlling strategic positions in the West Bank and the Golan Heights. Israel prefers a situation of "no peace, no war" while exercising control over these territories to a withdrawal from all or most territories. (Israel claims that it does not trust the Palestinians' commitment to peace after an Israeli withdrawal).[19] The conflict is, therefore, between two principles: "peace in exchange for territories," which is America's first priority, and "no peace but territories and security," which is Israel's first priority.

The second approach assumes that both nations rank peace as their highest priority.[20] Peace serves Israel's most vital strategic, economic, and political interests. *Strategically*, peace would relieve Israel of the permanent threat to its existence. *Economically*, peace would enable Israel to devote its scarce resources to a desperately needed economic recovery. In order to arrest a 400 percent annual rate of inflation, Israel had to adopt severe austerity measures and price controls. It spends 30 percent of its gross national product (GNP) on defense, and its external debt, over $20 billion, is higher than its GNP. *Politically*, peace would gain Israel much-awaited Arab recognition. Israel is technologically advanced and its economy would gain tremendously if Arab and African markets opened up for its goods and services. Hence, Israel and the United States share a strong need for peace. The main conflict between the two allies concerns the strategies and tactics of the peace process, that is, how, when, and in exchange for what should Israel withdraw.

Both approaches can be convincingly argued. The first approach is usually argued by critics of Israel's policies. It assumes that Israel's consistent rejection of U.S. peace initiatives is the ultimate proof that Israel rejects the principle "territories for peace."[21] The second approach is used by Israel's supporters who argue that its withdrawal from the Sinai proves that it adheres to the "exchange of territories for peace" principle.[22] However, it is clear that America and Israel do not see eye to eye on many issues. The 1987 debate over an international peace conference has accentuated these disagreements. The United States tries to exert leverage whenever its policies are rejected by Israel. However, U.S. leverage has been very elusive. Not surprisingly, the U.S.S.R. has encountered the same difficulties when dealing with its client states in the region.[23] Hence, because of regional and global dilemmas, this frustrating lack of leverage has become an integral part of U.S.-Israel relationships.

REGIONAL DILEMMAS

The Israeli-Arab conflict, which began with the establishment of Israel, created two inevitable, regional dilemmas, both caused by and resulting from conflicting

American interests in the region. The desire of the United States to pursue an
"evenhanded" policy in the Middle East has been a cornerstone of American
policy. It aspires to support both Israel and the moderate Arab states. Neither
domestic upheavals nor interregional conflicts, which plague the area, have
changed this long-term policy. The United States has been committed to (1) the
security of Israel and its right to exist in peace, and (2) to a just solution of the
Palestinian problem, that is, an "exchange of territories for peace."[24] In the
long term, the United States wishes to create in the Middle East what former
Secretary of State Alexander Haig entitled a "mini NATO" or a "strategic
consensus," which would include the "Gang of Four," that is, Egypt, Jordan,
Saudi Arabia, and Israel—all friendly to the United States. The concept relies
heavily on military rather than political aspects of the possible alliance; thus
military aid and strategic cooperation agreements are considered the most important features of this concept.[25] However, the United States appears to have
ignored or underestimated the incompatibilities that exist between Israel and the
moderate Arab states. Hence, the "strategic consensus" cannot materialize in
the foreseeable future.[26]

Tensions between the potential Gang of Four mounted with Israel's annexation
of the Golan Heights (1981) and its invasion of Lebanon (1982). The Arab states
made it clear that their friendship and cooperation were conditioned by the ability
of the United States to influence Israel to make territorial concessions. The United
States was faced with the need to be able to "deliver Israel," and leverage was
sought to achieve this. However, Israel made it clear that it was not yet ready
to consider territorial concessions. It demanded that its strategic superiority be
established and its security needs be satisfied before it would consider territorial
concessions. Consequently, the United States has been supplying Israel with the
quality and quantity of arms necessary to bring about Israeli concessions that
would satisfy the demands of the Arab states. This situation creates a basic
dilemma. Arming Israel is a prerequisite for any Israeli withdrawal. However,
it undermines American leverage and helps Israel resist American pressures more
successfully. Thus Israeli concessions are less likely. This, in turn, alienates the
Arab states, whose cooperation and friendship are essential for U.S. economic
and strategic interests.

The second regional dilemma concerns the U.S.-Israeli relationship. The
United States has traditionally supported Israel for ideological, humanitarian,
and strategic reasons. The affinity between the two nations is based on shared
social and political values. They are both capitalistic, liberal democracies. Moreover, the United States feels an obligation to protect Israel and to make sure
that another holocaust never occurs.

The highest priority is, however, strategic. The last decade has put vital U.S.
interests in the Middle East and the Persian Gulf at stake. The lingering Iran-
Iraq war requires a strong Western presence in the gulf. Soviet presence in
Afghanistan and the horn of Africa makes the situation all the more dangerous.
It is essential for the United States to have a strong and reliable ally in the

Isreal.
US
Military
interst.

region. Israel answers both requirements. It is militarily strong and a reliable American ally. Thus strengthening Israel and maintaining its military superiority become vital American interests.[27] This situation, however, results in a dilemma. The strategic consideration to strengthen Israel and establish it as the most important U.S. regional ally makes Israel less vulnerable to U.S. pressures. Paradoxically, American leverage is undermined by American support of Israel.

GLOBAL DILEMMAS

The global environment mainly applies to the system of balance of power and the competition for power between the United States and the U.S.S.R. This competition has been especially dangerous in the Middle East where the stakes are extremely high and no demarcation lines were created to divide the region between West and East. Unlike Europe, the future of the Middle East was not determined by the end of World War II. This situation created two dilemmas; both derive from, and result in, conflicting global interests.

U.S. Middle East policy has always been guided by global considerations. Both superpowers consider influence in the region to be a vital national interest. Hence, the United States is apprehensive about a possible Soviet reaction to either an increase or decrease in American support for Israel. Strong arguments exist for an against increased U.S. support of Israel. The argument against increased aid is based on the belief that it encourages increased Soviet aid to extremist Arab states. This ''aid competition'' intensifies both the hostility among the regional rivals and tension between the two superpowers. One-sided support for Israel provides the U.S.S.R. with a pretext to penetrate deeper into the region and works against containment. In addition, it enhances Israel's power to resist substantial moves toward peace while alienating the friendly Arab states. A better way to achieve containment, and at the same time avoid the danger of a major confrontation between the superpowers, is to limit support for Israel and if needed even to pressure Israel ''to behave.''[28]

The second theory argues that the opposite is true. The need to ''create'' a half a world—a free half—without blowing the whole to pieces in the ''process''[29] requires the strengthening of Israel. Henry Kissinger, who influenced American policy in the Middle East perhaps more than any other politician, argued that containment is best served through support for Israel. In fact, limiting support for Israel never enhanced containment. The American expectation that diminished support for Israel would be reciprocated by reduced Soviet support for its client states never materialized.[30] In reality, the opposite occurred. An American ''evenhanded'' policy of reduced support of Israel usually induced the U.S.S.R. to adopt a more daring and dangerous policy. It was probably interpreted by the U.S.S.R. as a sign of weakness.[31]

Despite upheavals and political changes in the region, Soviet vital interests in the Middle East have not changed. The Soviet Union, although proclaiming self-sufficiency in oil today, may become dependent on Middle Eastern oil in the future.[32] In addition, gaining control over the West's energy sources is an irresistible temptation for the U.S.S.R. Second, the Middle East is of vital strategic importance to the Soviets. This region is considered a Soviet "back-yard," and the unprecedented American naval presence of improved carrier-borne aircraft, combined with improved nuclear submarines, pose a new threat to the Soviets. The U.S.S.R. considers this region to be part of its defensive perimeter and has a strong drive to turn it into its sphere of influence.[33]

During the 1950s Soviet interests were primarily defensive, that is, they tried to weaken the military network of interlocking alliances that the West was creating around them. Then in the 1960s and 1970s, as a result of favorable circumstances, they adopted more ambitious and expansionist trends. The U.S.S.R. under Gorbachev is flexible and proven to be in tune with regional dynamics. It responds to specific needs and situations and has been adopting a businesslike policy by providing specific "aid packages" to individual Middle Eastern states.[34]

The American answer to the aggressive Soviet policy has been increased support for Israel and the friendly Arab states. The reflagging of twelve Kuwaiti ships in 1987 is a case in point. The U.S.-Arab cooperation in the gulf has not altered Israel's position as a major arm of U.S. foreign policy helping to counter dangerous Soviet maneuvers. The two superpowers are continuing to supply their clients with increasingly sophisticated weapons and missile systems. The Soviet Union supplies arms to Iraq, Libya, and Syria (Iran receives arms from China and North Korea); the United States supplies arms to Israel, Egypt, Jordan, and Saudi Arabia. Lately, Iraq's massive acquisition of arms set new records with over $5 billion in arms annually, since 1983. Libya doesn't lag far behind. Saudi Arabia's arms transfers amount to almost $3.5 billion per year, whereas Syria received almost $2 billion in annual military aid from the U.S.S.R.[35]

U.S. policy in the Middle East must, therefore, be assessed in the context of the power competition between the United States and the U.S.S.R. The situation has been aggravated in 1987 with the escalation of the hostilities in the gulf and the heavy American presence there. This situation results in an ever-growing U.S. commitment to the security of its allies in the region, especially Israel. Support for Israel, however, creates a major global dilemma. It undermines American leverage and gives Israel an edge over the United States. America has to refrain from pressuring Israel through a decrease or suspension of military aid, lest such acts undermine the power position of the United States in the region. Israel, aware of the U.S. dilemma, can take advantage of it and manipulate American aid to serve its political purposes.

The second global dilemma results from U.S. pursuit of spheres of influence. The United States has to maintain its credibility as a patron state with present and future client states throughout the world. It could not and would not abandon a client state in a time of crisis, since the Soviet Union could exploit such an act to attract prospective client states and to change the global status quo in its favor. (President Sadat's decision to break away from the Soviet Union and renew his ties with the United States was influenced mainly by his belief that the United States was a much more reliable and credible patron state than the U.S.S.R.) The use of coercive leverage could undermine or even destroy America's reputation while enhancing Soviet credibility in the eyes of prospective client states.[36]

It is clear that these regional and global dilemmas allow Israel to continue to enjoy a high level of independence in its foreign policy decisions. U.S. power to coerce Israel to adjust its policies and to conform to American desires will continue to be limited. U.S. massive military and economic aid to Israel will not change in the near future regardless of significant conflicts and disagreements over issues and interests.

LEVERAGE IN PATRON-CLIENT RELATIONSHIPS: CAN IT WORK?

The growing number of approaches to foreign policy has created neither clarity nor standard methods for analyzing leverage and influence.[37] It is, therefore, helpful to define influence and leverage in the context of patron-client relationships. The assumption is that the client state's dependence on its patron state will result in leverage that could then be measured and evaluated.

When the United States became the sole supplier of arms to Israel in 1967, the two had developed a very special relationship of dependence. However, Nixon realized early in his presidency that he could not manipulate arms transfers to create leverage. This fact is as true in the 1980s as it was in the 1960s.

However, since the aborted Rogers peace plan of 1969, the United States persisted in its efforts to promote an Israeli-Arab peace with various levels of success and failure. Israel has always been suspicious of U.S. peace initiatives. Its greatest fear has been an imposed agreement reached between the United States and the Arab states. Hence, peace efforts always created tensions between the United States and Israel. Consequently, the United States has been using tactics of coercion and inducement to achieve an Israeli compliance. Not surprisingly, the tactics yielded very little success.

For example, during the Lebanese crisis of 1982–84, the U.S. foreign policy suffered a succession of setbacks that resulted from lack of leverage and complete inability to influence the policies of either its friends or its foes. Hence, it is paramount to understand how leverage and influence should be identified, explained, and predicted. The existing literature offers only limited guidance for this task. Sustained attention to peaceful forms of pressure has only recently begun.[38] Quantitative analysis can hardly provide an insight. The instances of influence are too few in any particular international relationship to permit a valid quantitative analysis of statistical significance.

The case of U.S.-Israel relationship proves this point. The structural features of the international system—bipolar, balance of power, spheres of influence—determine the nature of the interaction between the patron and its client. Other nations that are an integral part of the environment also play a major role. All these actors pursue their own national interests and foreign policy goals. They make their policy choices and, consequently, they effect U.S. leverage.

Political leverage assumes correlations between arms transfers and the patron state's ability to use it to coerce or induce its client state.

Leverage is defined as manipulation of the arms transfer relationship in order to coerce or induce a recipient-state to conform its policy or actions to the desires of the supplier-state. Coercion involves the denial of ongoing or future aid while inducement depends upon the promise of increased aid.[39]

In the analysis of leverage, it is pertinent to distinguish among power, influence, and leverage. Although leverage is always defined in terms of power and it implies either coercion or inducement, it is nonetheless a distinct form of power. Leverage, when correctly used, may result in more power. However, unlike power, leverage excludes the application of brute force and assumes *two co-operating actors* in a relationship of dependency.

Hence, patron-client relationship is a prerequisite of leverage. Power, on the other hand, requires neither cooperation nor dependency relationships. A more powerful state can invade or take over a weaker country and the sheer use of force yields compliance. Leverage, when attained, makes the use of force unnecessary. In order to gain and maintain leverage, the patron state encourages long-term dependency relationships. However, under certain circumstances the tables might turn and the asymmetry between the patron and the client in economic and military powers might become irrelevant.

Whereas power and leverage are by definition coercive, influence can be noncoercive. Indeed it may enrich rather than limit the weaker actor's choices. Moreover, influence can result in mutual benefits for both the patron and the client states.[40]

Leverage always implies a strategy aimed at controlling another country's policy choices. Influence need not be a strategy. It is a process of interaction in a framework of either friendly or unfriendly relations. By contrast, leverage means manipulation of aid, which is coercive and aimed at limiting the policy choices of the client state. Influence, unlike leverage, does not depend on a patron-client relationship and does not require dependency. Influence may or may not be coercive, whereas leverage is always coercive. Leverage is measured by the level of compliance achieved and is considered successful when the level of compliance is high.

Leverage is based on two primary tactics used by the influencer to achieve compliance: (1) *coercion* (a threat or an actual punishment), and (2) *inducement* (a promise or an actual reward). It is believed that the proper manipulation of these two tactics is responsible for the existence or absence of leverage.

For example, leverage is achieved when and if actor A, which seeks to modify

Table 3
Top Recipients of U.S. Arms (in Billions of Dollars)

Country	1955–69	1970–80	1981–85
Saudi Arabia	0.779	30.01	6.4
Iran	0.657	21.00	—
Israel	0.535	12.35	4.1
Egypt	—	3.61	3.0

Source: U.S. Arms Control and Disarmament Agency, *World Military Expenditures and Arms Transfers* (Washington, D.C.: Government Printing Office, 1985–86); U.S. Department of Defense, *Foreign Military Sales and Military Assistance Facts* (Washington, D.C.: Government Printing Office, 1979–85); Andrew J. Pierre, *The Global Politics of Arms Sales* (Princeton, N.J.: Princeton University Press, 1982), pp. 148–49.

On the other hand, massive surpluses of petrodollars, caused by the sharp rise in oil prices, created a large Arab demand for arms, which accelerated the transfer of American and Soviet arms to the region. As for individual countries, Saudi Arabia has always been the number one purchaser of U.S. military equipment (Table 3).

NOTES

1. George Shultz, "International Security and Development Cooperation Program," Department of State Special Report (April 1984), p. 1.

2. Andrew Pierre, *The Global Politics of Arms Sales* (Princeton, NJ: Princeton University Press, 1982), p. 3.

3. Shultz, "International Security," p. 1.

4. Defense Security Assistance Agency (DSAA), *Foreign Military Sales and Military Assistance Facts*, 1983 and earlier editions.

5. Ibid.

6. Pierre, *Global Politics*, p. 15.

7. Defense Institute of Security Assistance Management (DISAM), *The Management of Security Assistance* (Wright-Patterson, OH: Defense Institute of Security Assistance Management, 1981), pp. 1–22.

8. Roger P. Labrie, John G. Hutchins, and Edwin Peura, *U.S. Arms Sales Policy* (Washington, DC: American Enterprise Institute for Public Policy Research, 1982), p. 1.

9. Public Law 87–195, *Legislative and Foreign Relations*, September 4, 1961, Chapter 2, Sec. 503, 1982, Vol. 1, p. 435.

10. The Marshall plan included no military aid. The numbers apply to economic aid only; see DSAA, *Foreign Military Sales*, 1965 ed., p. 5.

11. Senator Humphrey's speech, *New York Times*, October 19, 1975, quoted in Michael T. Klare, *American Arms Supermarket* (Austin: University of Texas Press, 1984), p. 2.

12. See Labrie et al., *U.S. Arms Sales Policy*.

13. Congressional Research Service, *Changing Perspectives on U.S. Arms Transfer*

Policy. Report to the Subcommittee on International Security and Scientific Affairs, U.S. House of Representatives, September 25, 1981, p. 5.

14. This view is expressed by Sheehan, Ball, and Tillman, among others.

15. An example of this view is Shultz's letter to Congress, "International Security."

16. Klaus Knorr, *The Power of Nations* (New York: Basic Books, 1975), p. 195.

17. See, for example, Seth Tillman, *The United States in the Middle East: Interests and Obstacles* (Bloomington: Indiana University Press, 1982), pp. 233–234. He argued that a strong coalition among Congress, Jewish leaders, and other influential individuals practically controls U.S. policy.

18. Ibid., pp. 230–274.

19. See discussion in Steven Rosen and Mara Moustafin, "Does Washington Have the Means to Impose a Settlement on Israel?" *Commentary* (October 1977), pp. 25–32.

20. See detailed discussion in Abba Eban, *An Autobiography* (New York: Random House, 1977), and Yitzhak Rabin, *The Rabin Memoirs* (Boston: Little, Brown, 1979).

21. This view is expressed in detail in Sean McBride, *Israel in Lebanon* (London: Ithaca Press, 1983), pp. 1–9; also see interview with King Hussein, *New York Times*, March 14, 1984.

22. In summer 1970 the Israeli Cabinet accepted Security Council Resolution 242, which stated that territories conquered during wars would be exchanged for peace. The Likud party, then a member of the Cabinet, left the coalition and the government was dissolved.

23. See discussion in Knorr, *Power of Nations*, pp. 180–206.

24. The Reagan administration reiterated the principle of "even-handedness" in many public addresses during that period, as in the Shultz news conference of August 20, 1982; the President's peace plan of September 1, 1982; the Shultz address before the UJA on September 12, 1982; the statement by Shultz before the Senate Foreign Relations Committee and House Foreign Affairs Committee, September 10, 1982, among others.

25. For a discussion of the strategic consensus concept, see Amos Perlmutter, "Reagan's Middle East Policy: A Year One Assessment," *Orbis* (Spring 1984), p. 27.

26. Ibid., pp. 26–29.

27. See article by Shoshana Bryen, "Advancing U.S.-Israel Strategic Cooperation," *Middle East Review* (February 1984), and Steven Spiegel, "Israel as a Strategic Asset," *Commentary* (June 1983), pp. 51–55.

28. Israel's foes usually advocate this view; for example, see William Brubeck, *The Path to Peace Revisited* (New York: Seven Springs Center, 1982), and George Ball, "How to Save Israel in Spite of Herself," *Foreign Affairs* (Summer 1977).

29. Former Secretary of State Alexander Haig's address before the U.S. Chamber of Commerce, Washington DC, April 27, 1982, *Department of State Bulletin* (June 1982), pp. 40–44.

30. For example, during 1969–70, Nixon followed the recommendations of Secretary of State William Rogers and pressured Israel to accept the Rogers peace plan by suspending arms shipments. It boomeranged when the U.S.S.R. intensified its activities and sent thousands of Soviet personnel—including pilots—to Egypt. During Ford's reassessment policy, the U.S.S.R. again tried to strengthen its power position in the region.

31. Thomas Wheelock, "Arms for Israel: The Limits of Leverage," *International Security* (Fall 1978), p. 125.

32. Drew Middleton, "Russian Presence and Economic Interests in the Mediterranean and the Indian Ocean," in Seymour Finger (ed.), *The New World Balance in the Middle*

East: Reality or Mirage? (Teaneck, NJ: Farleigh Dickinson Press, 1975), pp. 43–49; also John C. Campbell, "Soviet Policy in the Middle East," *Current History* (January 1981), pp. 1–4, 42–45.

33. Alvin Rubinstein, "The Soviet Presence in the Arab World," *Current History* (October 1981), pp. 313–316, 338–339.

34. Ibid., p. 313.

35. Pierre, *Global Politics*, p. 8.

36. Secretary Shultz's statement to the Senate Foreign Relations Committee, October 24, 1983, *Department of State Bulletin*, No. 520.

37. See, for example, Robert Dahl, 1957; Klaus Knorr, 1975; Hans Morgenthau, 1978; Andrew Pierre, 1982; Thomas Schelling, 1976, among others.

38. David Pollock, *Politics of Pressure* (Westport, CT: Greenwood Press, 1979), p. 7.

39. Marvin Feuerwerger, *Congress and Israel* (Westport, CT: Greenwood Press, 1979), p. 11.

40. Wheelock, "Arms for Israel," p. 123.

41. For a classical statement on these concepts, see Jack Nagel, *The Descriptive Analysis of Power* (New Haven: Yale University Press, 1975), pp. 29–30; Robert Dahl, "Power," in *International Encyclopedia of the Social Sciences* (New York: Macmillan Press, 1968); B. Blechman and S. Kaplan, *Force Without War* (Washington, DC: Brookings Institute, 1979).

42. See Dahl, 1957; Knorr, 1975; Wheelock, 1978; Pierre, 1982.

43. Knorr, *Power of Nations*, pp. 166–206.

44. Wheelock, "Arms for Israel," p. 124.

45. See Tillman, 1982; Eveland, 1980; also interview with King Hussein, *New York Times*, March 14, 1984.

46. Pollock, *Politics of Pressure*, p. 4.

47. The Foreign Assistance Bill of 1983 was debated when the relationships between the United States and Israel were at one of their lowest points. It did not affect Congress's decision to approve the same level of aid as was requested before the invasion —$785 million in economic aid and $1.7 billion in military aid. It was signed by the President on December 21, 1982.

48. This statement is based on personal interviews with AIPAC officials during an annual AIPAC meeting in April 1984.

49. With a total annual budget of only $3.5 million (a 1984–85 figure) and a small staff of lobbyists, AIPAC pursues its goals in a low-key manner, especially after its major failure on the AIWACS issue; see the *New York Times*, March 24, 1984.

50. Kenneth Waltz, *Theories of International Politics* (Reading, MA: Addison-Wesley, 1979), pp. 79–128.

51. Knorr, *Power of Nations*, pp. 176–201.

52. Pierre, *Global Politics*, p. 18.

53. A 1976 report to the Senate Foreign Relations Committee noted that large-scale arms sales to Iran invariably involved a commitment to provide support for the weapons. The absence of such commitment could have provoked a major crisis in the U.S.-Iran relationship. Consequently, 24,000 American personnel in Iran could have become hostages had Iran become involved in a war then. Indeed, because of the close supplier-client relationship, "it was not clear who really has influence over whom in times of an ambiguous crisis situation," concluded the report. Quoted in Pierre, *Global Politics*, p. 18.

54. Report by the Comptroller General of the United States, *U.S. Assistance to the State of Israel*, June 24, 1983, p. 1.

55. "Foreign Assistance Program: FY 1986 Budget and 1985 Supplemental Request," United States Department of State Special Report, May 1985, pp. 3–11.

56. Ibid., p. 12.

57. Iraq, Israel, Oman, Libya, and Saudi Arabia spent over 30 percent of their GNP on defense. Information from U.S. Arms Control and Disarmament Agency, *World Military Expenditures and Arms Transfers* (Washington, DC: Government Printing Office, 1985).

58. Ibid., pp. 3–11.

59. Klare, *American Arms Supermarket*, p. 130.

60. In the year 1957 alone, Iraq received *$13.2 million* worth of arms; DSAA, *Foreign Military Sales*, edition 1981.

2

The Rogers Peace Plan of 1969: The Wrong Idea at the Wrong Time, for the Wrong Actors

The Six-Day War of 1967 was a turning point in the history of the Middle East. It changed the nature of the Israeli-Arab conflict as well as the context of the U.S.-Israeli relationship. The countries in the region and their respective patron states were faced with new realities that they could neither predict nor control. Israel's victory changed the regional and the global balances of power. It strengthened the power positions of both Israel and the United States and counterbalanced Soviet political gains of the early sixties in Egypt and Syria. Israel's victory proved its military superiority. No longer was Israel considered a weak client state and a burden. It became America's most important regional ally and a strategic asset.[1] The new realities compelled the Arab states to reassess and change their attitudes. Instead of thinking in terms of destroying Israel, they had to start thinking about coexisting peacefully with Israel.

Other changes, however, were less encouraging. Libya, South Yemen, and Iraq underwent anti-Western revolutions. Egypt and Syria moved closer to the Soviet bloc in a drive toward a new era of pan-Arabism. The Middle East became an arena for a fierce American-Soviet rivalry over power and influence, and the United States more often than not was less aggressive than the U.S.S.R. in this competition.

The struggle for spheres of influences—namely, the fight for control over the region's resources—became extremely dangerous as the stakes grew higher. The regional and global dilemmas that control the region's politics created confusion and uncertainty concerning policy choices. Both patron states found it difficult, if not impossible, to control their client states' behavior. The escalation of violence after 1967 spilled over and created dangerous tensions in U.S.-U.S.S.R. relations. Hence, President Johnson, and with more vigor Nixon, found it important to try and settle the Israeli-Arab conflict.

The period between January 1969 and August 1970 was marked by the most important peace initiative, known as The Rogers Plan for a Comprehensive Settlement, made public on December 1969. An analysis of the events must include (1) the timing, that is, why the United States chose that particular moment in history to initiate a settlement, (2) the nature of the proposed settlement, that is, the substance of the proposal and what it offered to Israel and the Arab states in terms of peace, security, and withdrawal from territories, and (3) why it failed. It is essential to understand the procedures that the United States followed in its efforts to implement the plan and that contributed to the plan's failure.

Two major features characterized American policy during that period. First, the United States followed an unambiguous and consistent set of long-term goals that characterized America's containment policy since the end of World War II. These goals were reiterated by every American president, and there seemed to be a "unanimity and the consistency in American perception of both its national interests, and its policy objectives."[2]

The second feature is that the United States has always been sharply divided on the strategies and tactics that should be employed to attain these goals. In contrast to the consistent, clear, long-term objectives, the U.S. short-term policy was ambiguous and ambivalent. Issues and implementation processes were vigorously debated. The controversy involved mainly the State and Defense departments and the White House. "Debate and differences of opinion about U.S. Middle East policy have been an almost continuous feature of the American political scene."[3] The volatile political situation in the region added to the difficulty of formulating a consistent foreign policy.

Washington was sharply divided on the interpretation of U.N. Resolution 242, which became the basis of all Middle East peace initiatives, and on implementation processes, namely, a comprehensive peace plan versus step-by-step diplomacy. The Soviet Union's role in the peace process was another important area of disagreement. In the late sixties the comprehensive approach advocated by the Department of State prevailed. The Department's approach, however, was based on several misperceptions, among them the assumption that the United States enjoyed leverage over Israel and the friendly Arab states. This was the basic premise of the Rogers plan. Another misperception concerned the State Department's belief that the United States and the Soviet Union had a mutual interest in stabilizing the Middle East. In reality, all efforts to bring about American-Soviet cooperation not only failed, but proved to be detrimental to U.S. interests. The State Department also ignored the dilemma that any settlement favored by Israel would be unacceptable to the Arab states (especially the radical Arab states), and vice versa. Indeed, U.S. Middle East policy during that period was based on misperceptions, which in turn exacerbated the conflict and reduced the chances of a settlement. Ironically, U.S. policy aided the Soviet Union and helped it to expand its influence.

Two separate peace initiatives, one American and one a U.N. resolution, preceded the Rogers plan and served as its theoretical framework. On June 19, 1967, President Johnson announced his "Five Principles for Peace." Later that year the United Nations adopted Resolution 242, which also called for peace among the fighting sides. These two documents, however different, probably inspired the Secretary Rogers peace plan. Of the two documents, President Johnson's Five Principles is the lesser known. The second, U.N. Resolution 242 of November 22, 1967, received much attention and has been mentioned in all discussions concerning peace in the Middle East.

Johnson's Five Principles stated that (1) every nation in the area has a fundamental right to live and to have this right respected by its neighbors, (2) justice for the refugees is a human requirement, (3) maritime rights must be respected, (4) the wasteful and futile arms race in the Middle East must be contained through a bilateral agreement between the United States and the U.S.S.R. (Johnson called on U.N. members to report shipments of arms to the United Nations and to keep them on file for all the people of the world to observe), and (5) the political independence and territorial integrity of all the states in the area must be respected.[4]

Johnson was the first American President to sign a major arms deal with Israel. The most important item on the deal was the sale of fifty advanced Phantom F–4 fighter-jets to be delivered in September 1969. However, bothered by the escalation of the Middle East arms race, Johnson took a surprising and unexpected act. He suspended all arms deals with Israel after the Six-Day War, hoping to reach an accord with the Soviet Union on an arms freeze to the region. He believed that a freeze would lead to peace. He assumed that a mutual withholding of arms was possible and that the United States and the U.S.S.R. had a shared interest in bringing peace to the region. Both assumptions, which guided U.S. policy during 1969–70, proved wrong. Hence, following the Six-Day War,

the United States suspended the delivery of arms to Israel, including spare parts and ammunition. . . . In addition to turning down new orders, the Americans delayed shipment of orders that had already been approved and signed. The reason for violating these signed contracts was the vain hope that the Soviet Union would reciprocate by cutting down arms shipments to the Arab states. . . . But the Soviet Union, interpreting the suspension of arms deliveries as an act of weakness, speeded up their arms deliveries to Egypt and Syria.[5]

President Johnson's efforts to reach an agreement with the Soviet Union failed, as was the case with the Rogers plan a few years later. Israel at that time accepted the Johnson peace initiative as the first step in a long march toward the desired peace, and not as a final document. The countries of the region as well as the superpowers were slowly moving away from any dialogue, each believing that time was to their advantage. The most substantial gains were those of the Soviet Union, which skillfully manipulated the ill-conceived American policy during that period to expand its role and to increase its influence in the region. Naively, the United States neither comprehended the Soviet policy nor tried to contain it. In the words of Henry Kissinger:

The Soviet Union, which in the late Forties had written off the Middle East as beyond its capacity to influence (Andrei Zhdanov in a report to the conference of Communist Parties, September 1947, essentially treated the Middle East as in transition from the British to the American sphere of influence), had leaped . . . by a sale of arms and . . . by the dispatch of thousands of military advisers to Egypt. The Soviet presence constituted a major geopolitical change since World War II. For fifteen years it helped exacerbate the conflict.[6]

The State Department underestimated the growing Soviet aggressive involvement in Egypt, Syria, Iraq, Algeria, Sudan, Libya, and South Yemen. It continued to hold the misperception that the Soviet Union, desperate to avoid a superpowers confrontation, had a vital interest in settling the Israeli-Arab conflict. This incorrect assumption inevitably led to conflicts between the United States and Israel. The latter considered American trust of the U.S.S.R.'s peace efforts to be extremely naive and short-sighted.

Surprised by its own show of force, Israel adopted political objectives that did not coincide with those of the United States. Israel's most vital interests were securing its existence, territorial integrity, and economic well-being, all of which were threatened by its hostile neighbors. Israel insisted on direct negotiations with the Arab states and a contractual peace before any withdrawal took place. The United States was ready to compromise on an Israeli withdrawal in exchange for less than a contractual peace, and it did not consider Israel's demand for direct negotiations to be essential. The United States accepted the Arab demand for indirect negotiations mediated by a third party, a condition that Israel considered humiliating and unacceptable.

No one captured the situation better than Henry Kissinger who said:

By 1969, Israel had existed for twenty years unrecognized by its neighbors, harassed by guerrillas, assaulted in international forums, and squeezed by Arab economic boycott. . . . [I]t was only nine miles wide at the narrowest point. . . . With implacable adversaries on all its frontiers, Israel's . . . cardinal and ultimate objective was what for most other nations is the starting point of foreign policy—acceptance by its neighbors of its right to exist.[7]

The Israeli victory of 1967 created big hopes in Washington and Jerusalem and was perceived as an opportunity to reach a settlement in the long and painful Israeli-Arab conflict. Moreover, the United States hoped that peace would allow it to support Israel without antagonizing the Arabs. In turn, it would decrease Soviet influence in the region. Paradoxically, the United States believed that it was paramount to enlist Soviet cooperation in a pursuit of a settlement. The United States hoped that together the two superpowers would pressure their respective client states to accept the agreed-upon settlement. As U.S. Ambassador to the United Nations Arthur Goldberg stated, "the Middle East is a region in which detente between the Soviet Union and ourselves is essential."[8]

Only one week after the war had ended, Ambassador Goldberg expressed great hopes that the General Armistice Agreements would be replaced "at the very least, by a termination of any state of war and of any claims to the exercise of belligerent rights."[9] Israel shared the American hope that its decisive victory would bring about a genuine and contractual peace. Israel's mistake was that, like the United States, it ignored the global and regional dilemmas that rendered this desired outcome impossible. According to one observer:

The Israelis first believed their victory to have brought peace very near or at least to have put war very far . . . but they did not take into account the possibility that the interested outside forces that had been forced by the pace of events to remain passive during the war might reassert themselves after its end to inhibit its consequences.[10]

Former Prime Minister Rabin, who at that time served as Israel's Ambassador to Washington, recalled in his memoirs that on June 19, 1967 (the same day that President Johnson delivered his peace plan) the Israeli government reached a major decision.

It communicated to the government of the United States that in exchange for a peace treaty Israel was prepared to withdraw to the international border with Egypt. In addition, the Sinai peninsula was to be demilitarized, and appropriate measures would guarantee Israel's freedom of navigation in the straits of Tiran and the Suez Canal. On the same terms, Israel was prepared to withdraw to the international border with Syria, with the Golan Heights to be demilitarized, and proper security arrangements made in the area. The future of the West Bank and the Gaza Strip would be considered separately, as well as the problem of the Palestinian refugees. This was conveyed to Secretary of State Dean Rusk by Foreign Minister Eban on June 22, 1967.[11]

However, the Israeli hope of a possible settlement of the conflict did not coincide with the desires of the Arab states. This division was manifested in the Khartum resolution adopted on September 1, 1967, in an Arab nations summit meeting. The resolution reaffirmed the three classical negatives: *No peace, no recognition of Israel, no negotiations with Israel.*[12]

The Khartum resolution created a political deadlock. Israel adamantly adhered to its three principles: direct negotiations, contractual peace, and territorial adjustments; the Arab states rejected these demands and insisted on their "three principles." The only hope for any dialogue between both the regional and the global actors lay with U.N. Resolution 242, adopted on November 22, 1967. Although the resolution was universally accepted, each nation interpreted it according to its respective political goals. The resolution evaded the conceptual differences that existed among the various actors by adopting ambiguous language and calling for "withdrawal of Israeli armed forces from territories"— not "the territories—occupied in the recent conflict." It did not call for withdrawal of Israeli armed forces from all territories, leaving the option of territorial adjustments open to negotiations. Ambassador Goldberg explained: "Boundaries must be accepted and other arrangements made, superseding temporary and often-violated Armistice lines. . . . Historically, there have never been any secure or recognized boundaries in the area. Neither the Armistice lines of 1949 nor the cease-fire lines of 1967 have answered this description."[13]

The Soviet Union, however, expressed a different interpretation of the resolution. Reflecting the Arab position, the U.S.S.R. said that the resolution called for a total and unconditional withdrawal of Israeli forces to positions they had held before June 5, 1967. The procedures envisaged by the resolution for working toward a settlement were, likewise, stubbornly disputed. Israel regarded the resolution "as a statement of principles in the light of which the parties should negotiate peace."[14] The Arabs, however, "considered that the resolution provided a plan for settlement of the Middle East dispute, to be implemented by the parties according to modalities to be established by the Special Representative."[15] Israel's demand for direct negotiations was rejected by the Arab states, whereas their demand for indirect negotiations was rejected by Israel.

Other disputes concerned the nature of the assurances that the United States offered Israel in exchange for a withdrawal, and Israel's implied obligation to make a commitment in advance of negotiations of its willingness to withdraw from any of the occupied territories. At the heart of the dispute over Resolution 242 was Israel's right—enjoyed by all sovereign nations—to recognition of its sovereignty, territorial integrity, and political independence, within secure and recognized borders. The concept of a bargain of troop withdrawal in exchange for recognition and the right to live could be perceived as invalid and illusory. "It is juridically invalid, because the right is fundamental and inalienable, hence,—by definition—not subject to negotiation."[16] Israel considered it morally wrong to exchange territories for its natural right to "life, liberty, and the pursuit of happiness." The United States, however, saw nothing wrong with that.

The disagreement between Israel and the United States exhibited strong differences in the two nations' vital interests. Israel's insistence on direct negotiations was not a technical demand. Direct negotiations would constitute a de facto Arab recognition of Israel. The United States, however, eager to reach a settlement, viewed this demand as excessive and preferred indirect negotiations under the auspices of U.N. special representative Gunnar Jarring (Swedish ambassador to Moscow). The trouble with direct negotiations, Secretary Rusk said in July 1967, was that "there is some question as to whether any of the governments in the area can, in fact, do that and survive."[17]

The second conflict of interest between the United States and Israel concerned the resolution's emphasis on the "inadmissibility of the acquisition of territory by war," which Israel refused to accept verbatim. Israel demanded border adjustments necessary to answer its security needs, whereas the United States adhered to the principle that the border adjustments must be minor. However, Israel revised its position, and in December 1967, Jarring was received officially in Jerusalem and was presented with an Israeli agenda for discussions.

In early 1968 the Israeli government publicly announced its acceptance of the Rhodes formula for indirect negotiations, which had produced the Armistice

Agreements of 1949. (In the Rhodes talks some form of face-to-face negotiations did take place.)

Israel's surprising move followed a Soviet peace initiative, which was being negotiated between the two superpowers and which completely excluded a contractual peace between Israel and the Arab states. In addition, Secretary Rusk initiated a "Seven Points Plan," which suggested an Israeli withdrawal in exchange for a formal termination of hostilities; a solution to the refugee problem based on giving each refugee the option to return to the home he or she had occupied before the establishment of the state of Israel; and the signing of some as yet unspecified document by Egypt and Israel.[18] Another unresolved issue on the U.S.-Israeli agenda was the sale of the Phantoms.

Israel understood that in something of a pre-election gambit, on October 9, 1968, President Johnson had announced the administration's decision to sell the fifty planes to Israel. Yet when Foreign Minister Eban arrived in the United States and met with Dean Rusk on October 22, it was clear that the administration was resorting to delaying tactics. Paul Warnke requested that Israel specify in writing why it needed the Phantoms. Washington's condition for selling the planes was that Israel sign an unprecedented document, consenting to a U.S. presence in and supervision of every Israeli arms manufacturing installation and every defense institution engaged in research, development, or manufacture—including civilian research institutions.[19] The year 1968, however, did not end with a sad note for Israel after all. The Phantoms deal was finally signed, and the U.S. reaction to the Soviet peace initiative was favorable from Israel's viewpoint.

Five days before the end of the Johnson presidential term, Rusk handed the Soviets a letter stating that "peace can only be achieved by a process of negotiations between the sides . . . The parties must sign a contractual agreement that binds each side vis-à-vis the other."[20] Egypt rejected Rusk's Seven Points on the ground that they were too generous to Israel, thus relieving Israel of the need to reject it on the ground that it was too generous to Egypt.

Finally, Washington reached a series of important decisions favorable to Israel, including the commitment to sell Israel fifty Phantom F–4 jets and three squadrons of A–4 Skyhawks (seventy-five airplanes). In July of 1968, the first major sale of a new expanded Hawk air defense missile was announced, whereas shipment of the Phantoms was scheduled to begin in late 1969.[21] As the year 1968 was nearing its end, Israel, the Arab states, and the U.S.S.R. were waiting to see what would be the new administration's policy.

NIXON'S MIDDLE EAST AGENDA

In 1969 both Washington and Jerusalem experienced a change in government. The new administrations were confronted with the urgent need to develop foreign policies that would cope with changing environments and situations. In addition, "when a new Administration comes to office it is taken for granted that it will 'tackle' the important world problems; new Presidents always chide their predecessors for leaving issues not yet conclusively solved."[22] Nixon and his new Secretary of State were ready for a vigorous, innovative Middle East policy. However, they soon realized that they were facing several long-standing dilemmas.

The first dilemma was how to maintain friendly relations with both Israel and the moderate Arab states. Part of that dilemma was how to militarily strengthen Israel—which was necessary in view of the strong Soviet presence in Egypt and Syria—without antagonizing the Arab states, which perceived a strong Israel to be a direct threat to their security. Moreover, arming Israel could be considered an American act of hostility against the Arabs. Egypt's association with the U.S.S.R. presented another problem, since its radical policies were detrimental to the interests of both Israel and the United States. The largest Arab nation in the Middle East, Egypt (population over 40 million), posed the greatest threat to Israel's security. Its unprecedented alliance with the Soviet Union, which allowed the U.S.S.R. to gain, for the first time in history, power positions in the Middle East, alarmed the United States and created tensions that could spill over to other regions.

Hence, the Israeli-Arab conflict created for the United States both regional and global dilemmas. During 1969 and through 1970, the State Department, under the leadership of Secretary Rogers and Assistant Secretary Joseph Sisco, decided to develop a new American approach, vigorous and comprehensive, to settle the Israel-Arab conflict. After a year and a half in office, in December 1969, Rogers publicly announced his new initiative, which became known as the Rogers peace plan. However, because it was based on misperceptions, its life was not only short, but plagued with difficulties from its inception. It is surprising, however, that such embarrassing failure was never completely shelved. Indeed, the plan came to life, wearing a different title but carrying the same message, when on September 1, 1982, President Reagan announced his new peace plan. It was almost a clone of the Rogers plan. Needless to say, the fate of Reagan's initiative was not unlike that of the Rogers plan. It was quietly buried only a few weeks after its birth.

The Rogers plan was based on the principles articulated in President Johnson's Five Principles. Following Johnson's footsteps, Nixon stated that his administration would adhere to, and would try to implement U.N. Resolution 242. He suggested that the time had come to translate these abstract proposals into concrete policies. The new bureaucracy was asked to develop a new and effective peace plan. In his initial press conference, on January 27, 1969, Nixon stressed both the importance of the Middle East to America's national interest and the danger to world peace that the unresolved Israeli-Arab conflict posed: "I believe we need new initiative and new leadership on the part of the United States in order to cool off the situation in the Middle East. I consider it a powder keg, very explosive. It needs to be defused."[23]

Nixon defined his new initiative to mean that the United States would continue to support the Jarring mission, to carry on bilateral and four-power talks in the United Nations, to maintain discussions with Israel and the Arab states, and to offer regional economic assistance. The State Department, however, departed from Johnson's principles and developed a concept based on the principle of "evenhandedness," which basically meant restraining the political support of Israel as well as the delivery of arms.

The State Department urged the President to review the existing arms deals with Israel and to exercise restraint until a territorial withdrawal would be agreed upon. As to the quality of the peace agreement, the standards to be applied to Arab commitments were not overtly rigorous. From the Israeli perspective, an even-handed American policy was tantamount to being pro-Arab.[24] The State Department believed that shift in the U.S. approach was needed because the foreign policy strategists of their predecessors had missed opportunities to achieve more substantial progress toward a stabilizing settlement of the Arab-Israeli conflict.[25]

Interestingly, when Nixon assumed office in January 1969, the Middle East was not his first priority. He was totally consumed by the Vietnam War, which he had promised during his election campaign to bring to an end. His second priority was U.S.-U.S.S.R. relations and how to secure global stability. His third priority was China. In an article published in 1967, he wrote: "Any American policy toward Asia must come urgently to grips with the reality of China."[26] The Middle East ranked fourth on Nixon's foreign policy priority list. He decided to engage himself and his newly appointed National Security Adviser, Henry Kissinger, in the global issues and the resolution of the Vietnam War, leaving the regional problems of the Middle East to the Department of State, headed by his old friend, William Rogers. Nixon's early approach to the Middle East was influenced by his underestimation of the seriousness of the Soviet involvement in the region. Also, he believed that any solution should be worked out through international diplomacy and in cooperation with France, England, and the Soviet Union. He assumed that the State Department bureaucracy was best equipped for such diplomatic activity. But perhaps the most important factor was Nixon's skepticism of the State Department's hope that a resolution of the conflict was within reach.

Nixon was ready to consign the Middle East to the State Department partly because success seemed very elusive and risks of domestic reaction were high. He feared that any active policy would fail. "In addition it would almost certainly incur the wrath of Israel's supporters. So he found it useful to get the White House as much out of the direct line of fire as possible."[27]

THE ROGERS PEACE PLAN TAKES SHAPE

Following the "blank check" that the Department of State had received from Nixon to develop a new Middle East policy, it embarked on, and became intensely involved with, a comprehensive peace initiative. From its inception, Henry Kissinger, the national security adviser, was opposed to it. On February 1, 1969 the NSC held a meeting dedicated to Middle East policies. Three proposals were discussed: (1) to leave the search for a settlement to the parties and to Ambassador Jarring, (2) adopt an active and independent policy involving U.S.-Soviet talks, and (3) assume that a peace settlement is impossible and concentrate efforts on objectives short of a settlement.[28]

The second alternative was decided on, with the third, which was Kissinger's preference, remaining available as a fall-back plan. The State Department insisted on this policy because it wrongly assumed that the Soviet Union would cooperate with the United States even at a cost of straining its relations with Nasser. This premise was based on the misperception that the U.S.S.R. would trade off regional interests for global interests. In other words, Rogers assumed that the Soviets would sacrifice their interests in the Middle East for the sake of improving their relations with the United States. Kissinger and others in the NSC were highly skeptical. They assumed that the U.S.S.R.'s position of influence in the Middle East was dependent chiefly on providing arms to its key clients. If peace was established, these arms would no longer be needed in large quantities. "The Soviets, therefore, had an interest in preventing a real peace agreement, preferring instead a state of controlled tension."[29]

A similar difference of opinion concerned the State Department's belief that both superpowers had the leverage and the will to coerce their respective clients to accept a comprehensive settlement. By mobilizing France and England, Rogers and Sisco hoped to achieve a universal consensus, followed by a universal determination to use all tactics available (mainly the withholding of arms) to coerce Israel and the Arab states to reach a settlement.

As a result, Rogers was willing to withhold arms shipments to Israel, disregarding the fact that it would weaken both U.S. and Israeli power positions. Moreover, Rogers wrongly believed that a settlement was in the Soviet interest; in effect the U.S.S.R.'s interest was to prolong "controlled tension." In the short run the State Department could overlook its conflict of interest with the U.S.S.R. and could pressure Israel even at the risk of dangerously weakening an important ally. In the long run, however, the United States had to face the "facts of life" and move away from policies that were detrimental to Israel and ultimately to the United States, namely, ending the tactic of withholding arms as leverage.

The new American approach had an immediate effect on the delivery of arms to Israel. The first issue was the delivery of the fifty F–4 Phantoms promised by the Johnson administration. Since the actual delivery of the airplanes was scheduled for late 1969, Nixon chose to uphold the deal. However, he decided to withhold all Israeli requests for new weapons as a bargaining chip with the Soviets, assuming that the Soviets would reciprocate by withholding deliveries of arms to their clients. In reality the opposite occurred.

The "evenhanded" policy and the intensive search by the State Department for a U.S.-Soviet accord was perceived in Israel as an erosion in American support. Israel became very anxious and suspicious of American policy, and refused to change its position on the withdrawal issue. The Arab states and the Soviet Union were encouraged by this development. They decided to advance SA missiles along the canal and reinforce their troops. Their political expectations had naturally risen. The State Department ignored these developments and continued to believe that the "Big Four" talks would sooner or later yield a settlement.

Charles Yost, U.S. representative to the United Nations, expressed the official view when, on November 18, 1971, he said that because the issues are "inextricably linked, it follows that their ultimate resolution will come only as part of an over-all settlement."[30] The question was, however, whether the deeply rooted conflict that involved several nations with conflicting needs and interests could realistically be expected to find a resolution in a comprehensive-all-encompassing settlement. The hostility between the Jews and the Arabs involved more than territorial disputes. It was rooted in the schism between the two national groups.[31]

Other crucial factors ignored by the architects of the comprehensive settlement concerned the nature of the "package deal" they were creating. They wrongly assumed that it was possible to create a "package deal" that would satisfy the Big Four and the regional actors. Their approach was naive and completely invalid.

Indeed, Washington failed to see that (1) the U.S.S.R. had a vested interest to exacerbate and manipulate the tensions, not help alleviate them, (2) the United States had very little leverage and could not "deliver Israel," i.e., Israel could not be coerced to make concessions; hence, a settlement became practically unattainable, (3) the gap between the Israeli and the Arab demands and interpretation of Resolution 242 could not be bridged at that time, and (4) the U.S. and Soviet conflicting national interests in the Middle East made an accord between them impossible to achieve. Only after the Soviets intensified their military involvement in Egypt and Syria while negotiations were in progress did the State Department acknowledge it.

The Rogers bureaucracy insisted on a comprehensive settlement and rejected Kissinger's suggestion to move cautiously and in small steps. This approach was based on the misperception that only a comprehensive settlement would solve each single issue, since no single issue is soluble unless all are. Moreover, each issue in dispute was viewed as merely one aspect of the overall dispute, which had, therefore, to be resolved in its entirety.

The Rogers approach suffered from an additional flaw. It prescribed solutions before negotiations between the parties began. Israel felt that any suggested peace plan approved by the Big Four would be an imposed settlement, thus making the process of peace negotiations meaningless. In fact, it is surprising that Nixon did not realize that the Rogers initiative was an inevitable political failure before late 1970.

Unlike the State Department bureaucracy, which looked for an American-Soviet rapprochement, Kissinger was alarmed by the Soviet military build-up in the region and did not accept the "linkage theory," which argued that the U.S.S.R. would trade off interests in the Middle East in exchange for American concessions in Vietnam.

It has been suggested that Rogers, a lawyer by profession who had served as attorney general in Eisenhower's Cabinet, was neither particularly experienced in foreign policy nor a strong, assertive personality.[32] Joseph Sisco, who became one of the major actors in the Rogers comprehensive settlement plan, was "not a conventional Foreign Service Officer. He had never served overseas; only the insistence of Dean Rusk had earned him promotion to the highest rank of the service."[33] It was perhaps this lack of experience that led the State Department to underestimate two major changes that took place in the Middle East during that time and that ultimately resulted in the collapse of the American peace initiative. First, the Soviet Union was pursuing an aggressive policy, gaining influence in Egypt, Syria, Iraq, Libya, and South Yemen. Second, President Nasser's increased militancy thwarted Washington's efforts. As early as February 1969 Israeli sources reported 1,288 incidents of sabotage and terrorism inspired and supported by Egypt and Syria in the year and a half following the Six-Day War. Israel's casualties were 234 dead and 765 wounded among military personnel and 47 dead and 330 wounded among civilians—"a staggering total, . . . equivalent to over 20,000 dead and 100,000 wounded for a nation the size of America."[34]

Egyptian aggressiveness was nurtured by increased Soviet aid, especially by the massive transfer of quality and quantity of the most advanced arms, among them some new weapons never before seen outside the Soviet Union. By late 1968 Egyptian and Syrian inventories included new Soviet shipments of at least 150 MIG-21 fighter-jets, and 50 SU-7 later model jet-fighters. The Egyptian ground forces were enhanced by the arrivals of T-54/55 tanks, which were gradually replacing older models supplied right after the Six-Day War. Syrian forces also seemed to improve in both quality and quantity of arms.[35] This massive military build-up was down-played by Washington, which continued to voice impatience with the stalemate and to blame it on Israel's refusal to make territorial concessions.[36]

Governor William Scranton, Nixon's special envoy to the Middle East, declared after a nine-day visit to the region that "it is important that U.S. policy become more even-handed. . . . The U.S. should deal with all countries in the area and not necessarily espouse one."[37] Scranton expressed the prevailing State Department approach, which was advocated mainly by the critics of Israel. The alternative approach criticized the Big Four forum, arguing that "the number of parties and other interested actors who had to be satisfied, and the number of issues that had to be resolved rendered this objective too complex and too difficult"[38] The United States learned the hard way that it should have negotiated with Egypt directly rather than through the Big Four forum. Kissinger, who strongly opposed the prevailing State Department approach, believed that this particular negotiating forum promised hardly any results. Moreover, it was likely to produce a lineup against the United States. He warned against

the constant and fundamental premise—stated explicitly by one of the State Department representatives at the February 1, [1969], NSC meeting—that the U.S. . . . [should] pressure an ally on behalf of countries which . . . pursued policies generally hostile to us, and were clients of Moscow. I therefore doubted the advisability of American pressure . . . until we could see more clearly what concessions the Arabs would make and until those who would benefit from it would be America's friends, not Soviet clients.[39]

In several memoranda that Kissinger had sent Nixon, he argued that the United States would better pursue attainable goals: (1)"a partial settlement, such as one with Jordan, which had a long and honorable record of friendship with the U.S.," (2) conduct exploratory talks with both the Soviet Union and the Arab states before launching a campaign that included detailed peace terms, (3) be patient and wait until Egypt would finally realize that the only hope for a settlement lay with some form of alignment with the United States.[40]

Rogers did not accept Kissinger's view and continued his efforts to reach a universally agreed-upon comprehensive settlement. The American initiative alarmed Israel, even though it was still informal and not conclusive. The timing was also not promising. Prime Minister Eshkol died of a heart attack on February 22, 1969. Golda Meir headed the government until the elections, which were held in November. When Secretary Rogers made his plan public, Israel was in the midst of building a ruling coalition, trying to bridge the rivalries between the prospective partners of a government of National Unity. The new threats to its security resulting from the massive rearming of its defeated adversaries and the Khartum resolution buried Israel's early hopes of reaching individual settlements with Egypt and Syria. Bewildered and anxious, Israel was hardening its position, shifting away from its decision to withdraw to the international borders with Egypt, and uncertain about the American position.[41] It was a real possibility that American support of Israel would decrease, if Israel refused to make concessions demanded by the State Department. Israel, however, rightly gambled that this would be a short-term policy.

THE INEVITABLE FAILURE OF THE
ROGERS PEACE PLAN

The developments that occurred in Egypt during 1969–70 proved that Israel had gambled correctly. During February and March 1969, the State Department was accelerating its negotiations with the Soviet Union. In its zeal to reach a swift, substantive, comprehensive settlement, Washington initiated a succession of proposals, which was exactly what Israel hoped would not happen. The State Department "feared that a deteriorating situation would increase Soviet influ-

ence.'' Kissinger argued that the opposite was true. A settlement accepted by
the U.S.S.R. would show the radical Arab states that the United States was
vulnerable to Soviet pressures. Instead, the United States should demonstrate
that a settlement "could not be extorted from us by Soviet pressure.''[42]

While the State Department was pursuing unrealistic agreements, Nasser embarked on a new campaign against Israel. "It was again President Nasser who
lit the fuse.''[43] In April 1968 Nasser proclaimed a three-stage war against Israel:
(1) reconstruction of the Egyptian army, (2) active defense, and (3) the liberation
of the Israel-held territories. As early as September 8, 1968, Nasser tested his
strategy by launching a massive artillery barrage along the Suez Canal, attacks
that continued through October. Only a strong Israeli retaliation convinced Nasser
that the Egyptian Army was not yet ready for stages two and three of his strategy.
In February 1969, however, on his return from Moscow and on the occasion of
visiting troops along the canal, Nasser proclaimed the beginning of the second
phase in the war against Israel: constant military activity. This declaration began
the war of attrition, which continued until August 1970.[44]

The active phase of the war of attrition began in March 1969, with four months
of massive artillery barrages. The two sides "dealt each other heavy blows, but
the outcome was indecisive. . . . [T]he Egyptians executed many raids . . . but
failed to capture a single stronghold. . . . On the other hand Israel suffered heavy
casualties.''[45] Nasser showed no signs of exhaustion despite Egypt's heavy
losses. It seemed that he was prepared to continue the war indefinitely; Israel,
frustrated and hurt, could not.

With the Soviet Union increasing its penetration into the area and Nasser
intensifying hostilities along the canal, Israel needed American support to counter
these developments, which were hurting both countries. Israel perceived an
overlap of interests, especially in the need to curb Soviet influence and Arab
radicalism. Hence, when Ambassador Rabin met with Kissinger on March 4,
1969, his objective was to secure U.S. support, especially to ask the United
States to accelerate the delivery of arms requested by Israel. Another important
issue was to clarify U.S. policy on borders. Rabin made it clear that Israel,
which then held some important cards in its hand, would not withdraw in return
for nebulous arrangements about the future. Rabin left Washington with the
impression that Kissinger was supportive on both issues. As for the question of
Resolution 242, Kissinger accepted the Israeli position that "withdrawal cannot
be separated from political quid pro quo of the Arabs. There is no substitute for
a contractual agreement between the sides in the Middle East, and peace negotiations must lead to a specific, binding agreement.''[46]

In a meeting between Secretary Rogers and Foreign Minister Eban, which
took place a few weeks later, Rogers reiterated the same theme. However, the
clouds of the U.S.-U.S.S.R. talks, which were conducted between March and
July 1969, were hovering over U.S.-Israeli relations and causing anxiety in Israel.
Because it was not part of the negotiations, Israel feared that Soviet pressure
eroded the American position. Although Rogers assured Eban that there would

be no imposed settlement,[47] there were signs that the United States was contemplating just that, at the same time expecting the Soviet Union to reciprocate by exerting leverage over Egypt. On March 5, 1969, Kissinger, who was aware of the State Department's plan, wrote a memorandum to Nixon explaining why the political dilemmas would make an agreement impossible.

In his memorandum Kissinger explained that the Soviets clearly understood and were aware of the problems of leverage, because of their own experience: "The Soviets—who know the limits of their own influence in Cairo and Damascus—realistically understand the limits of our influence in Jerusalem."[48] He suggested that the State Department be more realistic in its pursuit of a comprehensive peace. Israel, on the eve of an election, was limited in its ability to promise concessions. Washington actually made things worse. Quandt supported this opinion. He argued that the State Department's error "was its underestimation of Israel's will and ability to resist American pressure." He added that Nixon was misguided by his bureaucracy to adopt a possibly dangerous policy, namely, "to try to improve its relations with adversaries—the Soviet Union and Egypt—by pressuring one's own friend, Israel."[49]

While the White House and the State Department were at odds over U.S. policy, the war of attrition was escalating along the canal. Israel and Egypt hardened their positions, whereas the Soviet Union exacerbated the confrontation by intensifying the military build-up of Egypt and Syria. Secretary Rogers, yet unwilling to face the regional and global realities that rendered his peace efforts futile, continued to pursue his unrealistic peace initiative. On March 10, 1969, Rogers presented Nixon with his latest proposal, entitled "General Principles" or the "Nine Points" proposal. This was the rough draft of his famous peace plan, which he made public on December 9 of that year.

Rogers aspired to achieve a binding, contractual agreement, though not necessarily a peace treaty. His Nine Points proposal included major concessions to answer Soviet demands. He was ready to accept indirect negotiations, hoping that direct contact would occur at some future time. His plan allowed for minimal changes from pre-existing borders, and such changes "should not reflect the weight of conquest" (a euphemism for insisting on near-total Israeli withdrawal). Rogers was fully prepared to pressure Israel as much as would be necessary to impose a settlement.[50] Rogers also favored an imposed agreement, violating past American promises to Israel.

Nixon approved the plan, although he was skeptical about its chances of success. He told Kissinger that "it would give State something to do, while he handled Vietnam, SALT, Europe, and China." Kissinger assumed that Nixon probably gave Rogers an opposite explanation.[51]

After receiving Nixon's approval, Rogers and Sisco went ahead with full steam. Between March 18 and April 22, Assistant Secretary Sisco met with Soviet Ambassador Dobrynin on nine occasions,[52] while along the canal the situation deteriorated significantly. Backed by massive inventories of Soviet arms, Nasser announced the abrogation of the 1967 cease-fire. The State Department ignored the concerted Soviet-Egyptian aggression and continued to pursue Soviet cooperation on a settlement.

During the second week of May, Sisco conveyed a Nine Point proposal to Dobrynin. It was a revision of previous proposals rejected by the Soviet Union for being too generous to Israel. Each proposal included additional American concessions. In mid-October Israel learned that the State Department intended to modify one of the main points in the proposal that Sisco had submitted to Moscow that summer. Instead of suggesting that Israel would not "exclude" the international boundary as a future border between Egypt and Israel, the United States was now proposing that this border would be the final line, negotiations notwithstanding. Sisco acknowledged that the change was included in a new draft submitted to Moscow.[53] Israel argued that the new proposal was an unnecessary capitulation to Soviet pressure.

The Soviet sophisticated political strategy was based on intimidation tactics. While negotiating a peace settlement, it was supporting Egypt's war of attrition along the canal. The Soviet strategy, which seemed to escape the comprehension of the State Department, successfully linked the escalation of the war with their diplomatic activities in the two superpowers, and the Four Powers talks. The scheme was simple. Fear of escalating military activities would soften the American position and would result in more U.S. concessions.

Consequently, during May and June Egypt stepped up the hostilities along the canal. This had a direct impact on the Soviet-American talks, while it weakened and inflicted great damage on Israel. The ultimate goal of the coordinated Egyptian-Soviet aggression was to undermine America's position and influence in the Arab world. The Russians were exploiting the fighting to wear down American resistance to their demands. Simultaneously, the Palestine Liberation Organization (PLO) was gaining ground in Jordan and posing a threat to King Hussein; King Idris's regime in Libya collapsed; extremist elements were trying to overthrow the Saudi monarchy; and it seemed likely that the oil resources would slip out of Western hands and right into Russia's lap.[54] Israel tried in vain to convince the State Department that its concessions were not reciprocated nor did they promise a termination of the war of attrition. It expressed strong objections to the latest U.S. proposal of the summer of 1969, arguing that the U.S.S.R. was serving as the Arab's advocate, using the war as an intimidation tactic.

Satisfied with U.S. concessions, Dobrynin suggested to Kissinger, on April 14, that he would recommend the U.S. proposal to Egypt if it would be more specific on each of the principles. Kissinger felt that Dobrynin was in effect asking the United States to accept the Arab position, and Kissinger's theory was reinforced by the Egyptian press. It "readily admitted that hostilities were being manipulated by Cairo to raise the diplomatic stakes."[55] Secretary Rogers disagreed with Kissinger and argued that a detailed American peace plan was necessary to enhance the U.S. position in the Arab world "even if it were rejected."[56]

He was confident that the Big Four talks would produce an agreement, whereas Israel believed that it was a futile diplomatic exercise. Moreover, it raised Arab and Soviet expectations and induced Nasser to intensify the hostilities. During 1969–70 Nasser was more militant and noncompromising than the U.S.S.R. When a Soviet delegation arrived in Cairo, in July 1969, with a compromise formula, Nasser, who was inflicting heavy casualties on Israel, refused to go along.[57] Finally, no American concessions could save the Big Four talks, which had begun in April. By June they were put on an intermittent basis.

After the United States submitted numerous proposals to the U.S.S.R., Dobrynin presented a counterproposal to Sisco on June 17, 1969. Surprisingly, it included some concessions. First, the U.S.S.R. rescinded its demand for an early Israeli withdrawal. Second, it agreed to a linkage, that is, a simultaneous implementation of all provisions of the settlement. Finally, it agreed to the Rhodes formula, which included some form of face-to-face negotiations. On the substantive issues, however, the Soviets continued to object to direct negotiations, opposed any border adjustment, even minor, and demanded a unilateral Israeli withdrawal. The questions of demilitarization of the Sinai, Israel's right of free navigation, and a contractual peace remained ambiguous.[58]

Rogers was optimistic, considering the Soviet proposal an important move toward peace. He was sure that the Soviets were ready to trade off Israeli concessions on borders with Arab concessions on contractual peace. He ignored the fact that the negotiations were deadlocked and that the Soviets never accepted the trade-off formula. Encouraged by the success of the Soviet diplomatic maneuvers, Nasser announced on July 23 that Egypt "was [now] passing into the 'stage of liberation' in its war with Israel. . . . [He strongly] condemned the United States and Britain for supporting Israel."[59]

Ignoring these developments, Rogers continued to pursue an accord with the U.S.S.R. He was ready to coerce Israel, if needed, to accept the agreed-upon proposal. He considered withholding of weapons as a legitimate and effective tactic. The war of attrition had made Israel more dependent on the United States than ever before. Following this policy, the United States tested its leverage when Prime Minister Golda Meir visited Washington on September 25, 1969. "Her themes with Nixon were simple: [Nasser should not be allowed to] avoid responsibility for making peace by getting others to settle the terms; the Soviet Union had to know that the U.S. would not permit Israel to be destroyed. . . . Only this would bring peace."[60]

Prime Minister Meir reiterated Israel's demands and linked Israeli withdrawal with arms, asking for an additional 25 F–4 Phantoms and 100 A–4 Skyhawks (the two most advanced fighter-bombers at that time). Israel also requested $750 million in economic aid for the following five years.[61] Rogers suggested to Nixon that he use the request as leverage to attain otherwise unacceptable territorial concessions. With these policy recommendations before him, Nixon developed his new policy of "hardware for software." This meant that Israel's arms requests would be approved if the Israelis showed more flexibility in the negotiations. Nixon's ''hardware for software'' formula ''was leaked to the press in a way that implied that arms aid would . . . be conditional.''[62]

Prime Minister Meir was furious. Summoning Ambassador Rabin, she asked to speak to Kissinger.[63] She rightly targeted her outraged protest on the State Department,[64] and expressed dismay at its myopia. Denying Israel arms meant weakening an ally at a most crucial time, when the Soviets were strengthening their positions and massively arming Egypt and Syria. It was a show of American weakness vis-à-vis Soviet political pressure. Israel argued that only the combination of a militarily strong Israel with a politically strong America would curb Soviet adventurism and advance the cause of peace.

The State Department rejected Israel's arguments regardless of the fact that no progress was made in the negotiations. The position taken by Rogers exacerbated the conflict between the United States and Israel. While fighting a long and bitter war along the canal against Egypt and the Soviet Union, Israel felt very frustrated by American withholding of arms. Israel's main contention was that the United States should not dictate the terms for peace. In a press conference, Rogers argued that the United States had the right and the intention to do just that:

Q: Mr. Secretary, the Israeli criticism is that it should not be the American function to suggest specific proposals which the Israelis feel prejudice their case?

A: Well, we just don't agree to that. . . . We have to conduct our foreign policy in a way that we think is best for our national interest.[65]

Although Rogers denied any linkage between the pending request for additional arms and the peace process,[66] the United States was holding up all new Israeli aid requests. This policy antagonized both Israel and the Arab states; Israel because its new arms requests were denied, and the Arab states because Israel began to receive, on September 1969, the fifty F–4 Phantom jets promised by Johnson. These plans enabled Israel to launch deep penetration air raids against Egypt.

After a year of negotiations, it was clear that neither the Soviets nor Egypt were planning to make meaningful concessions. Rogers, however, caught in misperceptions, continued to stress the need for Israeli concessions on borders, indirect negotiations, and a contractual agreement short of a peace treaty. He still believed that the U.S.S.R. would reciprocate by delivering Nasser, and he genuinely felt that his proposal was fair and generous to both sides. The State Department ''gambled [that the plan] would be attractive enough to persuade Israel to withdraw and to convince the Soviets to press Egypt. Both hopes were to be disappointed.''[67]

The government of Israel was hoping that the Rogers plan in its October form would never become the official American policy. Kissinger, too, repeated his objection to Nixon saying, ''It cannot produce a solution without massive pressure on Israel."[68] Kissinger's argument was that the Soviet aggressive policy threatened vital American interests in the region. Containment required a strong and reliable ally there; hence, withholding arms to Israel was against American interests. On the regional level, the State Department underestimated Nasser's militancy and his pan-Arab aspirations. Both were enhanced and promoted by Nasser's war against Israel. A premature Israeli withdrawal could, therefore, be a grave strategic mistake. Only a strong Israel could contain the Soviets and curb Arab radicalism. (When in 1970 Israel was requested to stop a Syrian invasion of Jordan, it proved this point.) While the controversy concerning U.S. policy was going on, Rogers made his peace plan public.

The speech by Rogers further complicated Israel's already difficult political situation. Besides the real war with Egypt and the proxy war with the U.S.S.R., Israel was now faced with a political war with the United States (which began pressuring Israel to accept a proposal that threatened its security).

On December 9, 1969, at the Galaxy Conference on Adult Education, Secretary Rogers announced his peace plan. Only a few weeks earlier, Israel's newly elected government had called for retention of Israel's control over Jerusalem, the Gaza Strip, and the Golan Heights, and for a territorial link to Sharm-al-Sheik. Rogers chose not to inform Israel of his proposal, and the "timing and sudden manner of its revelation created a sense of crisis . . . provoked a predicated diplomatic backlash . . . and contributed to the formation of new 'national unity' coalition, in which Begin and other Israeli 'hawks' retained a role."[69]

The speech was entitled: "A Lasting Peace in the Middle East: An American View," and it suggested comprehensive solutions to the issue of peace, security, withdrawal, and territory. On the first issue, *peace*, Rogers avoided the Israeli demand for a contractual peace and suggested navigation rights and a universal respect for sovereignty. On the second issue, *security*, Rogers talked vaguely on "demilitarized zones and related security arrangements." Shunning the issue of direct negotiations, he suggested that "the parties themselves, with Ambassador Jarring's help . . . work out the . . . details of such security arrangements." On the third issue, *withdrawal and territory*, Rogers referred to Resolution 242 and called for an Israeli withdrawal "from territories occupied in the 1967 war . . . [and] the nonacquisition of territory by war. . . . [A]ny changes in the preexisting lines . . . should be confined to insubstantial alterations required for mutual security." Rogers declared: "We do not support expansionism." He insisted that both sides had to make concessions, although the concessions that he demanded of the Arab states were trivial compared to the substantial concessions Israel was asked to make.

For reasons known only to him, Secretary Rogers chose to join together the two most controversial issues: "refugees and Jerusalem." He strongly urged a just settlement for those Palestinians who had been made homeless in the wars of 1948 and 1967. The United States contributed about $500 million for the Palestinian refugees and was prepared to contribute generously along with others to solve this problem. On the question of Jerusalem, the Secretary suggested that the city should not be divided. "Jerusalem should be a unified city. . . . Arrangements for the administration of the unified city should take into account the interests of all its inhabitants . . . and there should be roles for both Israel and Jordan in the civic, economic, and religious life of the city." Rogers avoided Israel's claim that Jerusalem was the civil capital of Israel. He ended his speech with praise for the comprehensive settlement approach, saying that "these questions of refugees and Jerusalem, as well as other aspects of the conflict, can be resolved as part of the overall settlement."[70] Israel wondered whether it could reject the Rogers plan without creating a major crisis in U.S.-Israel relations.

The realities of the Middle East, namely, the history of the Israeli-Arab conflict, could not support the comprehensive approach. The question of the refugees was not related to the border dispute between Israel and Egypt; as Syrian hostility to the very existence of Israel was not related to the problem of a united Jerusalem. The different problems involved different actors with different political aspirations and different national interests. Nothing indicated that a comprehensive settlement was the right approach. To the contrary, a nonambitious, step-by-step diplomacy using a strategy that separated the issues as much as possible and sought bilateral agreements looked much more promising.

Israel did not regard the dispute over direct or indirect negotiations as a technical question because it symbolized Arab nonrecognition of Israel. It also put in question the good faith of the Arab states in the negotiations. If the Arab states were ready to make peace, why wouldn't they talk to the Israelis? The Arab position reinforced the rejectionist approach expressed by the Khartum resolution, which was never denounced. To expect Israel to withdraw under these circumstances was at best very naive. As expected, only a few hours after it had been announced, the Rogers plan was universally rejected. Israel argued that it was too generous to the Arab countries; the Arab states felt that it was too generous to Israel. The Egyptian press defined the plan "as an American trick to pretend to Arabs that the United States was impartial, as well as to undermine Soviet-Egyptian relations."[71]

The Soviet Union, probably caught by surprise, issued an initial positive response saying that "the Rogers speech was long overdue."[72] Later, however, the U.S.S.R. shifted its position to be in line with the Egyptians. "The Soviets, in the wake of a high-level visit to Cairo in December 1969, had reversed their conditional acceptance of the compromise Rogers proposal."[73]

The strongest reaction came from Israel. The American proposal convinced the Likud party to join the newly elected government in order to create a unified front against possible U.S. efforts to force the proposal on Israel. The part in the Rogers plan that surprised Israel the most was the suggestion about the future of the West Bank and Jerusalem. Israel's first reaction was an official cabinet announcement dated December 10, rejecting the plan in all its parts. "Mrs. Meir was 'bitterly disappointed' and 'heartbroken' and thought the situation 'a scandal' and 'calamitous.' "[74]

On December 22, the Israeli government issued a statement saying: "Israel will reject any attempt to impose a forced solution upon her. . . . The proposal . . . is . . . an attempt to appease the Arabs at Israel's expense."[75] Israel dispatched Foreign Minister Eban on December 16 to Washington to meet with Secretary Rogers. The atmosphere of their talk was far from cordial. Rogers insisted that the U.S. policy had not changed; Israel had changed by retreating from its decision of June 19, 1967, to restore the whole of the Sinai to Egypt. "Israel can't expect to decide on changes and have the U.S. conform to her policy," Sisco chided the Israeli delegation.[76]

Israel argued in vain that the hardening in its position was in response to Arab intransigence, specifically to the Khartum resolution. The State Department refused to accept the argument that the key to a settlement was Arab concessions. During a National Security Council meeting of December 10, the State Department presented an expanded, new proposal "to put forward a plan on Jordan comparable to that on Egypt."[77] It is difficult to comprehend the motivation to expand the Rogers peace initiative in view of its rejection by all involved. Moreover, in his meeting with Foreign Minister Eban, Rogers was informed that Israel was conducting direct negotiations with King Hussein and preferred to continue them without U.S. interference.

"We are talking with the Jordanians about territorial changes, principally in the Jordan valley . . . if the U.S. publicizes its view that Israel must withdraw from all the territories—including those on the Jordanian border—that will put an end to the contacts."[78] This was, however, exactly what Rogers had done. His reasons, as Kissinger had put it, were inexplicable: "What possessed the Department to persevere when all the evidence indicated certain failure must be left to students of administrative psychology. Perhaps when enough bureaucratic prestige has been invested in a policy it is easier to see it fail then to abandon it."[79]

The new Rogers proposal included eleven points, among them a demand for an Israeli withdrawal from the West Bank, an option to the Palestinian refugees to return to Palestine, and a suggestion of a joint Jordanian-Israeli administrative body that would run a unified Jerusalem. The proposal was presented by Charles Yost to the representatives of the Big Four in the United Nations on December 18, 1969. The plan resembled the first Rogers plan and suggested that "the permanent border would approximate the armistice demarcation line existing before the 1967 war, but would allow for modifications based on administrative or economic convenience."[80]

The State Department made two puzzling decisions: (1) not to tell Eban that Yost had been instructed to submit the proposal only a few hours later, and (2) to introduce a proposal only three days before the Arab summit meeting at Rabat. It was bound to create unnecessary pressure on the moderate Arab states to reject it.

Sisco, the architect of the Jordanian plan, claimed that the timing was intended to shatter Arab unity and to strengthen the moderate Arab states by providing them a plan that actually meant the "delivery of Israel." In the short term, Sisco was right. The Rabat meeting ended unresolved, and Nasser left Rabat frustrated and vowing, "I will fight alone."[81] In the long run, however, the situation only got worse. The American concessions did not induce the Soviets or the Egyptians to do the same. In fact, the Soviet Union rejected the new American proposal in its entirety.[82] Kissinger was not surprised; rather, he believed that "a steady stream of American concessions would increase Soviet temptations to act as the lawyer for [the] Arab radicals."[83] At the NSC meeting on December 10, 1969, Kissinger suggested that the United States should stop the flow of proposals and stop pressuring Israel to accept them. A stalemate in the situation would convince the Arab radicals that their only hope for a settlement was the United States. "The longer the stalemate continued the more obvious it would become that the Soviet Union had failed to deliver what the Arabs wanted."[84] This strategy, however, was adopted only in 1970, or as Kissinger said, "over the corpses of various State Department peace plans."[85]

Israel was outraged by the Jordanian plan. It found itself in an unprecedented situation. The United States was initiating settlement proposals that would weaken Israel along its eastern and southern borders. It was clear that Jordan could not cooperate because of the Khartum resolution. Hence, Rabin, the Israeli ambassador to Washington, suggested an Israeli countermeasure. Following the principle that "offense is the best defense," he suggested that Israel would escalate the war of attrition and carry it into the Egyptian heartland. As early as September 1969, Rabin suggested deep penetration air raids into Egypt.

The NSC had given careful consideration to the possible effect of the raids on the stability of Nasser's regime. Israel argued that it was likely to lead to far-reaching results, that is, that Nasser's standing could be undermined, which would weaken the Soviet position in the region. Some even argued that the raids might result in Nasser's overthrow. Rabin believed that the Nixon administration favored the air raids and considered them "the most encouraging breath of fresh air the American administration has enjoyed recently."[86]

It is difficult to determine exactly how the idea of the deep air raids was born. Although Rabin attributed it to himself, many in Israel disagree. They mention the pivotal role of General Mordechi Hod, then the Air Force Chief of Staff. The role of the United States has been another source of controversy. It was unclear whether the United States would support the raids. Rabin, who was sure of U.S. support, if not openly, at least tacitly, said that "a man has to be blind, deaf, and dumb not to sense how much the administration favors our military operations." Moreover, the United States would supply Israel additional arms necessary to step up the military activity with the aim of undermining Nasser's standing. Thus the U.S. supply of arms depended more on stepping up Israel's military activity against Egypt than on reducing it. Israel's hidden agenda in escalating the war of attrition might have been to end American peace initiatives and justify Israel's rejection of the Rogers plan.

The Israeli and Soviet rejections of the plan put a sudden end to the first

Middle East initiative of the Nixon administration. With it died Nixon's effort to create linkage between Vietnam and the Middle East, which he hoped would help provide the key to peace in the Middle East.[87] The termination of the Rogers initiative was perceived in Israel as a green light for an escalation of the war of attrition. But in feeling that any decline in Nasser's prestige would undermine the Soviet position or that bombings might result in Nasser's overthrow, Israel, as it learned later, could not have been more wrong.

It was unclear "who was the horse and who was the carriage" in the Arab-Soviet pursuit of escalating the war of attrition. In 1969 most members of the Israeli Cabinet believed that the Soviet Union was more moderate than Nasser. Thus they hoped that "the bombing would instigate a Soviet reaction to restrain Nasser's radical policies."[88] But Nasser survived the war and even gained strength.

A crucial factor in Israel's decision to launch the air raids was the assumption that the Soviets would not get too involved. Those who opposed the escalation of the war (members of the leftist Mapam party) disagreed. On January 7, 1970, Israeli F–4 Phantom jets crossed the cease-fire lines and bombed the heartland of Egypt. Only ten days earlier, on December 28, a group of Israeli paratroopers landed beyond the Egyptian border and captured a new, sophisticated Soviet antiaircraft radar installation. (The radar was transferred to Israel by helicopters.) The sky was clear on January 7 and Israel bombed targets as close as fifteen miles from Cairo and the Nile Delta. Israel believed that the bombing demonstrated Nasser's impotence and would force him to end the war. However, the bombing was counterproductive; the Soviets did not keep a low profile and Israel was faced with grave, unintended consequences. The U.S.S.R. seized the opportunity, stepped up its own involvement in the region, and increased its power and influence.

"At the end of January, Nasser suddenly paid a secret visit to Moscow. Thereafter, the problems of the Middle East began increasingly to merge with the relations of the superpowers."[89] Egypt and the Soviet Union were coordinating their reaction to the new Israeli strategy, which took them by surprise. The first Soviet move was to deliver a strong protest letter, dated January 31, 1970, from Premier Kosygin to the leaders of the Big Four, warning them that if the raids continued "the Soviet Union will be forced to see to it that the Arab states have means . . . [to rebuff] the arrogant aggressor." The Soviet letter demanded a complete and speedy withdrawal of Israeli forces from all the occupied Arab territories.[90]

Second, the Soviet deployed SAM–3 surface-to-air missiles in Egypt and dispatched over 10,000 advisers, including Soviet combat pilots, flying air cover missions over Egypt. Consequently, the Nixon administration was faced with two urgent problems. First, it needed to reduce the dangerous tension between Israel and Egypt before it spilled over into a superpower confrontation. Second, it had to address the broader issue of peace, following the failure of the Rogers plan. In fact, Nixon had to assess the impact of the Israeli air raids in both global and regional terms. Moreover, he had to assess the impact of the massive transfer of Soviet arms and military personnel on the region's strategic balance. This analysis was necessary for the development of U.S. policy toward Israel. The American "evenhanded" approach and the question of leverage had to be answered. Nixon could not determine whether the United States should pressure Israel and whether this would be reciprocated by the Soviets. Would the Soviets stop, or at least limit, the delivery of arms to the Arab states? Should the United States stop arms shipments to Israel?

Israel requested an additional 25 F–4 Phantoms and 100 A–4 Skyhawks. Nixon was pressured from both sides. Domestic pressures mounted to abandon the Rogers plan and to move away from the "evenhanded" approach that catered in vain to the radical Arab states and the Soviet Union. On the other hand, the State Department wanted to suspend all arms shipments to Israel until it stopped the deep penetration bombing, accepted a cease-fire, and made concessions toward a comprehensive settlement.

In early 1970 the United States adopted a compromise policy. On February 4, Nixon sent a very strong and unequivocal reply to the Soviet protest letter rejecting Soviet allegations that the Rogers plan was a cover for the Israeli air raids. It stressed the point that Egypt had initiated the war of attrition and was deliberately escalating the hostilities. The President warned that "the Soviet threat to expand arms shipments, if carried out, could draw the major powers more deeply into the conflict."[91]

Nixon, however, wished to induce Soviet cooperation, so he decided to withhold Israel's request for additional arms. On January 30, Israel was informed that its request was being withheld for 30 days. The message to the Soviets was clear: either they stop the flow of arms to Egypt and Syria or the United States would waive all restrictions and answer all Israeli arms requests.

The State Department assumed that it would be possible to use withholding of arms as leverage. However, U.S. policy on that question was ambiguous, and conflicting statements were issued by the State Department and the White House saying that "the time has passed in which great nations can dictate to small nations their future where their vital interests are involved."[92]

Nixon's policy of hardware for software exemplified this approach. Should Israel soften its position on territorial concessions, shipments of arms would follow. Aid commitments were periodically announced simply to soften the blow of unattractive political proposals. Hence, withholding of arms to Israel served two purposes: (1) to bring the Soviets to suspend all arms shipments to Egypt, and (2) to coerce Israel to stop the bombing and accept a cease-fire. The first goal was not achieved. The second was achieved almost a year later, but for reasons not related to U.S. policy.

The withholding announcement created anger and frustration in Jerusalem. "Arms sales became the symbol of U.S.-Israeli relations."[93] The fact that the delay was also an ultimatum to the Soviets and the Arab states did not reduce Israeli anger. "This . . . was an attempt to exercise influence on more than one target. . . . Decisions about arms transfers to Israel were made with an eye not only on Israel and the Arabs, but also—on the Soviet Union.''[94] The policy did not attain its goals. As noted earlier, the Soviet Union stepped up its arms shipments to Egypt.

During the spring of 1970 the Israeli-Egyptian war of attrition intensified. Israel expanded its bombing raids deep into the Egyptian interior, and the Soviets reacted by accelerating their military build-up in Egypt. In March Israel reported that 16,000 Soviet military personnel were deployed in Egypt, including fighter pilots, some of whom engaged in air battles with Israeli pilots. Nixon's deadline of thirty days had long passed, but no official response was given to Israel concerning its request for planes. Washington was still hoping that the U.S.S.R. would cooperate.

During February and March, while Washington and Moscow were negotiating a cease-fire and containment of the hostilities along the canal, the U.S.S.R. continued its massive arms shipments to Egypt. These included SAM–3 anti-aircraft missiles, never before given to a foreign country, not even to North Vietnam. ''The missiles were accompanied by 1,500 Soviet military personnel. . . . Never before had they put their own military personnel in jeopardy for a non-Communist country.''[95]

The American reaction was more than surprising. On March 23, only a few weeks after the promised decision on arms to Israel was due, Secretary Rogers said that ''the President has decided to hold in abeyance Israel's request for additional aircraft.''[96] To Israel's dismay, Rogers added that ''in our judgment, Israel's air capacity is sufficient to meet its needs for the time being.''[97] Rogers expected Israel to stop the air raids and was not ready to admit that his peace initiative failed. Kissinger criticized strongly this approach.

Indeed, two diametrically opposed opinions emerged in Washington. Rogers and other State Department officials blamed the impasse in the peace process on Israeli intransigence. They were convinced that if Israel would receive a new large-scale military aid package, as it requested, it would ''blow the place apart.'' The opposite opinion was that if Israel did not receive the aid, the chances of a Middle East explosion would increase. Kissinger, who advocated the latter view, got in touch with John Haldeman, Nixon's Chief of Staff, and asked him to convey to the President his deep concerns about the plan to cut off Israel's military aid. Kissinger argued that ''this would head us into a simultaneous confrontation with the Soviets and the Israelis.'' Kissinger believed that the Soviets were planning some unspecified military move and that this was not the right time to withhold arms to Israel ''against which this imminent Soviet move was directed.''[98]

Ambassador Rabin, the strong advocate of the deep penetration raids, incorrectly assumed no link between the withholding of arms and the bombing. The F–4 Phantoms were only ''a pawn in the interpower chess match.''[99] In fact the bombing provided the U.S.S.R. with a golden opportunity to enhance their influence through the increased transfers of arms and military personnel. However, Rabin was partially correct about Egypt. Having suffered heavy blows that threatened his prestige, Nasser urged Moscow to stop the Israeli bombing through a bilateral agreement with the United States. He also asked for additional military aid.[100]

In answer, Dobrynin presented to the White House, on March 10, a proposal for tension reduction measures that included some Soviet concessions: (1) a de facto cease-fire along the canal if Israel stopped the bombing, (2) the U.S.S.R. would accept the principle that a settlement would not only end the state of war but would establish a state of peace, and (3) the Arab governments would control the guerrilla forces operating from their territories.[101]

The State Department was elated. "Our policy of relative firmness has paid off on all contested issues."[102] State Department efforts to mend fences with Egypt gained new momentum. Between April 10 and 14, Sisco visited Egypt and offered Nasser U.S. evenhanded mediation. In his May speech, Nasser rejected the offer saying: "The U.S., in taking one more step on the path to securing military superiority for Israel, will . . . effect the relations of the U.S. and the Arab nations for decades, and maybe, for hundreds of years. . . . There will be either rupture forever, or . . . another serious and defined beginning."[103]

Nasser's ultimatum reinforced the State Department's desire to withhold all arms shipments to Israel. Washington embraced Egypt's position without realizing that Nasser offered nothing in return for Israeli and American concessions. Nor did the hailed Soviet proposal address the crucial question of continued shipment of advanced weapons to Egypt while the United States was withholding arms to Israel. The shift in the strategic balance was inevitable, especially with the presence of Soviet military personnel in Egypt. The time of euphoria in Washington, thus, did not last long.

Israel and the United States could not have been more divided on the issue of a cease-fire. The United States viewed it as a stabilizing act, reducing tensions between the regional and global actors. It might even bring Nasser back home to the West. Israel, however, believed that a cease-fire as demanded by Nasser would only save his neck, help restore his prestige, and strengthen the Soviet position. Not only was the U.S. policy of withholding arms not reciprocated, but the U.S.S.R. accelerated its arms shipments to Egypt. It seemed that the Soviets stepped up their involvement in Egypt with each act of withholding of U.S. arms. This produced deep concerns in Israel.[104]

On April 29, the Israeli daily *Ha'aretz* published, in a special edition, what Israeli intelligence knew for many weeks: that Soviet pilots were flying Egyptian air force planes. The Israeli government viewed this as a dangerous development in the Middle East.[105] Israel assumed that the Soviet Union would refrain from engaging its pilots in air battles with Israeli pilots, and that Soviet military personnel would not operate the SAM missiles. Both assumptions were incorrect.

A *New York Times* report of June 26 explained the U.S. policy, arguing that the State Department's approach was a result of three considerations. First, withholding of arms would coerce Israel to be more restrained in its military activity. Second, it would coerce Israel to comply with American demands for political concessions. Third, the United States hoped that "if American arms supplies could be kept within modest limits, the Soviets might be comparably retrained." The State Department feared that a new arms deal with Israel might provoke the Soviets to increase their military activities in Egypt.[106]

Nixon's policy gained very little success. Israel continued its air raids and Egypt continued its war along the canal. A cease-fire became Nixon's first priority. However, Israel rejected a cease fire at that juncture because it assumed that a new status quo would give Egypt a strategic advantage.

It became clear that the United States could not approach Israel with a request for a cease-fire while rejecting its weapon requests. Kissinger claimed that he came up with the compromise formula. He suggested to Nixon to define new arms shipments to Israel as "replacements" of lost weapons with up to eight Phantoms and twenty Skyhawks in 1970. This should satisfy Israel's request and would not cause Arab protests.[107]

Ambassador Rabin had a different account. At the March 18 meeting, Nixon suggested replacing "any of your planes put out of action." Kissinger then suggested, "Why don't we reach prior agreement on the numbers going out of action?" Nixon objected to an agreed-upon number of replaced planes, and Rabin understood that Israel's only chance to get the additional Phantoms was to agree to a cease-fire.[108]

In April Rabin advised his government to stop the air raids. Moreover, the deployment of the SAM-3 missiles had resulted in heavy losses to Israel's air force. An additional concern was the possible risk of engaging Soviet pilots and missile crews in air combat with Israeli forces. The air raids had become a military and political risk. Nasser's regime was not undermined and Soviet influence was getting stronger. A change in policy was clearly needed.

In Washington the picture did not look good either. The evenhanded policy had not improved U.S.-Arab relations. To the contrary, Soviet influence had spread to Syria, Libya, Iraq, South Yemen, and Ethiopia. The weakening of Israel by withholding of arms seemed dangerous and unwise.

On April 30 (the same day that Nixon announced the Cambodian operation), Kissinger informed Ambassador Rabin that the White House was carrying out an "immediate and full" review of the situation. Kissinger was authorized to tell Rabin that the United States would probably provide Israel with additional planes, despite Nixon's earlier decision.[109]

This commitment was reiterated by Nixon when he met with Foreign Minister Eban on May 21. Nixon asked Eban not to make the renewed arms shipments public. It was important to the peace process that the quantities not be revealed. Under these conditions Nixon promised Eban four airplanes per month, enough to satisfy Israel's needs.[110] Simultaneously, Israel ended the deep penetration air raids, and the road to a cease-fire opened. In mid-June the first positive signals were seen from both Egypt and Israel. The United States worked directly with the parties because the situation was "sufficiently serious and at the same time sufficiently promising to warrant this dramatic departure from the Big-Four format."[111]

On June 19, 1970, Secretary Rogers made his new initiative public, proposing that Egypt, Jordan, and Israel "stop shooting and start talking, for at least ninety days."[112] Rogers also suggested that the parties use Jarring as a go-between. He wished to achieve not only a cease-fire but a resumption of the Jarring talks. Rogers hoped that a reduction in Israeli-Egyptian tension would weaken Soviet influence and strengthen the U.S. power position in Egypt and the other Arab states.[113]

Although Israel was not informed or consulted about the new peace initiative, it was expected to embrace the formula of software for hardware, namely, a cease-fire exchange for Phantoms. This was a far cry from the American demand a year earlier for an Israeli acceptance of the Rogers comprehensive peace plan. Clearly, the regional and global dilemmas were responsible for the shift in U.S. policy. Indeed, Nasser's pan-Arabism and radical policies shattered U.S. hopes for mending fences with Egypt. The support of Israel proved once again to be the best tactic of containment of both Soviet and Arab radicalism.

Hence, when Israel accepted the cease-fire proposal in August 1970, it was not as Rogers expected, because of U.S. leverage, which proved to be extremely limited. The decision to withhold the shipment of arms as leverage did not effect Israel's decision to stop the air raids. During 1969–70 Israel gambled rightly that the United States would have to lift the arms ban and abandon the evenhanded policy.

On May 26, Prime Minister Meir discussed in the Israeli Knesset the political dilemmas ignored by Rogers. She blamed the escalation of the conflict on the Soviet Union and chided the United States for withholding arms. Meir stressed the need for direct negotiations and, in a surprise move, announced that her government had decided to accept the controversial U.N. Resolution 242.[114] This statement meant that Israel was ready to make territorial concessions in exchange for peace. Meir, however, did not react to the cease-fire proposal, which was still debated in Israel.

The Rogers cease-fire proposal was considered in Israel worse than his initial peace plan, mainly because it subscribed to indirect negotiations through Gunnar Jarring. "When Golda Meir read the new Rogers document she almost hit the ceiling."[115]

Hence, the administration's efforts to gain Israel's cooperation on its cease-fire proposal failed. During July, President Nixon, Secretary of Defense Laird, and other administration officials tried in vain to convince Israel that the cease-fire proposal would not change the Israeli claim for defensible borders. They pointed out the many benefits—increased military aid, assurances that Israel's strategic superiority would be maintained, and, last but not least, that the original Rogers plan would be practically abandoned.

Israel, however, was not yet convinced. Kissinger, critical of the administration's proposal, had written a memo to Nixon on June 16, explaining that the

Rogers initial plan resulted in stepped-up Arab military activity and opened the doors for a massive influx of Soviet personnel. The new cease-fire proposal might involve the same dangers. He argued that the United States should not pressure Israel to return to the prewar borders or to give up its territorial buffers. It was inconceivable that Israel would make such concessions to Nasser in exchange for six aircraft and perhaps additional planes later on. "To the Soviets," Kissinger argued, "the proposal would be a weak gesture in the face of their continued expansion of influence."[116] Kissinger argued that the most important issue was missing from the second Rogers initiative, namely, Soviet presence in Egypt.

For a while, the second Rogers initiative followed in the footsteps of the first. Israel, Egypt, and the U.S.S.R. rejected it, each claiming that it was too generous to the others. Dobrynin expressed outrage at the "unilateral American attempt to take over Middle East diplomacy." The proposal suggested nothing new, he argued.[117]

Kissinger criticized the Rogers initiative, demanding that it include a pullout of Soviet military personnel from the Middle East. He was worried about the "Soviet technique of using military presence to enhance geopolitical influence."[118] Moreover, Israel did not trust Egypt and demanded assurances that SAM-2 and SAM-3 missiles would not be deployed and advanced during the cease fire. In addition, Israel asked for the delivery of the requested Phantoms and Skyhawks (under the replacement formula), and wanted the planes to be equipped with new electronic countermeasures (ECMs) that could meet the challenge of Egypt's new Soviet-manned air defense missile batteries.[119] Israel suffered mounting casualties and substantial losses of sophisticated combat airplanes. It needed new weapon systems and was ready to accept a cease-fire.

How to induce Nasser to accept the cease-fire was another problem. Clearly, the U.S. threat to supply Israel with the most sophisticated offensive and defensive weapons influenced his decision. The U.S. proposal was in the case of Israel, "the carrot," and in the case of Egypt, "the stick." Rumors about Israel's nuclear capability contributed to Nasser's anxiety. Finally, Nasser planned to use the cease-fire to enhance his strategic positions along the canal, which he actually did later, gravely violating the cease-fire agreement. Hence, he was first to announce, on July 22, that he accepted the American-sponsored cease-fire. Israel was not surprised, arguing that the cease-fire would be more useful to Egypt than to Israel. Washington, however, was elated by Nasser's announcement.

Rogers claimed credit for having initiated it. Sisco privately disputed it. "Nixon was convinced that his tough statement on July 1 had done the trick, [while Kissinger, admitting that] humility not being [his] strong suit . . . was not loath to ascribe some of the success to [his] conversations with Dobrynin." Probably all were somewhat right.[120] At this point Nixon insisted on Israel's cooperation. On July 24 Ambassador Barbour hand-delivered to Meir a personal message from Nixon. The message included detailed clarifications regarding security arrangements for the cease-fire and American guarantees that if the cease-fire was violated, the United States would be committed to Israel's security and the balance of power in the Middle East.[121]

On July 25, in a meeting with her "Kitchen Cabinet," Meir decided to accept the cease-fire proposal, although she could not attain unanimous support of the full Cabinet. This ultimately lead to the walk-out of the Gahal party, headed by Begin, from the coalition, dissolving the National Unity government. The question of whether the withholding of weapons coerced Israel to accept the cease-fire cannot be answered easily.

Indeed, the United States used withholding of arms, combined with inducement—increased aid—to coerce Israel, which was in great need of the Phantoms. However, in the best case the planes were due to be supplied a year or more later, which allowed Israel to resist U.S. pressures.

As noted earlier, Israel gambled that the growing Soviet involvement in the region would force the United States to renew its arms supply before the year was over. Moreover, Israel expected the evenhanded policy to end soon. Hence, the withholding of arms, which began in January 1970, was not a major factor in Israel's decision to accept the cease-fire. More important were the high toll of the war of attrition, the retraction of the Rogers peace plan, and strong domestic pressures demanding to end the war.

On July 30, in a press conference, Nixon announced that cease-fire negotiations would begin along with a resumption of the Jarring mission. On August 6 Israel formally announced its acceptance of the cease-fire. On August 7 the cease-fire went into effect. The Rogers peace plan of December 9, 1969, was not mentioned any longer. It was officially considered dead.

OVERVIEW

When Nixon assumed office in January 1969, the situation in the Middle East promised both problems and opportunities. The most pressing problems were Soviet growing involvement and the large shipments of arms to Egypt and Syria, and the renewed armed struggle between Israel and Egypt. The combination of the two might lead to an all-out war, which could result in a U.S.-Soviet confrontation.

The Rogers plan offered an attractive solution. Following the Six-Day War, Israel was in control of vast Arab territories, which could be traded off for peace. The Big Four forum was created to ensure universal support of the plan. Israel was viewed as the linchpin of the plan. In addition to being the most reliable American ally in the region, Israel was perceived as a check on forces and events detrimental to U.S. interests. Moreover, Israel was the only force that could contain Nasser and prevent him from gaining hegemony in the Arab world. The United States and Israel wished to stop Nasser's use of his growing prestige to bolster Soviet positions in the region.[122]

The Arab defeat in the Six-Day War created stronger Arab dependence on

Soviet arms. The victorious, hated Israel was associated with the United States. Washington believed it should change its image and policies, thus adopting the evenhanded policy and developing a comprehensive peace plan that would return most of the occupied lands to the Arabs. During Nixon's first term, Secretary Rogers was the architect of the U.S. Middle East policy. This, however, changed during Nixon's second term, when Kissinger controlled the political scene. Rogers, inexperienced and optimistic, made the mistake of trying to impose a settlement on Israel using withholding of arms as leverage. His second mistake was to believe that the U.S.S.R. would be willing to pull back and decrease its involvement in the region's politics. Indeed, Rogers believed that his plan would be attractive to all, and thus had an excellent chance to succeed. Kissinger, less optimistic and more suspicious of the Soviets, doubted the wisdom of the plan from its inception.

The timing was another mistake. In 1969 the Arabs were extremely anxious to regain control of their lands, whereas Israel was not so anxious to attain peace. Hence, Kissinger argued, the United States and Israel should have "played it cool" and waited for the Arabs and the Soviets to come to them with proposals and concessions. Instead, Rogers and Sisco were bombarding the Soviets with peace plans, offering them more concessions with each version. Ultimately, Nasser came to believe that he could regain his lands without making any concessions at all. The U.S.S.R. which did not enjoy any leverage over Israel, had no difficulty manipulating Washington to do the job. The Soviets were desperate to achieve an Israeli withdrawal in order to gain prestige and credibility within the Arab world. This was exactly the reason, argued Kissinger, why the U.S. *should not have pressured Israel* to withdraw. A unilateral Israeli withdrawal would enhance the Soviet position immensely. A wise U.S. policy would lead the Arab states to come to the United States with concrete proposals for improving relations with both Israel and the United States. The Rogers approach achieved the opposite.

Hence, Kissinger believed that American avid pursuit of a settlement was counterproductive. He suggested to play the game calmly and show the Arab radicals that the United States was indispensable to any progress toward peace. It was important to assert that a settlement could not be extorted from the United States by Soviet pressure. Kissinger believed that a political deadlock was in fact desirable; it would coerce Nasser to face reality and admit that Soviet tutelage and a radical foreign policy were obstacles to progress and that only the United States could bring about a settlement. Indeed, the deadlock demonstrated Soviet impotence and ultimately impelled a fundamental change in Egypt's foreign policy.

Another mistake in the Rogers plan was the linkage factor, that is, the effort to link global issues to regional ones. The idea of using detente to enhance U.S.-Soviet cooperation in the Middle East actually backfired. The U.S.S.R. was not ready to give up its political gains in the Middle East and even used detente to enhance them. American acquiescence of massive Soviet arms shipments and deployment of military personnel led them to believe that they could attain most of their political and strategic goals with very little cost.

The Rogers plan was not clearly defined either in terms of objectives or of outcome. It was difficult to determine what and how concessions should be reached and implemented. No common ground between the fighting parties was established, whereas the two superpowers had adverse goals. Transfer of arms was used by the Soviets to increase their influence; suspension of arms was used by Washington to increase its leverage. The Big Four forum, of which Rogers was so hopeful, was doomed even before it convened. His proposal appealed to none and angered all.

The Arabs rejected the Rogers proposal because it required recognition of the State of Israel, a written commitment to the security of Israel, and an unsatisfactory solution to the problem of the refugees. The U.S.S.R. rejected the proposal because any Israeli-Arab agreement was against its interests (see their harsh reaction to the Camp David Accords). The Palestinians rejected the proposal because it did not answer their demands. It seemed that the only supporter of the Rogers plan was Secretary Rogers himself.

The 1969–70 events proved that U.S. leverage was a myth. The patron-client relationships between the United States and Israel did not yield leverage. Moreover, the expectation that a withholding of arms would help create a more constructive relationship with the Soviet Union, the linkage between global and regional policies, was abandoned by the United States when it realized, after two frustrating years of negotiations, that the opposite happened. Indeed, in 1970 massive military aid to Israel was approved and justified.

As Nixon's first term was nearing its end, it became clear that the Rogers peace plan had backfired. Moreover, the assumption that Israel was strong enough to deter Arab threats, yet sufficiently dependent on American arms so that leverage could be effectively applied without endangering Israeli security was abandoned in 1970. Indeed, Washington realized that the U.S.S.R. had no intention of reducing the level of its involvement in the Middle East. To the contrary, Moscow was looking for new clients. With the high stakes involved, the United States could no longer afford to weaken Israel by denying its arms requests.

The analysis of American search for peace during 1969–70 demonstrated that although Israel's swift victory of 1967 had changed the political map of the Middle East, it did not necessarily make a comprehensive peace settlement possible. The ambitious Rogers plan had to give way to a more modest policy, based on "step-by-step" diplomacy. The unrealistic expectations based on misperceptions and wishful thinking had to be abandoned. Moreover, the evenhanded policy induced neither reciprocity nor cooperation from the Soviets. Indeed, by the end of 1970, Rogers's approach was not only abandoned, but was completely reversed. The 1970 Syrian invasion of Jordan convinced Nixon that a militarily strong Israel was an asset and a vital U.S. interest. Hence, Nixon had to admit that the complex reality of the Middle East rendered a comprehensive settlement impossible.

NOTES

1. This change was best exemplified in the U.S. appeal to Israel to intervene in the Syrian-Jordanian conflict of September 1970.

2. Alfred L. Atherton, "Arabs, Israeli, and Americans: A Reconsideration," *Foreign Affairs* (Summer 1984), p. 1194.

3. Ibid.

4. T. G. Fraser, *The Middle East, 1914–1979* (New York: St. Martin's Press, 1980), p. 114.

5. Yithak Rabin, *The Rabin Memoirs* (Boston: Little, Brown, 1979), p. 132.

6. Henry Kissinger, *White House Years* (Boston: Little, Brown, 1979), p. 346.

7. Ibid., p. 343.

8. See Ambassador Arthur Goldberg's statement of May 24, 1968, *Department of State Bulletin* (July 1968), p. 27.

9. Ambassador Goldberg's statement, U.N. Security Council, July 9, 1969, quoted in David Pollock, *The Politics of Pressure* (Westport, CT: Greenwood Press, 1979), p. 20.

10. Nadav Safran, *Israel the Embattled Ally* (Cambridge: Harvard University Press, 1978), p. 261.

11. Rabin, *Rabin Memoirs*, p. 135.

12. Resolution adopted at the Khartum conference, September 1, 1967.

13. Statements in the U.N. General Assembly and the U.N. Security Council, September 21 and November 15, 1969.

14. *Report of the Secretary General*; S/10070, January 4, 1971, p. 18.

15. Ibid., p. 28.

16. Ibid., p. 30.

17. Secretary Dean Rusk's news conference, July 19, 1967; *Department of State Current Documents on U.S. Foreign Policy*, 1967, pp. 505–506.

18. Rabin, *Rabin Memoirs*, p. 140.

19. The United States consistently denied any attempt to pressure Israel through the suspension of arms. Rabin, however, argues that this was a well-established tactic; see *Rabin Memoirs*, pp. 141–142.

20. Ibid., p. 141.

21. *A Chronology and Selected Background Documents Relating to the Middle East*, December 27, 1968.

22. Kissinger, *White House Years*, p. 349.

23. *Public Papers of the Presidents of the U.S.: Richard Nixon, 1969*, p. 18; see also Bernard Reich, "United States Policy in the Middle East," *Current History* (January 1971), p. 3.

24. William Quandt, *Decade of Decisions* (Berkeley: University of California Press, 1977), p. 81.

25. Pollock, *Politics of Pressure*, p. 57.

26. Richard Nixon, "Asia After Vietnam," *Foreign Affairs* (October 1967), pp. 115–125.

27. Kissinger, *White House Years*, p. 348.

28. See Quandt's analysis, *Decade of Decisions*, p. 82.

29. Ibid., p. 87.

30. See discussion by Ernest Gross, "The Arab-Israeli Dispute, a Study for Discussion," 1976 (unpublished paper), p. 28.

31. Malcolm Kerr, "The Arab and Israelis: Perceptual Dimensions of Their Dilemma," in William A. Beling (ed.), *The Middle East, Quest for an American Policy* (Albany: State University of New York Press, 1973), p. 5.

32. Quandt, *Decade of Decisions*, p. 74.

33. Kissinger, *White House Years*, p. 348.

34. Ibid., p. 349.

35. Sources include *IISS Survey*, 1967; *IISS The Military Balance*, 1968–1969, pp. 45–46; *SIPRI Year Book*, 1968–1969, p. 63.

36. Charles Yost, "Israel and the Arabs," *The Atlantic Monthly* (January 1969).

37. *New York Times*, December 12, 1968.

38. Saadia Touval, *The Peace Brokers* (Princeton, NJ: Princeton University Press, 1982), p. 167.

39. Kissinger, *White House Years*, p. 351.

40. Ibid., see detailed discussion pp. 352–355.

41. Rabin, *Rabin Memoirs*, p. 145.

42. Kissinger, *White House Years*, p. 354.

43. Rabin, *Rabin Memoirs*, p. 143.

44. Ibid., p. 143.

45. Safran, *Israel*, p. 264.

46. Rabin, *Rabin Memoirs*, p. 146.

47. Ibid., p. 147.

48. Kissinger, *White House Years*, p. 356.

49. See Quandt's discussion, *Decade of Decisions*, pp. 92–94.

50. Kissinger, *White House Years*, p. 357.

51. Ibid.

52. Quandt, *Decade of Decisions*, p. 84.

53. Rabin, *Rabin Memoirs*, p. 156.

54. Ibid., p. 148.

55. Articles in *Al-Ahram* and *Al-Akhbar* as reported in the *New York Times*, April 11 and 17, 1969.

56. Kissinger, *White House Years*, p. 364.

57. Gromyko's visit to Cairo was discussed in the *New York Times*, June 12, 14, 18, and 21, 1969.

58. See discussions by Quandt, *Decade of Decisions*, pp. 86–88; Rabin, *Rabin Memoirs*, pp. 145–150.

59. See detailed account in Kissinger, *White House Years*, p. 366.

60. Ibid., p. 370.

61. Dan Margalit, *A Communication from the White House* (Hebrew)(Tel Aviv: Otpaz Press, 1971), p. 20.

62. Kissinger, *White House Years*, p. 371.

63. Rabin, *Rabin Memoirs*, p. 155.

64. Kissinger, *White House Years*, p. 371.
65. Secretary Rogers's news conference, December 23, 1969, *Department of State Bulletin* (January 9, 1970), pp. 21–25.
66. Ibid., p. 23.
67. Kissinger, *White House Years*, p. 373.
68. Ibid., p. 374.
69. Pollock, *Politics of Pressure*, p. 65.
70. Excerpts from *Department of State Bulletin* (January 4, 1970).
71. Kissinger, *White House Years*, p. 375.
72. Ibid.
73. Pollock, *Politics of Pressure*, p. 68.
74. Kissinger, *White House Years*, p. 377.
75. Israel's Broadcasting Service, December 22, 1969.
76. Rabin, *Rabin Memoirs*, p. 159.
77. Kissinger, *White House Years*, p. 375.
78. Rabin, *Rabin Memoirs*, p. 159.
79. Kissinger, *White House Years*, p. 375.
80. Excerpts from Quandt, *Decade of Decisions*, p. 91.
81. Margalit, *A Communication*, p. 30.
82. See reports in the *New York Times*, January 13, 1970.
83. Kissinger, *White House Years*, p. 376.
84. Ibid.
85. Ibid.
86. Rabin, *Rabin Memoirs*, p. 151.
87. Quandt, *Decade of Decisions*, p. 92.
88. Margalit, *A Communication*, pp. 41–43.
89. Kissinger, *White House Years*, p. 558.
90. Ibid., p. 560.
91. Ibid., p. 561.
92. Nixon's news conference, March 4, 1969, *Department of State Bulletin* (March 1969), p. 240.
93. Margalit, *A Communication*, p. 69.
94. Pollock, *Politics of Pressure*, p. 68.
95. Kissinger, *White House Years*, p. 569.
96. Secretary Rogers' news conference March 23, 1970, *Department of State Bulletin* (April 1970), pp. 477–480.
97. Ibid.
98. Kissinger, *White House Years*, p. 566.
99. Rabin, *Rabin Memoirs*, p. 167.
100. Nasser talked about his secret visit to Moscow in his speech to Egypt's National Assembly, July 24, 1979, quoted by Pollock, *Politics of Pressure*, p. 69.
101. Kissinger, *White House Years*, p. 567.
102. Ibid., p. 568.
103. Excerpts from text published in *Arab Report and Record*, May 1–15, 1970, p. 276; quoted by Quandt, *Decade of Decisions*, p. 98.
104. Pollock, *Politics of Pressure*, p. 70.
105. Margalit, *A Communication*, p. 106.

106. Nasser's statement on June 25, 1970, as reported in the *New York Times*, June 26, 1970.

107. Kissinger, *White House Years*, p. 568.

108. Rabin, *Rabin Memoirs*, p. 173.

109. Kissinger, *White House Years*, p. 572.

110. Margalit, *A Communication*, p. 115.

111. *Department of State Bulletin* (August 1970), pp. 178–179.

112. Secretary Rogers' news conference, June 25, 1970, reported in the *New York Times*, June 27, 1970.

113. Touval, *The Peace Brokers*, p. 166.

114. Margalit, *A Communication*, pp. 116–118.

115. Ibid., p. 128.

116. Kissinger, *White House Years*, p. 578.

117. Ibid., p. 579.

118. Ibid., p. 581.

119. Interviews with Israeli Air Force officers.

120. Kissinger, *White House Years*, p. 582.

121. See discussion in Pollock, *Politics of Pressure*, p. 76.

122. Safran, "American-Israeli Relations: An Overview," *Middle East Review* (Winter 1977–78), pp. 30–34.

3

The Disengagement Agreements: A Framework for Peace

Following the quiet but official burial of the Rogers peace plan in 1971, two conflicting trends were shaping up in the Middle East. The first was President Sadat's determination to end the status quo, that is, gain back the Sinai and reopen the canal. The second was the Israeli and American persistence to maintain the status quo. Thus Israel and Egypt were locked in opposing positions. The PLO had not yet established its political and military strength, and neither Jordan not Syria were strong enough to challenge Israel without Egyptian support. Israel was slowly moving away from defining its interest in terms of peace and was developing strategies based on territorial security. Consequently, a military confrontation became inevitable.

UN Resolution 242 became the symbol of the political deadlock. Although universally accepted, it had as many interpretations as actors involved. Egypt became more and more impatient, but neither the United States nor Israel was perceptive enough to read the writing on the wall.

Israel's misperceptions were so widespread that when Ambassador Rabin's son, Yuval, who was on a weekend leave from his navy training center, was ordered, on Yom Kippur, to return to his base immediately, his father did not suspect war.[1] On October 4, just two days before the attack, Kissinger and Foreign Minister Eban met in New York and Kissinger was "jocular and relaxed." He believed that a prolonged stalemate was the best policy because "it would move the Arabs toward moderation and the Soviets to the fringes of the Middle East."[2] The turning point was Sadat's unexpected act of July 6, 1972, when he ordered all Soviet personnel and all Soviet-owned equipment to be pulled out of Egypt within a week. "No war could be fought while Soviet experts worked in Egypt. The Soviet Union, the West, and Israel misinterpreted my decision . . . and reached erroneous conclusions which in fact served my strategy."[3]

It was an opportunity lost by both the United States and Israel. Kissinger, almost ignoring the act, continued to advocate extreme caution, namely, to do as little as possible. A new American peace initiative was viewed as unnecessary and dangerous. Clearly, the failure of the Rogers initiative reinforced the attitude of "wait and see." The Israeli government, for different reasons, shared the American attitude.[4]

For three years Sadat expected Nixon to give the Middle East a higher priority. Kissinger, however, now assuming the pivotal role in Middle East politics, believed that Resolution 242 created an insurmountable deadlock. His premise was that if all would wait patiently, the Arabs would moderate their position and would ultimately recognize Israel, whereas Israel would then moderate its position and agree to make territorial concessions.

The early months of 1973 saw intensive diplomatic activities in Washington. On February 6 King Hussein arrived carrying a proposal to establish a United Arab Kingdom on the East and West banks of the Jordan River, subject to approval in a referendum among the Palestinians.[5] On February 23 Sadat's national security adviser arrived in Washington with a proposal to exchange an Israeli withdrawal for security arrangements and a possible Egyptian recognition, which would come at an unspecified future date. Three days later, on February 28, Golda Meir arrived in Washington delivering a new "shopping list" of sophisticated weapons. Meanwhile, the clouds of Watergate began to accumulate. On April 30 Nixon accepted the resignation of Haldeman and Ehrlichman. Kissinger's role in U.S. foreign policy was growing rapidly, and his step-by-step approach became the official policy. With the Middle East on the back burner, Kissinger devoted almost all his time to detente. During his May visit to Moscow, he informed Brezhnev about his talks with the various Middle East leaders. In June Brezhnev arrived for his first visit to the United States and talks again focused on the Middle East.

Brezhnev was surprisingly candid about the situation and warned Washington that Egypt and Syria were seriously considering the option of war. He said that as much as Moscow was against it, there was not much that it could do to stop them. He suggested that only a new American initiative, and specifically pressure on Israel to withdraw, could prevent a war.[6]

This, of course, did not happen. The Arab states and Israel were locked in their respective dilemmas and were not willing to pay the price of peace, that is, implement the principle of territories for peace. The Palestinian issue was also deadlocked. Israel's security demands required its continued control of the West Bank. The Arab intransigence rejection of the Jewish state did not allow for any reconciliation process to develop. Indeed, Syria rejected the very existence of Israel in any form. When Kissinger flew to Damascus from Tel Aviv, the Syrian press reported that he "had arrived from occupied territories."[7]

The PLO added to the tense atmosphere by a surge of dramatic terrorist attacks.

In May 1972 it launched a bloody attack at the Tel Aviv air terminal, and in September it massacred a group of Israeli athletes participating in the Munich Olympic Games. The Arabs, desperate to regain their lost lands, were nonetheless reluctant to choose the negotiation path. Israel, caught in its misperception, was unwilling to make any commitments to induce talks. The United States adopted a myopic approach, believing that things were moving in the right direction. The U.S.S.R. was faced with its frustrating dilemma; it wished to advance the Arab cause but realized that Washington held the key to any progress.

By the summer of 1972, war became imminent. In October Sadat decided to move. In January 1973 the war plans were completed. Indeed, the Yom Kippur War was mainly an attack on the status quo,[8] and Sadat's objectives were never to conquer the Sinai. His objectives were to change the political environment, restoring Egypt's honor and reactivating the negotiation process.[9] How the clear writing on the wall escaped Washington and Jerusalem still demands explanation.

THE 1973 WAR: A PRELUDE TO A SETTLEMENT

The concerted Egyptian-Syrian attack on Israel was launched on Saturday, October 6, Yom Kippur, the Jewish holiest day. The war caught Kissinger and Eban in New York, where they were attending the UN annual General Assembly meeting. At 6:15 A.M., only ninety minutes before the war broke out, Kissinger was awakened by Joseph Sisco, who delivered him a message from Golda Meir that the war would begin within a few hours. From that moment on and until he completed his term, Secretary of State Kissinger was engaged almost exclusively in Middle East politics.

Two major consequences followed the war: (1) Israel realized that its strategic superiority and its most preferred borders (the Suez Canal and the Golan Heights) did not provide security against a surprise attack,[10] and (2) Egypt and Syria realized that defeating Israel, even under the best of conditions, was impossible. Thus the ground was ready for the disengagement agreements.

Especially interesting was the shift in Israel's politics. Before the Six-Day War, Israel was nervous and not sure of its strategic superiority, but its legendary victory provided it with the best possible borders, creating in the nation a sense of security and a feeling that if war again broke out, the outcome would be similar. "The idea that Israel would not be able to deal the Arabs a fatal blow with its existing weaponry had not entered anybody's head."[11]

Sadat did not share these beliefs, which were common not only in Jerusalem, but in Washington and Moscow as well. Sadat knew that a total defeat of Israel was impossible. However, Sadat fought a *political war*, and his military objectives were very limited. Sadat attributed the idea of the war and the actual war plans to his own understanding of the regional and global environments, and claimed that he personally drew up the general strategic plan for the battle. He believed that if Egypt would "recapture even 4 inches of Sinai territory . . . and establish ourselves there so firmly that no power on earth could dislodge us, then the whole situation would change—east, west, all over. First to go would be the humiliation we had endured since 1967.''[12]

Unaware of Sadat's plans, the United States and Israel shared the misperception that an all-out Arab attack was a military suicide, therefore very unlikely. Much to their surprise, Israel suffered major setbacks and needed urgent American military aid in order to regain its military superiority and ultimately to win the war.

Kissinger began to plan the cease-fire agreement while Israel was fighting desperately to stop the advancing Egyptian Army. His planned step-by-step policy, which began with the cease-fire, was moving toward a long-term settlement. This had led many in Israel to believe that Kissinger was actually responsible for Israel's strategic difficulties. Moreover, Washington requested that Israel not launch a pre-emptive air strike two hours before the invasion, as was proposed by Israel's chief of staff, General "Dado" Elazar.[13] Many Israelis believe that a pre-emptive air strike would have exposed the surprise effect, stopped the Egyptian invasion, and changed dramatically the course of events. However, the United States strongly objected to the air strike and communicated that feeling to the Israeli Chargé d'Affaires in Washington, Eban in New York, and Meir in Jerusalem (through Ambassador Keating). On the morning of June 6, Meir decided to respect the U.S. desire. She rejected General Elazar's request and refrained from launching a pre-emption strike.[14]

Indeed, the Israeli Commission of Inquiry concluded that Minister of Defense Dayan even opposed a large-scale mobilization because he thought that it could be interpreted as an act of provocation, which might instigate a hostile Arab reaction. On this issue Meir decided against Dayan's opinion and ordered a partial mobilization just a few hours before the attack. It proved, however, to be too little too late.

During the fierce battles of the first week, Israel's pleas for replacement of lost weapons were deliberately delayed by Washington. Kissinger blamed the Pentagon, but Israel blamed Kissinger.

The war forced the United States to deal with two vital but conflicting interests. Washington had to contain the growing Soviet influence in the Middle East, but did not wish to undermine the spirit of detente. This required that the United States pursue its policy with great caution and diplomatic wisdom. Thus Washington tried to protect its economic and strategic interests in the Middle East with assertion and determination, hoping that the damage to detente would be minimal.

A more concrete and immediate problem ensued from the first. Nixon decided to become intensely involved in Middle East politics and to support Israel. But this clashed with the strong Soviet support of the Arab states, which led to an inevitable conflict between them. It culminated when, on October 25, 1973, the U.S.S.R. threatened with a unilateral military intervention to save the Egyptian Third Army, and the United States, for the first and only time in history, reacted with a nuclear alert. However, throughout the crisis, even after the alert, the

this would destroy any chance of a renewed American-Egyptian relationship. Moreover, a confrontation with the Soviets seemed inevitable.

A decisive Israeli victory conflicted with Washington, Cairo, and Moscow interests. Sadat, frantic to stop Israel's advance, called on the United States and the U.S.S.R. to send in troops to save the Third Army. Washington feared that the Soviets would seize this opportunity to send thousands of Soviet troops into the region. The Soviets intensified the crisis by announcing that they accepted Sadat's invitation and by reinforcing their troops. Seven airborne Soviet divisions stationed in East Europe were put on high alert. The CIA reported that the number of Soviet ships in the Mediterranean had grown to more than 100, an all-time high, and a flotilla of twelve Soviet ships including two amphibious vessels was heading for Alexandria.[33]

It was difficult to determine whether the Soviets were bluffing or how to call their bluff. Washington responded by putting the 82nd Airborne Division on high alert, and moving the aircraft carrier *FDR* from Italy to join the carrier *Independence* in the eastern Mediterranean. "The carrier *JFK* and its accompanying task force were also ordered to move at full speed from the Atlantic to the Mediterranean."[34] The climax of the crisis came on October 25 when Nixon declared a nuclear alert and sent a strong message to Brezhnev urging him not to pursue a unilateral action. The Soviet compliance was swift, although indirect. In an urgent message from Sadat to Nixon, he substituted his request for a U.S.-Soviet force with an international force to be sent to the war zone by the Security Council. The force would exclude troops from the five permanent members of the Security Council, that is, no American or Soviet troops would be deployed. The United States prevailed in the crisis but allowed the Soviet Union to save face. Security Council Resolution 340, of October 25, established UNEF II, which formally came into being on October 27. It served as an important tool in the disengagement agreements.[35] (According to an informal agreement, thirty-six Soviet and thirty-six U.S. observers were attached to the UNEF II force).

The cease-fire line included all the territories conquered by Israel until October 25, that is, it incorporated the Israeli siege of the Egyptian Third Army. Hence, the United States was unsuccessful in coercing Israel to accept its cease-fire proposal, namely, to stop along the October 22 line. Although heavily dependent on the United States for weapons, Israel decided to defy U.S. pressures and ignore its threats to withhold future military and economic aid.

A FRAMEWORK FOR PEACE: THE 1974–75 DISENGAGEMENT AGREEMENTS

On November 11, 1973, at the Kilometer 101, Israel and Egypt signed the first limited disengagement agreement. This six-point agreement was concluded in direct negotiations (the first since 1949) between General Aharon Yariv and General Mohamed Abdel Ghany el-Gamasy, the military representatives of Israel and Egypt. The agreement was followed by three important disengagement agreements: Sinai I, signed on January 18, 1974 at the Kilometer 101 by both countries' chiefs of staff; the Israeli-Syrian disengagement agreement, signed in Geneva on May 31, 1974; and Sinai II, signed in Geneva on September 4, 1975. With the November 11 agreement Israeli-Egyptian relationships entered a new era. The direct negotiations signified a de facto recognition of Israel, and the representatives not only negotiated issues relevant to the implementation of the cease-fire, but they also exchanged ideas informally about broader and more far-reaching disengagement agreements.

Thus the six-point agreement, although very technical and even subsidiary, signified for Israel a reversal in "the cycle of conflict and the set up of a process of negotiations."[36] Both Egypt and Israel were interested in reaching a substantial disengagement agreement. They preferred direct, bilateral negotiations with American mediation to the Geneva multilateral negotiating framework. The first indication of this attitude was Ismail Fahmy's visit to Washington on October 28. It was not a coincidence that Prime Minister Meir decided to visit Washington at the same time.

The presence of both Fahmy and Meir in Washington provided an opportunity for intensive negotiations. The talks, however, were not direct, because Egypt was not yet ready to conduct formal, direct talks with Israel.[37] During his visit Fahmi announced that Egypt was willing to accept the fact that Israel was here to stay. "Egypt," he said "has no interest in putting Israel into the sea or invading Israel, irrespective of the Palestinian situations."[38] This was a major shift from the traditional Egyptian policy. It was now Israel's turn to reciprocate.

Although Prime Minister Meir declared publicly that during her visit to Washington she would discuss only U.S.-Israeli relations, namely, arms supplies, when she arrived on October 31, her talks with Nixon and Kissinger centered around the peace process. Nixon told Meir that Israel had to make territorial concessions or U.S. generous arms supplies would be discontinued.[39] Nixon also told Meir that Sadat was ready to reach a settlement and that Kissinger was charged with the responsibility to mediate a settlement. Meir's visit to Washington was relatively long (she left on November 5), and it was interpreted in more than one way. Many in Israel believe that Kissinger exerted great pressure on Meir to accept the six-point agreement.[40] Meir, old, sick, and exhausted, made the concessions.

Others, however, argue that the United States exerted very little pressure. Meir herself assured a group of reporters in a news conference on October 31, in Washington that there had been no pressure.[41] The major problem was Egypt's demand for a unilateral Israeli withdrawal, which was strongly rejected by Israel. However, both Israel and Egypt understood that the agreement benefited them, thus it was concluded within a few days and in a very friendly atmosphere.[42] Sadat made two major concessions. First, the direct negotiations would continue; second, a bilateral Egyptian-Israeli agreement would be signed. Israel made territorial concessions and agreed to assure the survival of the Third Army. The

United States became directly involved in the agreement by signing the first MOU (Memorandum of Understanding) with Israel promising to secure the free passage of Israeli ships in Bab el-Mandeb, and reassuring Israel that U.N. forces would not be withdrawn on the request of one side. U.S. mediation was rewarding. On November 7, during a visit to Cairo, Kissinger and Sadat announced to surprised reporters that Egypt and the United States had decided to renew their diplomatic relations, which were severed in 1967. Exchange of ambassadors was due in two weeks. Joseph Sisco and Harold Saunders were dispatched immediately to Israel to help step up the negotiations.[43]

The three parties were moving fast toward a settlement. After the conclusion of the November 11 agreement, Kissinger wanted to convene the Geneva Peace Conference (which was part of the October 19 U.S.-Soviet agreement). First, he wanted to relax the tension created during the last week of October. Second, he assumed that without a Soviet blessing Syria, Egypt's ally in the war, would not accept any American-Israeli proposal for disengagement. Kissinger learned later that he was wrong on both counts.

The idea of an international peace conference appealed to the Soviets and to Kissinger, but to none of the Middle East parties. Israel considered the forum hostile and biased because of West Europe's independence on Arab oil. The Soviet cochairmanship did not appeal to Israel either. The U.S.S.R. clearly was a representative of its adversaries. Egypt did not favor the idea because it could invite a renewed aggressive Soviet involvement in the Middle East. Syria rejected the proposal because it required direct negotiations with Israel. Hussein had a personal problem with the representation of the Palestinian people. Following the events of September 1970, he wished to avoid any direct confrontation with the PLO. The PLO also did not like the idea of a Geneva conference because it was not recognized as a member with equal status. Hence, apart from Moscow and Washington, no one considered the Geneva Peace Conference a good idea.

During his visit to Washington, on December 7, 1973, Israeli Defense Minister Dayan presented Israel's formal position and his own private position on disengagement. It was based on return to pre–1973 lines. He indicated that an Israeli-Egyptian agreement was within reach with no need to go to Geneva. Dayan "envisaged an Israeli withdrawal to a line ten kilometers west of the Mitla and Gidi passes—some thirty kilometers east of the Canal—in return for Egyptian agreement to substantial demilitarization of the forward areas, obligation to reopen the Suez Canal and rebuild the Canal cities."[44]

Dayan's visit to Washington established the basis for the Sinai I agreement reached a few weeks later. The Geneva conference was neither necessary nor helpful. This was not, however, Kissinger's opinion at the time. He urged Israel not to propose too substantial, far-reaching concessions at Kilometer 101, because he wanted the final accord to be reached in Geneva. The Israeli government followed his request and allowed the Kilometer 101 talks to adjourn sine die on November 29. The formal disengagement talks were transferred from Kilometer 101 to the Geneva conference.[45]

Although Kissinger never acknowledged his responsibility for the ending of the talks at Kilometer 101, it is difficult to explain it otherwise. The negotiations were making progress, and as early as November 26 Israel and Egypt seemed ready to agree on major Israeli withdrawals in return for a substantial reduction of Egyptian armored strength. The experiment in direct negotiations looked very promising.[46] However, Kissinger felt that the Israeli-Egyptian talks were proceeding too rapidly and that Syria had been left out. He feared that a bilateral Egyptian-Israeli disengagement agreement before Geneva might antagonize Assad. He therefore advised Israel to slow down at Kilometer 101 and to harden its position on disengagement until Geneva, where Syria could be an equal partner.

Washington's problem was clear. It wanted a settlement but feared that without the participation of Syria and the U.S.S.R. no meaningful Israeli-Egyptian agreement could be reached. Kissinger wrongly assumed that the Soviets were essential for any negotiations with Syria. Hence, although the Geneva conference was doomed, it nonetheless opened with great fanfare on December 21, 1973, at the Palais des Nations under the chairmanship of Kurt Waldheim, secretary general of the U.N. While the parties in the Geneva conference were arguing over trivial, procedural matters, meaningful negotiations were taking place in Cairo and Jerusalem between Sadat, Kissinger, and Meir.

The Geneva conference had a hidden agenda: oil. The oil embargo developed into a troubling energy crisis and Geneva was expected to bring it to a happy ending. No one expected oil prices to climb to almost $11 per barrel (before the war the price was lower than $3!). As the oil embargo continued, and after the Organization of Petroleum Exporting Countries (OPEC) had decided, on December 23, to double the prices, Kissinger and other Western leaders became extremely concerned with the war situation.[47]

The Geneva conference opened on December 21, right after the general elections in Israel, with the participation of Israel, Egypt, and Jordan. Syria's place remained unoccupied. It refused to participate in the peace conference and decided to reinforce its troops in the Golan Heights and put them on a high alert. Syria's message was clear—either an Israeli-Syrian disengagement agreement was reached, regardless of Geneva, or Syria would resume the fighting.

Sadat was aware of Assad's sensitivity to a bilateral Israeli-Egyptian agreement, and a few days before the opening of the Geneva talks, he met with the Syrian President. The two had agreed to go to Geneva, but Assad made it clear that he would go "only after the conclusion of disengagement agreements."[48]

Kissinger missed the Syrian message. First, Assad wanted bilateral Israeli-Syrian negotiations. Second, he wanted to keep the Soviets out of the political process. Not surprisingly, Israel, Egypt, and Syria, for different reasons, were eager to use American exclusive mediation. The fact that Israel and Egypt almost concluded the Sinai I agreement through direct negotiations at Kilometer 101 proved how meaningless the Geneva talks were.

Did the Sinai I agreement involve the use of American leverage? The question is intriguing because withholding of arms was used, and many believe that the heavy American pressure was crucial to the success of the negotiations.[49]

However, the nature and practice of the pressure are highly debatable. Israeli officials were more inclined to suggest that throughout the October War, the United States used arms leverage consistently to influence Israeli strategy. For example, "on the eve of the Sinai I shuttle, Defense Secretary Schlesinger privately intimated, according to Dayan, that the United States would provide Israel with some new arms, but that more would come only if diplomatic progress were achieved."[50]

Quandt also argued that only after Nixon and Kissinger began to exert heavy pressure on Israel was Israel willing to go to Geneva and to consider serious concessions needed to reach an agreement.[51] The facts, however, support the opposing view, that is, that very little pressure, if at all, was needed to conclude the Sinai I agreement, because both parties were very eager to reach a settlement. The war was a terrible trauma for Israel. Its defense strategy, which was based on the premise that the 1967 borders could not be crossed, that the Sinai desert was a perfect buffer zone, and that it had more than enough warning time to mobilize its reserves in case of an Egyptian attack, proved to be a myth. In effect Israel was more vulnerable strategically in 1973 than it was in 1967.

Egypt was preparing for a crossing of the canal—constructing bridges and mobilizing the largest invasion force in its history—while Israel refused to believe that this meant war. Indeed, Israel was completely surprised with the seizure of initiative and the early success of a complex amphibious Egyptian operation. Israel's deterrent power had failed, as well as its intelligence. The Israeli theory that Egypt faced one of two options: accept the status quo or change it by negotiations had proved baseless. Israel erroneously ruled out Egypt's third option, that is, changing the status quo by waging war.

The war left Israel bewildered, confused, frustrated, and angry, but most of all short of breath. It needed time to think things over, to analyze and understand what had happened, why, and how. The disengagement agreements provided Israel with exactly that; "time out" to reflect on the past and prepare for the future. It also promised Israel a period of peace with secure borders. Israel needed that for replenishing its depleted weapons arsenal, and training its troops with the new and sophisticated weapon systems received from the United States.

Egypt, too, had a strong interest in an agreement. Sadat knew that even under the most favorable circumstances, Israel could not be defeated or pushed out of the Sinai. When the war ended, Israeli troops were stationed only sixty-five miles from Cairo. Sadat realized that the only way to achieve an Israeli withdrawal was political, that is, through negotiations, and he was ready for direct talks. Hence, American pressure was not necessary; indeed Israel and Egypt were moving toward an agreement much faster than the American mediators even imagined.

The cease-fire had caught the Israeli and the Egyptian forces in awkward positions. They were both vulnerable and intertwined, spread along the two banks of the canal. Both were easy targets for surprise attacks from each other. Egypt had its Third Army trapped, and Israel was under heavy pressure. The continued and massive mobilization took its toll. Israel could not afford such long periods of mobilization that paralyzed its work force. In addition, both Egypt and Israel hoped to derive from disengagement important political-strategic advantages.[52]

The Israeli-Egyptian negotiations began with Dayan's visit to Washington, on January 4, 1974, during which he outlined a disengagement proposal that was later presented to Sadat during Kissinger's visit to Cairo on January 12. It should be noted that although Kissinger's role in the conclusion of the agreement was crucial, it was Moshe Dayan who first formulated the disengagement concept in 1970–71. The agreement concluded in 1974 resembled in many respects the formula he had proposed then.

Whereas Kissinger wished the negotiations to be concluded in Geneva, Sadat asked him to stay in the region and to help reach a settlement right then and there. Indeed, the final agreement was reached in only four days.

Hence, the common theory that U.S. leverage was needed and used in the negotiation process of the Sinai I agreement is not consistent with the facts. Moreover, Kissinger's mediation was necessary but not sufficient to bring about the agreement that was signed on January 16, 1974.

THE ISRAELI-SYRIAN DISENGAGEMENT AGREEMENT

On May 31, 1974, only four months after the completion of the Sinai I agreement, Syria and Israel signed a disengagement pact. Bringing together Israel and its fiercest enemy, Syria, in the Golan Heights disengagement agreement was the most impressive achievement in Kissinger's shuttle diplomacy. His success of May 1974 has not been repeated since, and it is difficult to predict when or even whether another Israeli-Syrian agreement will be reached. The agreement came as a surprise to all because the conventional wisdom suggested that the next peace settlement would be between Israel and Jordan. Kissinger tried to use the momentum of the Sinai I agreement to start an Israeli-Jordanian dialogue.

From Aswan Kissinger left for talks with King Hussein and only later met with President Assad. The major difficulty in the negotiations was that Israel had no strong incentives to make far-reaching territorial concessions to either Jordan or Syria in exchange for a settlement short of a peace treaty. Jordan did not take part in the October War and therefore the status of the West Bank did not change. Jordan had no dole to offer Israel. Moreover, Arab League resolutions prohibited Jordan from negotiating on behalf of the Palestinians.

An agreement between Israel and Syria seemed even less likely. Until 1973 Syria had refused any talks of peace. It claimed that it was dedicated to Israel's destruction and therefore did not care where Israel's borders were located. However, the October war changed the situation. Unlike Jordan, Syria did participate in the war, as a result of which Israel enhanced its strategic positions and moved its forces even closer to Damascus. Syria, however, did have two bargaining chips: it was holding Israeli prisoners of war, and it threatened to renew the fighting if an agreement was not reached. Indeed, Syria began to wage a war of attrition along the Israeli-Syrian border, which could have developed into a full-scale war.

Hence, unlikely as it seemed, Israel and Syria thought that an agreement would be beneficial to their respective interests. An Israeli-Jordanian agreement, on the other hand, was not reached, regardless of the king's political moderation and personal positive attitude, because no mutual interests that could instigate such a settlement existed on either side. American mediation played a crucial role in the Golan Heights disengagement agreement. Kissinger played an indispensable personal role as a mediator, a catalyst, an imaginative and resourceful diplomat, who did not "take no for an answer" from either side.

Golda Meir never forgot how, upon Kissinger's return from one of his trips to Jerusalem from Damascus, at about 1:30 A.M., he sent a message from his plane to say that he wanted a meeting with the Israeli Cabinet that morning at 2:30 A.M. At the meeting he turned up as fresh as though he had spent the past month in a summer resort, although everyone around him was wilting.[53]

Many believe that the United States used its leverage to pressure Israel to accept the disengagement agreement with Syria.[54] The facts, however, show that very little pressure, if any, was exerted by the United States to bring Israel and Syria to the bargaining table. In fact, throughout the negotiations, that is, during the first four months of 1974, the United States did not use withholding of weapons to Israel, even when the negotiations reached dead ends and although the process entailed "some of the bluntest exchanges with the Israeli leadership ever to take place."[55]

Long before a settlement was reached, President Nixon approved Israel's request for $2.2 billion in emergency assistance to purchase replacement for military equipment lost in the war, and he waived repayment of as much as $1.5 billion of it, without linking the military aid or the financial grant to any political concessions by Israel.[56] During his last months in office Nixon was very concerned with a political success in the Middle East. He admired Kissinger's diplomatic skills and trusted him with a free hand to follow his own political tactics and strategies, to get Israel and Syria to stop the fighting and start talking.

While Syria was intensifying the fighting along its border with Israel, Syrian Brigadier General Hikmat Shihabi was invited to Washington for talks with Kissinger on April 13. A few days earlier, on March 29, Israel's minister of defense, Dayan, was invited to Washington. Kissinger realized that both nations were eager to reach an agreement; however, their positions were too far apart to even establish a negotiation framework. Assad's initial offer demanded an Israeli withdrawal south of the 1967 cease-fire line. Assad also opposed the lifting of the oil embargo. Kissinger knew that Israel would never agree to such far-reaching concessions, not even for a peace treaty. Israel at that point did not specify what territories it was ready to give back, but insisted on maintaining control over the city of Kuneitra—the Syrian capital of the Golan Heights—which Syria demanded be returned. Assad's first proposal was that Israel give up all its gains from the October war plus half of the Golan Heights taken in 1967. It amused Kissinger to think of the fireworks that would come when Golda heard this proposition.[57]

Syria's leverage was that it was holding about sixty Israeli prisoners of war. Israel's first demand in any negotiations was their safe return. Meir announced: "there could be no negotiation until there was some sign that Israeli prisoners of war held in Syria would be returned."[58] The negotiations between Israel and Syria confronted strong opposition in both countries. The shaky coalition in Israel limited the power of the Prime Minister to make unpopular decisions. Meir's resignation, on April 11, just before Kissinger's shuttle began, was made under the pressure of criticism of her government's responsibility for Israel's unpreparedness and its intelligence failure.[59]

Conditions in Damascus were similar. The devastating military defeat could be erased only by a substantial political victory. Of the two nations, a disengagement agreement was far more important for Assad than for Meir. Hence, Assad initiated the trilateral talks in January, while Israel, Egypt, and the United States were busy negotiating the Sinai I agreement. Like the Sinai I agreement, the meaningful negotiations between Israel and Syria did not take place in Geneva. While "continuing working groups" of Israel, Egypt, and Jordan began their discussions in Geneva on January 7, 1974, the real Israeli-Syrian drama was taking place in Jerusalem and Damascus, with Kissinger playing the major role.

Israel was desperate to free its prisoners of war; Syria rejected all requests to let the Red Cross visit the POWs, or even to provide Israel, the United States, or the Red Cross with a list of the prisoners' names. This allowed Syria to torture or kill prisoners—which was a real fear in Israel—without taking any risks of being exposed. Another source of anxiety in Israel was Assad's threat to renew the fighting if a settlement on a partial Israeli withdrawal was not reached. In fact, during the first two months of 1974, the negotiations were accompanied by heavy shelling and numerous Israeli casualties on the Syrian front.[60] After two months of negotiations, Syria agreed to give Washington, but not Israel, a list of the POWs in exchange for a concrete Israeli proposal on disengagement. This opened the door to the final agreement.

The rapid pace of the negotiations caught the Soviets by surprise. Moreover, Moscow realized that it had been excluded from the talks. Displeased and angry, Gromyko, in a meeting with Nixon on February 4, threatened to obstruct the negotiations and to line up other Arab states against the peace process.[61] Kissinger, wrongly believing that Soviet cooperation was crucial to any settlement— "we also did not want a blowup with the Soviet Union"[62]—arrived in Moscow on March 24, and on March 26 held a three and one-half-hour meeting with Brezhnev. The meeting did not resolve the Soviet-American dispute. Brezhnev claimed that Washington was reneging on its commitment to hold the peace talks in Geneva under joint U.S.-U.S.S.R. auspices. Kissinger, on the other hand, accused Brezhnev of obstructing his efforts to achieve a Syrian-Israeli agreement. Brezhnev answered by accusing Kissinger of keeping the Soviets out of the negotiations, to which Kissinger answered that he was only following the parties' request.

Like Sadat, Assad wished to conclude the agreement bilaterally and have only the ceremonial signing in Geneva. He could not negotiate with Israel publicly and risk a failure. He had to be assured success before he could go to Geneva. A public failure could threaten his political survival. Nor did he want the Soviets "to be part of it, as he made clear by telling me proudly and in great detail how he had prevented Gromyko from visiting Damascus while I was there . . . hardly glorious treatment for Syria's principal weapon supplier.''[63]

Although Kissinger enjoyed unprecedented cooperation from Assad, several major questions remained unanswered. Could the United States coerce Israel to make the necessary concessions? Could Syria be brought to a more workable position? Should Sadat and other Arab leaders play a role? Would the Soviets cooperate or try to obstruct the negotiations? At home, Watergate created major problems. Nixon's closest aides had been indicated on March 1 for perjury, obstruction of justice, and illegal payments to suppress evidence.

Kissinger was very much on his own, trying to use national interests as incentives for a settlement. Israel wanted Assad to stop terrorist activities. This was a vital Israeli interest.[64] On the other hand, the fierce battles along the Syrian border and the memory of the war created strong opposition in Israel to any settlement with Syria. The government knew that any withdrawal on the Golan Heights must be matched by substantial Syrian concessions. Israel was not sure whether Assad was strong enough to commit Syria to such concessions.

Israel demanded a signed treaty committing Syria to nonbelligerence, containment of terrorist activities, and the return of POWs. Israel knew that Assad needed to turn his military defeat into a political victory, and Israel was willing to grant him that in exchange for its demands. However, Assad was faced with a dilemma. An agreement that would return part of the Golan Heights to Syria was for him a matter of national pride as well as personal esteem. His government was a tyranny of the minority (Alawites) over the majority (Sunnis). Assad assumed power in 1970 in a country that suffered many coups and upheavals. The presence of Israeli guns twenty-five miles from his capital of Damascus made him nervous and insecure. Assad also wished to reduce Syria's military expenditures and consequently decrease its dependence on the Soviet Union. A hard-headed, ruthless politician, Assad knew that a settlement with Israel would also provide him with a chance to enhance his relations with the United States, which he had severed in 1967. The prospects of being able to play "East" against "West" again appealed to Assad. Finally, he was defeated in a war that he initiated. The only way he could keep his promise to his people and regain control of the Golan Heights was to reach an agreement with Israel. Through an Israeli withdrawal he could reinforce his personal power. Although Syria was aligned with the Soviet Union, Assad knew that only the United States could help him save his neck. He hoped that the United States would pressure Israel to give up at least part of the Golan Heights. He was especially interested in resuming control over the city of Kuneitra, which was the symbol of Syrian control of the area. The city of Kuneitra and the hills controlling it became the center of the Israeli-Syrian negotiations. In her memoirs, Prime Minister Meir told how Kissinger learned about Kuneitra. She was extremely impressed with his steadfastness and patience. Although he never heard of the city before, once the negotiations began, "there wasn't a road, a house or even a tree there about which he did not know everything there was to know."[65]

Although both Israel and Syria were interested in a settlement, each had in mind a different outcome. After the successful resolution of the POW issue, the major difficulty was to bring Israel to make a reasonable offer that would lure Assad toward an agreement. On March 15 and 19 Kissinger met with Israeli Foreign Minister Eban and proposed that Israel give up the city of Kuneitra, withdraw to the October 6 lines if not farther, but maintain all the settlements on the Golan Heights and most of its territory. It was clear that Syria would reject any proposal that would not include a return of all Syrian territories taken in 1973 as well as a symbolic foothold beyond the old cease-fire line at Kuneitra. Assad's militant and intransigent attitude prevented any flexibility on these issues. Moreover, he was determined to gain from the disengagement agreement more than his armies had won in the field.[66]

The Israeli-Syrian talks began formally on March 18, the same day that the oil embargo was lifted. This was a strong statement that the Arab states supported an agreement. However, the map that Defense Minister Dayan brought with him to Washington on March 29 and the map that the Syrian Brigadier General Hikmat Shihabi brought with him to Washington on April 13 were still too far apart.

Dayan's disengagement line suggested a border east of the October 6 line, and it included Kuneitra. The plan suggested the application of a buffer zone, which Kissinger considered very helpful, flanked by two limited-forces zones to the east and west. Syria's answer was as expected. It presented a revised map showing a disengagement line running west of Kuneitra. Kissinger told Shihabi that he would try to persuade Israel to withdraw to the October 6 line and pull out from Kuneitra. He stressed the point that "that would be the most that Syria could hope for at this stage."[67]

Israel could hardly believe that Assad would agree to make substantial concessions.[68] Washington argued that any Syrian concessions would be considered an important political achievement. Indeed, the fact that Syria, the most hostile of Israel's neighbors, was negotiating with Israel was a political achievement. Moreover, an Israeli-Syrian agreement would take the pressure off Egypt, and would thwart the intensive Soviet effort to get itself involved in the Middle East.

Kissinger embarked on a mediation campaign without parallel in diplomatic history. Meir defined his efforts as "superhuman." He learned every detail of the topography so that he could be prepared for the negotiations. With the exception of Israeli military personnel, no Israeli Cabinet member was as familiar with and knew so much about Kuneitra as did Kissinger.[69]

Kissinger was a very good listener and he was prepared to spend as much time as was necessary to persuade Assad and Meir that they had to be more flexible. His determination to bring the negotiations to a successful conclusion was supported ironically by Nixon's difficulties at home. Nixon believed that a foreign policy success would help him rebuild his image as a strong, decisive, powerful president. Hence, "Occasional messages from the President served to prod Kissinger to continue even when he was close to despair, or when he thought that it was undignified for the American secretary of state to haggle over minor details as he was required to do."[70]

Problems to be resolved were: (1) the extent of the Israeli withdrawal, (2) demilitarized zones, (3) Syria's promise to stop terrorist activities across the cease-fire line, and (4) the role of the U.N. observer force. In fact, the basic plan was similar to the plan or the model of the Israeli-Egyptian disengagement agreement. The scheme was simple. A U.N. buffer zone of a few kilometers would be followed with a force-limitation zone ten kilometers wide (demilitarized zones); then a twenty-kilometer belt free of artillery; and a thirty-to-forty-kilometer belt free of surface-to-air missiles. In total, seven different zones would be established in an area at most twenty-five kilometers deep and extending to well beyond Damascus![71]

The stumbling block was, as predicted, the final line to which the Israeli forces would withdraw. Syria was prepared to make a strong commitment to deter terrorist penetration into Israel. The nature, size, and function of the U.N. force did not present any difficulty either. However, the precedent set by the Sinai I agreement, in which Egypt regained much of the territory it lost in 1967, hardened Syria's attitude. Hence, during the first week of May, negotiations were deadlocked.

For both Israel and Syria the negotiation was an anguishing experience. Israel felt that it was being sacrificed to save Assad's rule. Moreover, it refused to reward Assad for his brutal assault on Israel. Syria experienced its anguishes, too. Assad knew that signing an agreement with Israel on the Golan Heights was an acknowledgment of Israel's right to be there. Yet, the need for an agreement, cleverly used by Kissinger in his famous shuttle diplomacy, nicknamed the "flying State Department"—resulted in an agreement. Formal negotiations began on April 27, and a month later, on May 31, the agreement was signed.

The breakthrough came on May 8, when Assad began to talk seriously about a line close to that proposed by Israel.[72] The major problem remained the city of Kuneitra and the hills surrounding it. On May 16 Israel agreed to make major concessions. It agreed to a minor withdrawal west of the 1967 line. Syria, however, insisted on a pullout from Kuneitra. Israel demanded to maintain its control over the three hills surrounding the city. (These hills became known as the "Himalayas of General Gur.") Finally, Israel agreed to pull back to the base of the hills. On May 18 Kissinger flew to Damascus to convince Assad to drop his demand for controlling the hills. Assad agreed under the condition that Israel would not place guns on these hills that were capable of shelling Kuneitra. On May 19 Kissinger obtained Israel's assent. On May 20 Kissinger could fly to Damascus with a map of the agreed line.

The two remaining questions were the demilitarization of the area and the size and functions of the U.N. force. Syria wanted only a small U.N. force in the buffer zone; Israel preferred at least two to three thousand U.N. troops.[73] Kissinger began to lose patience. On May 22 he drafted a departure statement and planned to leave the area the next day. Assad, afraid of losing the important Israeli concessions, announced on May 23 that he would accept a large U.N. force, a wider buffer zone of ten kilometers, and a limited-force zone of fifteen kilometers. On May 24 Kissinger returned to Israel where he faced demands for a Syrian commitment to stop terrorist attacks from its border. Israel had two final demands: a U.S. commitment to condone Israeli antiterrorist actions originating from Syria, and a commitment that arms sale agreements would be made on a long-term instead of a year-to-year basis.[74] Although on May 27 Assad changed his mind and refused to give a written commitment to the deterrence of terrorists, he agreed to give an oral commitment, which was accepted by Israel. The settlement could be finalized.

With Syria's concession in hand, Kissinger flew to Israel, and on May 29 he was able to announce that Israel and Syria had reached an agreement. Two days later the military representatives of Syria and Israel signed the necessary documents in Geneva. All were exhausted but elated.

ARMS AND LEVERAGE: THE ROLE OF MILITARY AID

The Israeli-Syrian disengagement agreement was signed after four months of intense and difficult negotiations. Israel was asked to make far-reaching concessions in exchange for a settlement that was not much different from a cease-fire agreement. General Gur, expressing the view of many in Israel, argued that "withdrawal was a sacrifice of permanent security needs to temporary diplomatic convenience . . . General Sharon predicted catastrophic results for our security if we gave up Kuneitra."[75] It was a difficult time for Israel. Following Meir's resignation, general elections were held in March. Throughout those weeks Israel was tormented by an inquiry commission that was probing the events leading to the October war.

In April the commission's report was made public. "It was like a cloudburst, bringing the heavy, hot tension to the breaking point." The report revealed severe deficiencies, neglect, false appraisals, and inadequate reaction in the terrible days that followed the Egyptian and the Syrian attacks.[76] Israel was not in the mood for far-reaching concessions to an enemy that hardly offered anything substantial in return. The question of how much pressure, if at all, was needed to coerce Israel to make these concessions was never clearly resolved. The common view is that Israel was "indisposed toward concessions to its bitter Syrian opponent and would have never signed the agreement had it not been pressured by the U.S."[77] The facts, however, show that although Israel fought for the best bargain it could get, it nonetheless was not coerced into signing. Moreover, transfer of arms played very little role in the American diplomatic campaign.

Indeed, of the three parties involved—Israel, Syria, and the United States—Israel should have been the least interested in an agreement. "Kissinger and Nixon were as anxious for agreement as the Israelis were reserved."[78] Nixon hoped that a foreign policy achievement would offset the Watergate affair, could help end the oil embargo, and would buttress the Israeli-Egyptian accord. Assad hoped that Israeli concessions on the Golan Heights would make up for his humiliating military defeat. For Israel, the common theory argues, there were no major gains, only more frustrating capitulations. It was the strong and assertive American pressure, exerted through Kissinger's diplomacy, that brought about the Israeli-Syrian disengagement agreement.[79]

However, this argument is not congruent with the facts. During the first three weeks of intense combat in October and in light of the weapons gap revealed in battle, the United States airlifted to Israel large quantities of arms. But Israel's inventories were not yet replenished. For example, to counter the surprising success of Arab antitank and antiaircraft missiles, Israel's shopping list included large quantities of armored personnel carriers and mobile, long-range heavy artillery for destroying missile sites. Before the war, Israel was not supplied with a new generation of hand-held or vehicle-mounted personnel antitank missiles which the Arabs had used very successfully on the Egyptian front. These weapons were delivered to Israel on the last week of the war. Israel included in its shopping list long-range standoff airborne weapons, less vulnerable to intensive ground fire. Israel also wanted to upgrade its relatively small navy, which proved to be effective in coastal operations during the war.[80]

However, top on Israel's shopping list were Mavericks, television-guided "smart bombs," the most advanced in their category and the most effective in countering Arab antiaircraft missile fire. In addition to Mavericks, Israel asked for advanced electro-optical target consoles and assorted new ECM pods and decoy chaff missiles. It also ordered some 3,000 new TOW antitank missiles. These were to match the newly provided Soviet Saggers, and were urgently needed to restore the strategic balance.[81]

Israel's dependence on the United States grew with each arms deal. By the end of the decade almost half of Israel's annual military aid credit was used to pay off its existing military debt. The contradiction between Israel's dependence on U.S. aid and its independence in pursuing its foreign policy goals becomes even more striking. Halfway through the war, on October 19, 1973, Nixon presented to Congress an aid package to Israel of $2.2 billion. Half was used to cover the October airlift, and the remaining billion dollars paid off Israel's old arms debt and possibly some future weapon purchases. The credit/grant offer and the terms of payment were not specified, a fact that in the long run enhanced Israel's bargaining position and decreased U.S. leverage. "Since 1974, almost half of Israel's military assistance has been in the form of grants. . . . U.S. military assistance to Israel exceeds assistance to any other country and continues to rise."[82] As long as the Soviet Union was providing its clients with sophisticated arms, the United States had to ensure Israel's strategic superiority.

Throughout the five months of difficult and sometimes confrontational negotiations, the United States did not use transfer of arms as leverage to achieve Israeli concessions. Between January—when the Golan disengagement agreement talks began—and May 31, Israel was receiving almost all the military hardware it had called for. Moreover, on the eve of Kissinger's Damascus shuttle, Nixon waived repayment on $1 billion. Consequently, U.S. leverage became completely ineffective. In March 1974, during the toughest period of the negotiations, Defense Minister Dayan had visited Washington and presented a list conditioning Israel's concessions on American weapons. Israel was telling Washington what could be exchanged for what, thus linking its concessions with long-term American commitments on arms supplies.[83]

THE SINAI II DISENGAGEMENT AGREEMENT: WAS REASSESSMENT SUCCESSFUL?

The Sinai II disengagement agreement, which paved the way for the Camp David Accords, has been considered the best example of successful American leverage. The theory assumes that the Israeli-Syrian agreement convinced Washington that more could be achieved. Thus President Ford decided to pressure Israel to make additional territorial concessions while asking Egypt for a nonbelligerence commitment. He then exercised successfully his famous "reassessment" strategy, prevailing over strong congressional opposition. Hence, in the debate over the effectiveness of American coercive tactics, the Sinai II agreement presumably stands out as the living example of U.S. leverage. This theory also assumes that Israel and the Arab governments are relatively impotent and could "never by themselves be able to devise a compromise solution."[84]

Moreover, the United States had to coerce Israel since inducement became too expensive. "[To provide] military and financial aid, as Secretary Kissinger did in the case of the Sinai Agreement, would exceed even our financial possibilities."[85] To achieve compliance the United States had to use its leverage, that is, to withhold all military aid (or to threaten to do it). However, an analysis of the events that preceded the signing of the Sinai II agreement reveals a completely different picture.

Shortly after the Golan Heights disengagement agreement was successfully completed in 1974, the leaders in Jerusalem and Washington had to step down. Both political changes were painful. During the summer, Nixon was fighting for his political survival to no avail. On June 19, he completed a five-day tour to the Middle East, which he believed would help reinstate his image. On June 25, a day after the Judiciary Committee completed its hearings and issued four more subpoenas to Nixon, he left for Moscow.[86] On June 24 the Supreme Court ruled that Nixon must turn over sixty-four tapes, and on June 27 the House Judiciary Committee began voting the first of three articles of impeachment. Nixon gave in on August 8, and on August 9, he resigned.[87]

Gerald Ford, although not a newcomer to American politics, was a novice in U.S. foreign policy. He continued to employ Kissinger as secretary of state, with the Middle East first on his foreign policy agenda. Hence, U.S. Middle East policy experienced both continuity and change. Shortly, the question of a new peace initiative was revived, along with Kissinger's famous step-by-step diplomacy. It was unclear whether he would take the "West Bank Highway," that is, try to reach an Israeli-Jordanian accord, or would return to Egypt for another, more substantial accord.

It seemed that Kissinger wanted both. He wanted to take another step forward in the Sinai while pursuing an Israeli-Jordanian accord. Although Sadat had urged the United States to give priority to the Egyptian front, Kissinger was inclined to put more effort on the Jordanian front. In a hearing before the Senate Foreign Relations Committee, he said that

the sensible next step . . . would be Jordan, because it is the most moderate of the Arab governments . . . and because the best way to deal with the Palestinian question would be to draw the Jordanians [into] the West Bank and thereby turn the debate . . . into one between the Jordanians and the Palestinians rather than between the Palestinians and Israelis.[88]

Kissinger's prophecy was only partially correct. Jordan refused to join the negotiations and Israel refused to offer Jordan concessions that would allow the king to begin formal talks. However, the conflict predicted by Kissinger between the king and Arafat of the PLO did materialize, and it did, as Kissinger predicted, relieve Israel of some of the pressure.

However, this road proved to lead down a blind alley. The parties' stands on the issues of the West Bank, the Palestinians, and the future of Jerusalem were irreconcilable. The United States had to take a different road to peace. William Quandt argued that the Jordanian option failed not because of substantive or conceptual problems, but because of the Watergate affair and the crisis of authority in Washington. He suggested that the Watergate affair killed the peace prospects in the Middle East.

However, the issue of how much Watergate crippled Nixon's presidential leadership has yet to be determined. The realities of the Middle East make it difficult to assume that a strong president could have transcended the step-by-step diplomacy and move on to a more comprehensive negotiation, including the Palestinians, as was suggested by Quandt. To blame the failure of a comprehensive settlement on Nixon's crisis of authority is highly speculative.[89]

The myopic view of the Jordanian option became more evident as time went by. Each president since Truman tried to bring Israel and Jordan to the negotiating table and failed. Even the momentum gained by the Camp David Accords did not bring King Hussein or the PLO to the bargaining table. The only possible movement toward peace was again between Israel and Egypt, where the issues were less complex and an agenda for an agreement could be established.

Ford's style as president was very different from that of Nixon. "Gerald Ford was an unlikely president."[90] He was a long-time Congressman and his ambition had been to become Speaker of the House, not a chief executive. However, once appointed to the vice presidency in October 1973, he made a quick shift in style as well as in state of mind.

Ford gave special attention to the Middle East. He shifted his long-term legislative loyalty and said that if U.S. foreign policy was to be successful, the President could not be rigidly restricted by Congress. Excessive legislative restrictions "even if intended for the best motives and purposes, can have the opposite results."[91]

This statement, coming from a twenty-year veteran of the House, showed a radical change of perception. Ford decided to be an assertive chief executive, especially in the realm of foreign affairs. He launched a new peace initiative within days of becoming president. His attitude made Kissinger's Middle East diplomacy easier and more difficult at the same time. Kissinger enjoyed a special relationship with Nixon, which derived from a sense of mutual respect and understanding. Such a relationship never developed between Ford and Kissinger.

The futility of the Jordanian option became evident at the Rabat Arab summit, when on October 28, 1974, the PLO was recognized as the sole legitimate representative of the Palestinian people. Hussein was stripped of his traditional role as the guardian of the Palestinians, whereas Arafat gained additional international fame and prestige when he addressed the U.N. General Assembly on November 13, 1974.[92] The only alternative left was a second partial Israeli-Egyptian agreement.

Washington wished to maintain the momentum and the movement toward peace under American leadership. Hence, Kissinger turned again to his best friend in the Middle East, Sadat. He explained that Egypt could now regain control of the oil fields and remove the Israeli forces from the Gidi and Mitla passes, which were the gateway to the Sinai. Moreover, the atmosphere in Egypt was unfavorable. Sadat was severely criticized for allowing himself to be persuaded by the United States to trade off the assets gained by the Arabs in the October war for some minor returns. Sadat needed another substantial Israeli concession "in order to rebut his critics and vindicate his policy."[93]

Israel had an opposing view. It felt that Sadat was expecting too much in exchange for too little. However, Israel was interested in a second agreement in the Sinai. Upon his return from Washington on September 1974, after concluding a series of meetings with the new American president, newly elected Prime Minister Rabin began to plan for an interim agreement with Egypt. Ford asked Kissinger to visit the Middle East in October, hoping that the previous successes would be repeated. One pressing issue was the oil price, which had not been resolved after the embargo was lifted. The price for a barrel was over $10, compared with less than $2 a barrel in 1973. It was a heavy drain on everyone's economy, especially Europe and Japan. Inflation followed by a recession plagued the sluggish Western economies. The transfer of world wealth to the Middle East was another source of worry. The United States was faced with a dilemma: how to continue its support of Israel while enhancing its trade and influence with the oil-producing countries in order to recycle their petrodollars. A peace agreement might have alleviated the problem. Hence, all three parties— Egypt, Israel, and the United States—were interested in an agreement. However, major conflicts of interests posed severe problems. Consequently, the negotiations were lengthy and difficult. On March 1975 they even broke down and the feeling was that an agreement could not be reached.

The negotiations encountered difficulties and frustrations right from the beginning. Kissinger's trip to the Middle East in early October 1974 proved to be a total failure, but he was not discouraged and visited Sadat in November to explore the Egyptian position and intentions after the Rabat summit. Kissinger discovered that Sadat was willing to continue the negotiations in spite of the Rabat resolution. The mood in Jerusalem was similar. In early December Foreign Minister Allon visited Washington to present Israel's position.

Allon's message addressed Sadat's major demands, that is, an Israeli withdrawal from the two strategic passes in the Sinai and the return of the oil fields of Abu Rodeis. Sadat made it clear that the agreement would be purely military in character, at least in appearance, involving no overt political concession. Allon said that in exchange for a withdrawal, Israel demanded a commitment for nonbelligerency, demilitarization of zones to be evacuated by Israel, and the rehabilitation of the canal. Israel wanted, in effect, to make it impossible for Egypt to become involved in a war legally and practically.[94]

Israel and Egypt were anxious to reach an agreement, but each expected the other to make concessions perceived unacceptable. Since Sadat refused to make political concessions, Israel felt that he showed "very little inclination to offer much in return."[95] Israel was willing to withdraw thirty to fifty kilometers along various parts of the Sinai, but without giving up the passes and the oil fields. However, unofficially, Rabin said on December 1974 that a nonbelligerence commitment was not essential to the agreement. In an interview to the Israeli daily Ha'aretz, on December 3, 1974, Rabin said that the energy crisis and European dependence on Arab oil put Israel in a very unfavorable position. Israel has to survive, said Rabin, for about a decade until Western dependence on Arab oil would be reduced. It was important, therefore, to gain time, and emerge "safe and sound, from these seven lean years." An agreement with Egypt was important as a strategy, and Israel should pay the price for its conclusion.

Another factor influencing Rabin's policy was the need to mend fences with the United States. Washington was eager to revive the step-by-step diplomacy.

Rabin knew that any progress on the road to peace would reduce the possibility of an Egyptian-Syrian military link and help prevent Egypt from returning to the Soviet sphere of influence.[96]

As Israel and Egypt were trying to work out their differences, Syria became involved. It would not accept a second Israeli-Egyptian agreement that could isolate Syria to confront alone a militarily superior Israel. Assad began to build up his forces along the border with Israel. The Soviet Union understood that the new American initiative would further weaken its influence in the region, especially in Egypt. In the meeting between Ford and Brezhnev, which took place in Vladivostock in November 1974, the Soviet leader insisted on continuation of the Geneva process.[97] Ford decided to dispatch Kissinger again to the region, mainly to try and get a more acceptable Israeli offer. Kissinger was optimistic. Rabin's statement to a former mayor of New York, John Lindsay, that "in exchange for an Egyptian commitment not to go to war . . . and in an effort to reach true peace, the Egyptians could get even the passes and the oil fields,"[98] left Kissinger cautiously optimistic. His shuttle to the Middle East was scheduled for late February and early March of 1975. Ford was disturbed over the situation in the region and expected Kissinger to make substantial progress.

Ford's two highest priorities were the Middle East and Indochina. In the early months of 1975 his first priority was to stabilize what he considered to be a very dangerous stalemate. In an interview to *Time* magazine and NBC-TV, Ford said: "Every day that passes without a new accord in the Middle East becomes more dangerous."[99]

During the February visit Kissinger realized that his optimism was premature. Although Rabin was advocating flexibility, the gap between Israel and Egypt had not narrowed. Egypt demanded an Israeli withdrawal from the passes, which Israel considered unacceptable; Israel demanded a commitment for nonbelligerence, which Egypt considered unacceptable. Kissinger spent five days in the Middle East visiting Israel, Egypt, Israel again, Syria, Jordan, and Saudi Arabia. The negotiations were fruitless. The only progress came from a meeting between Kissinger and the shah in Zurich, on February 18, where the shah promised to sell oil to Israel if it gave up the Abu Rodeis oil fields. Kissinger decided to return in March, hoping that both sides would show more flexibility.

When Israel reviewed its position it realized the dilemma it was facing. A deadlock could lead to the resumption of the Geneva conference, which might strain relations with the United States and get the Soviets back into the process. However, Egypt's substantial territorial demands were unacceptable unless the state of war against Israel was terminated.

Kissinger began his March shuttle with a trip to Egypt on March 8, 1975. Sadat was prepared to (1) declare that the Israeli-Egyptian conflict would not be solved by military means, (2) promise that Egypt would not use force and would observe the cease fire, (3) commit himself that no military or paramilitary forces would be allowed to operate against Israel from Egyptian territory, (4) reduce the hostile propaganda against Israel, and (5) selectively ease the economic boycott.[100] Kissinger went to Israel on March 9, submitting the Egyptian proposal and receiving the Israeli proposal.

Israel demanded various assurances of nonbelligerency, as well as more political concessions. Specifically, permitting the passage of Israeli merchandise and Israeli-manned vessels under foreign flags through the Suez Canal. Another demand was to create a real buffer zone between the forces. On the issue of the depth of its withdrawal, however, Israel was divided and could not reach a consensus.[101]

It was clear that Israel wanted to reach a political agreement, whereas Egypt wanted a military agreement. The second problem was technical but nonetheless very disturbing. It involved the depth of Israel's withdrawal, control of the passes, and demilitarization zones. The oil fields were the easiest issue to solve. Kissinger's schedule consisted of abnormal hours; he would arrive at odd times, ignore the differences between day and night, and often conduct marathon talks.[102] By March 20 Egypt presented two proposals. Under the first, both countries would hold the passes; Israel would control the eastern part, Egypt the western. The two armies would be separated by a ten-to-twenty-kilometer buffer zone patrolled by U.N. forces. The second proposal was that Egypt and Israel would take positions outside of the passes, at an equal distance, and the zone between them would be controlled by U.N. forces. This meant that Israel would remove its early warning system from Um Hashiva and withdraw some fifty to seventy kilometers, whereas the Egyptian forces would advance some twenty to thirty kilometers.

On March 19 Kissinger submitted to Israel what he believed to be the best package he could get. It included an exchange of the passes and the oil fields for a formula of nonuse of force, a document that would make sure that conflicts between Israel and Egypt would not be solved by force but by diplomacy. Other Egyptian concessions concerned the duration of the agreement, that is, it would remain in effect until superceded by another agreement; only U.N. forces would control the passes; Egyptian troops would move a few miles east of the passes; Egypt would relax the economic boycott against Israel.

Kissinger was dismayed when the Egyptian proposal was rejected by Israel, which did not accept the "nonuse of force" and insisted on nonbelligerency. As time passed, Kissinger grew more and more impatient and Ford became more and more angry. On March 21 Ford sent Rabin a very tough message. He warned the Prime Minister that if Kissinger's mission failed because of Israel's intransigence he would "reassess" U.S. policy toward Israel.

Ford felt frustrated and could not understand why, with all the American aid, Israel did not feel secure and confident so that it could show more flexibility. He had felt that Israel was not ready for any quid pro quo. He remarked bitterly: "If we were going to build up their military capabilities, we in turn had to see some flexibility to achieve a fair, secure and permanent peace."[103]

Ford's message boomeranged. The next morning the Israeli cabinet held an emergency meeting, on a Sabbath. It adopted a much harsher tone, refusing to consider giving up any part of the passes in the absence of nonbelligerency.[104] Kissinger did not even bother to take the Israeli proposal to Egypt. He communicated with Sadat by telephone and received his flat rejection, as expected. Kissinger concluded that he was unable to bring the parties to an agreement, and on March 23 he departed for Washington. Reassessment was now officially declared.

President Ford issued a statement that Washington was reassessing its relationship with Israel because "we gave Israel ample supply of economic aid and weapons, so that Israel would feel strong and confident . . . and more flexible and willing to discuss a lasting peace."[105] Like many others in Washington, he expected the military aid to give the U.S. leverage. When this did not happen, Ford was angry and frustrated. He could not understand why regardless of the fact that "the Israelis were stronger militarily than all their Arab neighbors combined, yet peace was no closer than it had ever been."[106] Indeed, because Israel was strong and well supplied, it could defy American pressures and maintain its own independent policy. However, Ford continued to insist on a quid pro quo.[107]

The reassessment policy has been used by both advocates and opponents of the leverage theory. Ford, although a long time supporter of Israel in Congress, felt that in a conflict of interests "we have to judge what is in our national interest above any and all other considerations." Ford believed that Washington was holding 99 percent of the cards in this game and could force Israel to make concessions that it was not otherwise prepared to make.[108] Many in Washington argued that Israel's intransigence did not result from real security considerations, but from an unreasoning distrust and false sense of insecurity, which could be overcome by devising security arrangements.[109]

This approach led to several major misperceptions. First, Israel's security needs were dismissed with relative ease. Second, the difficulties in devising effective security arrangements were underestimated. Third, the level of American leverage was greatly exaggerated.[110]

Indeed, the "reassessment" of 1975 was fruitless and, therefore, abandoned. It did not yield leverage and Israel successfully resisted American pressures. "The ability of the United States to exert coercive leverage on Israel has diminished since 1970."[111] Ford had ignored the fact that Israel would adamantly resist attempts to pressure it to withdraw to borders considered unsafe and insecure. Indeed, the Department of State in a 1969 survey by the Bureau of Intelligence and Research concluded that attempts by the United States and other countries to use arms embargoes as a policy tool can have some influence in marginal policy areas, but aid does not provide enough leverage to force a recipient to take any actions contrary to its vital interests, and more often than not, embargoes aimed at vital interests fail completely, and have detrimental effects on the long-term relations between the supplying nation and the recipient.[112] In the specific case of the reassessment policy, a complete arms embargo was inconceivable because it would have weakened Israel dangerously. A partial withholding of arms (which the reassessment was actually imposing) was not threatening enough to coerce Israel to comply with Washington's policy.

Israel's arms pipeline was not cut off. Hundreds of tanks continued to arrive on time. Even training of Israeli F–15 crews continued, as did production of special order, conventional explosive Lance warheads. Interestingly enough, the withholding of arms became a domestic political issue. On May 21 when reassessment became public, seventy-six Senators, three-quarters of the Senate, signed an open letter to Ford urging "responsiveness" to Israel's arms requests. The Senators urged Ford to be responsive to Israel's request for $2.59 billion in military and economic aid. According to Ford:

Although I said publicly that I welcomed the letter . . . in truth it really bugged me. . . . We have given vast amounts of military and economic assistance to Israel over the years, and we had never asked for anything in return. . . . Quite apart from that, the letter—especially its tone—jeopardized any chance for peace in the Middle East.[113]

The extent of Congressional influence on aid to Israel has been addressed by numerous works.[114] The prevalent view has been that the Jewish lobby has almost complete control over the American Congress. It has been considered extremely effective, professional, and equipped with state of the art communication techniques and plenty of money. Its foes argue that the American Israel Public Affairs Committee (AIPAC), which has an annual budget of less than $1 million, closely monitors legislation in Congress and plays a critical role in advancing Israel's interests. Among the Israel lobby's many victory trophies from the legislative arena, one of the most conspicuous and consequential was the "letter of seventy-six." It was considered crucial in terminating the Ford-Kissinger reassessment policy.[115]

This view, however, has not been universally accepted. Indeed, the argument was that during the 1970s the Arab countries gained substantial influence in Washington, which was manifested mainly in large deliveries of arms. Andrew Pierre argues that Israel was surprised and dismayed at the large transfers of American arms to Arab countries, which included arms packages to Egypt, Jordan, and Saudi Arabia. West European arms were delivered to Iraq and Libya, and Soviet arms piled up in Syria, Iraq, and Yemen.

In fact, the Ford Administration introduced a new idea in U.S.-Arab relations. The dependence of the West on Arab oil, with all its implications for energy supplies, proved the vulnerability of Western economies. It also had its impact on American policy. Specifically, the willingness to sell arms to the Arabs in greater quantities and at higher levels of sophistication introduced a military dimension to the re-equilibration of the American stance in the Middle East.[116] The U.S. arms transfers to the Arab countries, which gained new dimensions in the seventies culminated with the 1981 sale of the AWACS systems to Saudi Arabia, in spite of fierce Jewish lobbying against it.

OVERVIEW

Although President Ford was furious with the "letter of seventy-six" and felt that Israel tried to show him "who's boss,"[117] Israel did not harden its position as a result of the letter. Israel was waiting for Sadat to make proper concessions in exchange for an Israeli withdrawal from the Mitla and the Gidi passes, and the return of the Abu Rodeis oil fields. Kissinger's mission collapsed over two issues: (1) the extent of the Israeli withdrawal from the passes and the Israeli's early warning posts, and (2) Egypt's refusal to declare an end to belligerence. Israel's position before and after the reassessment policy was that "the Middle Eastern crisis persisted not because of an Israeli refusal to evacuate territories, but because of an Arab refusal to make peace."[118]

Israel explained to Kissinger that Sadat offered only token concessions that could not be taken seriously. Israel was persistent and for three months the negotiations were deadlocked. Hence, "reassessment" failed not because of the "letter of seventy-six" but because the parties refused to compromise. Ford and Kissinger realized that a continued pressure on Israel, namely, a withholding of arms, was counterproductive. "The only viable strategy was to resume step-by-step diplomacy."[119] Moreover, Ford decided to personally explore the prospects for an agreement with Rabin and Sadat. On June 1 and 2 Ford met Sadat in Salzburg three times. During these meetings Ford confessed that he had no new ideas because "the Israelis said they had none." Sadat's surprising answer was: "We are willing to go as far as you think we should go. We trust you, and we trust the United States."[120] Once Sadat agreed to make the necessary concessions, Israel reciprocated. Constructive ideas began to develop. Sadat suggested a buffer zone around the Gidi and Mitla passes, in which the United States could keep a limited number of nonmilitary personnel. They would be responsible for surveillance. They would monitor troop movements. The idea was welcomed by all.[121] In return for Sadat's concessions, Ford promised to ask Congress to approve substantial military and economic aid to Egypt. The two leaders agreed to station civilian technicians in a Sinai buffer zone as an American proposal, fearing that Israel might reject it if it learned that it was an Egyptian proposal. On June 11 Prime Minister Rabin arrived in Washington. Now that reassessment was abandoned, Israel was more willing to cooperate.

U.S. pressure during the reassessment was counterproductive because the United States was pressuring its only reliable ally. Moreover, the Arab states relied upon U.S. coercion to obtain goals for which they would otherwise have had to make concessions. Hence, when Ford suspended the promised $2.2 billion of U.S. assistance requested by Israel in January 1975, Israel did not capitulate. In the short run, Israel's arms supply was more than adequate. Israeli forces were reported to have enough supplies on hand to survive an American withholding of arms.[122] Thus the "reassessment" did not bear the expected results. Only after the United States and Egypt proposed substantial political and strategic concessions did Israel cooperate.

Many in Israel believed that Rabin was giving up too much. However, he believed that in Austria Sadat showed a great measure of flexibility regarding the main issues, which opened up the channels of communication. Hence, in the middle of June, Sinai II began to evolve. Israel, according to Rabin, was interested in an agreement for various reasons, the least among them being Ford's tactic of withholding of arms. The President was still using his coercion tactics; he threatened to go to Geneva and to involve the U.S.S.R. in the negotiations if the renewed talks failed.

When Kissinger met with Rabin on June 12, he threatened to end the negotiations if Israel continued to insist on holding on to the eastern parts of the passes. "As a result, Geneva will become inevitable and I don't know what position the U.S. will adopt there!"[123] On June 13 tempers rose high. Israel would not bow to Egypt's demands. "Please don't threaten me with the Geneva Conference," said Rabin to Kissinger. But maps were unfolded and the negotiations began to progress. The United States suggested stationing civilian technicians in a Sinai buffer zone if Congress would agree. Rabin seemed intrigued. Israel's reaction to Sadat's proposal was positive. "So positive, in fact, that Henry thought he should return to the area soon. I gave him my okay, and on August 20, he left for Israel, Egypt, Syria, Jordan and Saudi Arabia."[124]

Israel's desire to resume negotiations was mainly determined by security and economic considerations. Israeli leaders were hardly susceptible to pressure of the Ford administration. Indeed, Israel assumed that the United States would be more responsive to its economic and strategic needs, whereas Sadat would be more flexible concerning the technical and military aspects of the agreement. The long-term effects of withholding of arms on Israel's security was an important consideration in Israel. This could have included deliveries of previously promised Lance missiles, F–15 jet airplanes, among other weapon systems. Finally, Sadat showed flexibility on the three annual renewals of the mandate of the U.N. forces, on the continued Israeli use of the intelligence facility (provided Egypt was given one facing the Israeli lines), and he also accepted the principle of easing the economic boycott and promised to tone down anti-Israeli propaganda. Moreover, he was willing to have most of the terms of the agreement published, which was a de facto recognition of the State of Israel. The agreement became a reality.

It remained for the United States and Israel to work out their own understanding. Israel had two demands: first, a written memorandum of understanding saying that before the United States moved in any direction affecting the future of the region, it would notify Israel. "I had no problem agreeing to that," said Ford.[125] The second request was more troublesome. Israel demanded a military aid package of $2 billion and a clear American commitment that the United States would prevent any Soviet intervention in the Middle East.[126]

Ford approved an arms package to Israel of $1.5 billion. Half of that would be a grant; the rest would be a loan with an understood forgiveness feature. The Israelis, however, wanted more. Their shopping list included sophisticated weaponry that even U.S. forces hadn't yet received. The United States approved most but not all of the requests. The most controversial were air-to-air and SA missiles and F–16 fighter planes. Israel also requested Pershing I missiles to counter the Soviet SCUDs. The F–16 jets were not yet available for export, and the Pershing request was later withdrawn because of Congressional objection. (The Pershing has nuclear capabilities.) Israel was promised M–60 tanks plus assorted heavy artillery, Lance missiles, twenty-five F–15 jets, improved TOW and DRAGON missiles, and Maverick TV-guided bombs. Israel also asked for and received an assortment of advanced electronic warfare technology including E–2C Hawkeye and CH–53 helicopter airborne intelligence platforms, plus late model ECM, weapon guidance systems, and data-processing modules for Israel's combat airplanes.[127] Israel's requests for satellite technology as well as COBRA helicopter gun ships were denied.

After ten days of extensive shuttle diplomacy, between August 21 and August 31, all seemed ready for an agreement. Sinai II was modeled after Sinai I, with a U.N. buffer zone separating the two parties and a limited armament zone drawn on both sides. Israel dropped its demand for a formal political statement ending the state of belligerence, and the two sides agreed to resolve any conflict between themselves by peaceful means. Egypt agreed to permit the transit of nonmilitary cargoes to and from Israel to pass through the Suez Canal. Israel agreed to withdraw from the passes and the oil fields. Egypt agreed that Israel would continue to operate its electronic early warning station at Um Hashiba. Israel promised not to attack Syria, whereas Egypt promised not to join Syria if and when it attacked Israel. The United States promised to be responsive to Israel's military, economic, and energy needs, and promised to supply Israel with oil in the event of a boycott. Finally, Israel received American assurances about future U.S. political and diplomatic activities.[128]

The conclusive discussion between the United States and Israel was held on the night of August 31, and lasted until 6:00 A.M. It was mostly a dialogue between Kissinger and Rabin. After a long and difficult night, an agreement was reached. The Israeli Cabinet approved it on September 1, and the formal document was signed in Geneva on September 4, 1975. There is no doubt that the Sinai II disengagement agreement paved the way for Sadat's historic visit to Jerusalem on November 19, 1977, and it served as the political framework for the Camp David Accords.

The crucial question is: why did the negotiations break down in March, and why were they successful in June? Was the withholding of arms and the reassessment policy responsible for that? American and Israeli analysts differ sharply on this question. Most Americans tend to give more weight to U.S. leverage. Israelis depict reassessment as "the limits of leverage." Indeed, Israel proved its remarkable capacity to resist American pressures and then to extract a high price for eventual compliance.[129] Moreover, Israel enjoyed a high level of support from American public opinion and it gained political leverage from domestic politics.

It has been argued that Israel, however, could not have resisted U.S. pressure for more than a few months. Consequently, it had to cave in to American demands.[130] The fact that Israel did become more flexible in its demands could be interpreted as successful leverage tactics. However, it seems that Israel changed its policy only after most of its vital demands had been fulfilled.

First, Kissinger's threats during his shuttle in March were fruitless. All the promises to withhold arms were not effective because Israel was in no immediate need for arms. Second, the American "accepted wisdom that arms for Israel would make its leaders sufficiently secure so as to feel able to make territorial concessions" proved to be wrong.[131] Although Israel felt secure and adequately supplied with arms, it refused to make concessions. Finally, although transfer of arms was a central feature in the process of negotiations, it did not determine its success or failure. Israel's policy was directly linked to changes in the positions of Egypt and the United States.

Clearly, there was a change from March to September in the terms offered not just by Kissinger, but by Sadat as well. Israeli sources emphasized, for example, the important compromise on the exact location of the new lines and duration of Sinai II. Second, Egypt agreed that American technicians would monitor the accord. Thus, the outcome was a compromise in which other factors besides arms and other actors besides the United States played a major role. It seems that because the American and the Egyptian political concessions were combined with a policy of reassessment, it was common to attribute the success of the August shuttle to the withholding of arms. In fact, Israel could successfully protect itself without the F–15 jets that were promised and then withheld.

The June negotiations were successful because of substantial changes in Sadat's position concerning the major issues that bothered Israel. For example, Sadat agreed that the early warning stations be manned by Israelis and Egyptians, with the U.S. flag flying over them and American sentries guarding their entrance.[132]

Israel then waived its demand for a statement of nonbelligerence. Instead, an MOU was signed by the United States and Israel promising American protection. Israel could then be more flexible on the depth of its withdrawal. Israel was satisfied with demilitarization of the Sinai. It could provide an adequate security and allow Israel to take advantage of its superiority in mobile warfare beyond the zone of Egypt's ground-to-air missile umbrella.

The memorandum of understanding included far-reaching commitments to support and protect Israel militarily, economically, and politically. The United States had changed its traditional policy and promised long-term arms supplies to Israel. The MOU promised Israel Pershing I missiles and F–16 jets, which were not yet available for export, and three years later only about half of the promised number were finally released (in an arms package with Saudi and Egyptian planes). The Pershing request was withdrawn because of Pentagon opposition.

Hence, the goodwill of the three parties involved, combined with mutual concessions that satisfied the security and the political needs of all, yielded the much-awaited agreement. Since none of those conditions could be duplicated on the West Bank, a formal agreement was never reached between Israel and Jordan.

NOTES

1. Yitzhak Rabin, *The Rabin Memoirs* (Boston: Little, Brown, 1979), p. 235.

2. Henry Kissinger, *Years of Upheaval* (Boston: Little, Brown, 1982), p. 196.

3. Anwar-el-Sadat, *In Search of Identity* (New York: Harper & Row, 1978), p. 230.

4. Abba Eban, *An Autobiography* (New York: Random House, 1977), p. 497.

5. William Quandt, *Decade of Decisions* (Berkeley: University of California Press, 1977), p. 154.

6. Ibid., p. 160.

7. Kissinger, *Years of Upheaval*, p. 197.

8. See Sadat's discussion in *In Search of Identity*, pp. 235–236.

9. Harold H. Saunders, *The Other Walls* (Washington, DC: American Enterprise Institute, 1985), p. 11.

10. See the excellent discussion by Merril A. McPeak, "Israel: Borders and Security," *Foreign Affairs* (April 1976), pp. 426–443.

11. Eban, *Autobiography*, p. 512.

12. Sadat, *In Search of Identity*, p. 244.

13. See discussion by Matti Golan, *The Secret Conversations of Henry Kissinger: Step by Step Diplomacy in the Middle East* (New York: Quadrangle Books, 1976).

14. Matti Golan, *Sihotav H'sodiot Shel Henry Kissinger* (Hebrew) (Jerusalem: Schocken, 1976), pp. 40–44; also Insight Team of the *Sunday Times*, *The Yom Kippur War* (London: Deutch, 1974), pp. 124–129.

15. Elaborated in Sadat's speech to the Egyptian National Assembly, February 4, 1971, published in an interview with *Newsweek*, February 22, 1971.

16. In his address of October 16, 1973, Sadat reiterated his request of 1971 that the United States assume the role of a "peace broker"; see Saadia Touval, *The Peace Brokers* (Princeton, NJ: Princeton University Press, 1982), p. 230.

17. Sadat, *In Search of Identity*, p. 24.

18. Comptroller General of the United States, *U.S. Assistance to Israel* (Washington, DC: General Accounting Office, 1983), p. 8.

19. During their Washington meeting in September 1969, President Nixon asked Prime Minister Meir for a quid pro quo "hardware for software." Meir, surprised and angry, rejected the proposal outright. For a complete account of the meeting, see Rabin, *Rabin Memoirs*, p. 155.

20. Comptroller General report, p. 7.

21. Interview with Israeli General (Ret.) Amos Gilboa, June 1986.

22. Kissinger, *Years of Upheaval*, p. 493.

23. Eban, *Autobiography*, p. 517.

24. Kissinger, *Years of Upheaval*, p. 495.

25. Interview with Israeli Air Force pilots (ret.), June 1986.

26. Kissinger, *Years of Upheaval*, p. 539.

27. Seth P. Tillman, *The United States in the Middle East* (Bloomington: Indiana University Press, 1982), p. 75.

28. Nadav Safran, *Israel the Embattled Ally* (Cambridge: Harvard University Press, 1978), p. 510.

29. Kissinger, *Years of Upheaval*, p. 551.

30. Safran, *Israel*, p. 508.

31. President Nixon had sent Prime Minister Meir a personal message urging her to accept the U.S.-Soviet cease-fire proposal.

32. Kissinger, *Years of Upheaval*, p. 568.

33. See discussion by Golan (Hebrew), pp. 85–86.

34. Kissinger, *Years of Upheaval*, p. 589.

35. Seymour Finger, "The Maintenance of Peace," in *National Security and Nuclear Strategy*, eds. Robert Connery and Demetrios Caraley (New York: Academy of Political Science, 1983), pp. 27–37.

36. Eban, *Autobiography*, p. 540.

37. Touval, *Peace Brokers*, p. 233.

38. Kissinger, *Years of Upheaval*, p. 618.

39. Golan (Hebrew), p. 101.

40. Ibid., pp. 103–108; see also Safran, *Israel*, p. 510.

41. Eban, *Autobiography*, p. 538; Touval, *Peace Brokers*, pp. 236–237; views confirmed by Israeli military officials.

42. The friendly atmosphere was first developed at the Kilometer 101.

43. *New York Times*, November 8; Also Golan (Hebrew), p. 108.

44. Safran, *Israel*, p. 515.

45. Touval, *Peace Brokers*, p. 242.

46. Golan (Hebrew), p. 120.

47. Ibid., p. 224.

48. Safran, *Israel*, p. 516.

49. Golan (Hebrew), pp. 109–118.

50. Pollock, *The Politics of Pressure* (Westport, CT: Greenwood Press, 1982), p. 180.

51. Quandt argues that the heavy U.S. pressure was successful; see *Decade of Decisions*, pp. 220–223. The argument is, however, more presumptuous than factual.

52. Touval, *Peace Brokers*, p. 242.

53. Golda Meir, *My Life* (New York: Putnam, 1975), pp. 442–444.

54. See Golan, Safran, Quandt, among others.

55. Quandt, *Decade of Decisions*, p. 239.

56. Ibid., p. 237.

57. Kissinger, *Years of Upheaval*, p. 850.

58. Ibid., p. 939.

59. Touval, *Peace Brokers*, p. 249.

60. Quandt, *Decade of Decisions*, p. 234.

61. Kissinger, *Years of Upheaval*, p. 941.

62. Ibid., p. 941.

63. Ibid., p. 956.

64. Interviews with Israeli military officials.

65. Meir, *My Life*, p. 443.

66. Eban, *Autobiography*, p. 567.

67. Quandt, *Decade of Decisions*, pp. 236–238.

68. During a meeting with Kissinger in Jerusalem on February 27, Dayan told him that the Syrian proposal offered nothing in return for Israel's concessions.

69. Meir, *My Life*, p. 443.

70. Quandt, *Decade of Decisions*, p. 239.

71. See Kissinger, *Years of Upheaval*, p. 964.

72. *New York Times*, May 9, 1974; Quandt, *Decade of Decisions*, pp. 240–243; Touval, *Peace Brokers*, pp. 250–255; Golan (Hebrew), p. 196.

73. *New York Times*, May 23, 1974.

74. Safran, *Israel*, p. 531; Quandt, *Decade of Decisions*, p. 243.

75. Eban, *Autobiography*, p. 574.

76. Ibid., p. 568.

77. See discussion in Pollock, *Politics of Pressure*, pp. 160–208.

78. Ibid., p. 161.

79. See Golan, Pollock, Rabin, among others.

80. See Louis Williams (ed.), *Military Aspects of the Israeli-Arab Conflict* (Tel Aviv: Tel Aviv University Publishing, 1975), p. 168.

81. See *Aviation Week*, October 29, 1973.

82. Comptroller General Report.

83. Golan (Hebrew), p. 210.

84. George Ball, ''How to Save Israel in Spite of Herself,'' *Foreign Affairs* (April 1977), p. 465.

85. Ibid., p. 458.

86. *New York Times*, June 26, 1974.

87. *New York Times*, August 9–11, 1974.

88. See discussion in Kissinger, *Years of Upheaval*, p. 1139.

89. Quandt, *Decade of Decisions*, p. 252.

90. Ibid., p. 253.

91. Gerald Ford, *A Time to Heal: An Autobiography* (New York: Harper & Row, 1979), p. 233.

92. *New York Times*, November 14, 1974.

93. Safran, *Israel*, p. 540.

94. Ibid., p. 541.

95. Rabin, *Rabin Memoirs*, p. 248.

96. Safran, *Israel*, p. 540.

97. A joint communique issued on November 24 said that the search for peace should be based on Resolution 338, *New York Times*, November 25, 1975.

98. Golan (Hebrew), p. 232; Quandt, *Decade of Decisions*, p. 263.

99. Ford, *Time to Heal*, p. 245.

100. *Jerusalem Post*, May 13, 1975.

101. Rabin, *Rabin Memoirs*, p. 253; Quandt, *Decade of Decisions*, pp. 264–265.

102. Rabin, *Rabin Memoirs*, p. 254.

103. Ford, *A Time to Heal*, p. 245.

104. Safran, *Israel*, p. 545.

105. Interview with President Ford, Hearst newspaper chain, March 27, 1975, as discussed in Ford, *A Time to Heal*, pp. 245–246; also *New York Times*, March 28, 1975.

106. Ford, *A Time to Heal*, p. 245.

107. Ibid.

108. This has been a long-standing position of Israel's critics in Congress and the

academic community; see, for example, Tillman's discussion in *The United States in the Middle East*.

109. Ball made this argument in "How to Save Israel."

110. See Steven J. Rosen and Mara Moustafin, "Does Washington Have the Means to Impose a Settlement on Israel?" *Commentary* (October 1977), pp. 25–32.

111. Thomas Wheelock, "Arms for Israel: The Limits of Leverage," *International Security* (Fall 1978), p. 124.

112. Rosan and Moustafin, "Does Washington Have the Means," p. 25; also see Klaus Knorr, *The Power of Nations* (New York: Basic Books, 1975), and Andrew Pierre, *The Global Politics of Arms Sales* (Princeton, NJ: Princeton University Press, 1982).

113. Ford, *A Time to Heal*, p. 287.

114. See the excellent discussion in Marvin Feuerwerger, *Congress and Israel* (Westport, CT: Greenwood Press, 1979).

115. See, for example, Tillman, *The U.S. in the Middle East*, pp. 65–67.

116. See Pierre, "Beyond the Plane Package: Arms and Politics in the Middle East," *International Security* (Summer 1978), p. 148.

117. Ford, *A Time to Heal*, pp. 287–288.

118. Eban, *Autobiography*, p. 584.

119. Quandt, *Decade of Decisions*, p. 270.

120. Ford, *A Time to Heal*, p. 290.

121. Ibid., pp. 290–292.

122. *New York Times*, April 25, 1975.

123. Rabin, *Rabin Memoirs*, p. 264.

124. Ford, *A Time to Heal*, p. 308.

125. Ibid.

126. Quandt, *Decade of Decisions*, p. 273.

127. Pollock, *Politics of Pressure*, p. 191; also interviews with Israeli officials.

128. Touval, *Peace Brokers*, pp. 265–267.

129. This argument is the essence of Pollock's book, *Politics of Pressure*, see p. 192.

130. Golan (Hebrew), pp. 242–246, 251; information confirmed by Israeli officials in interviews.

131. Pierre, "Beyond the Plane Package," p. 149.

132. Rabin, *Rabin Memoirs*, p. 270.

4

The Camp David Accords:
A New Beginning?

On September 17, 1978 Egyptian President Anwar Sadat and Israeli Prime Minister Menachem Begin signed two framework agreements at the Blair House in Washington. The historic documents were witnessed by U.S. President Jimmy Carter. It is common to attribute the Camp David Accords to Sadat's bold initiative and courageous visit to Jerusalem on November 19, 1977. In fact, all three leaders were heavily involved in the peace process many months before Sadat's visit.

Throughout the negotiations, the Egyptian President was the most outspoken and the least patient of the three. Begin, a self-righteous man, burdened the peace process with his intransigent adherence to political principles and legal procedures. President Carter, newly elected and eager to achieve results, was almost exclusively consumed by the peace process for more than a year. He was an able mediator, relentless, and with extreme perseverance. The negotiations were difficult and laborious because of personality incompatibilities. Moreover, each viewed the others' positions adverse to their national interests and, therefore, unacceptable.

POLICY OBJECTIVES AND CONFLICTS OF INTERESTS

Interestingly, it was Begin who first raised the issue of a peace treaty with Egypt at a Fourth of July party given by Samuel Lewis, the American Ambassador to Israel. At the party Begin approached the Rumanian Ambassador, Yan Kovatch, and asked him to arrange a meeting with the Rumanian leader Ceaucescu, whom he wished to recruit as an internuncio in bringing the Israelis and the Egyptians to the bargaining table.[1] Begin's initiative led to his meeting with Ceaucescu in Rumania on August 26, 1977. Following that, the Israeli government assigned Minister of Foreign Affairs Moshe Dayan to travel to India, Iran, Turkey, and Morocco. The leaders of these countries became involved in the peace process, especially King Hassan of Morocco, who hosted two historic meetings between Dayan and Egypt's vice president, Dr. Hassan Tohami. It was during these two meetings that Sadat's visit to Jerusalem was arranged.

Begin's interest in an Israeli-Egyptian peace treaty was twofold. An opposition leader for thirty years, he wished to be the first Israeli leader to bring peace to the Middle East. His second and perhaps strongest desire was to secure Israel's control of the West Bank, or what he called the regions of Judea and Samaria. Hence, he planned to trade off the Sinai for the West Bank.[2] Begin correctly assumed that the election of Carter would help him attain his goal. He was right about the timing but wrong about Sadat and Carter's political attitudes and views. These misperceptions resulted in long and frustrating negotiations.

The first major issue of contention involved the nature of the agreement. Begin expected a bilateral agreement between Israel and Egypt. Carter and Sadat, on the other hand, shared the opinion that the negotiations should lead to a three-pronged agreement including Egypt, Jordan, and Israel. Carter was skeptical about a bilateral Egyptian-Israeli agreement. He believed that it would undermine Egypt's position in the Arab world and reinforce the extremist Arab states. Hence, to Begin's chagrin, Carter insisted that the question of the West Bank and the Palestinians should be an integral part of the negotiations.[3] The Geneva forum was another issue of contention. Carter feared that if the U.S.S.R. would not be a partner to the negotiations, it would obstruct the process.[4] Both Israel and Egypt opposed the idea.

Although it was highly unlikely that Israel would comply with American policies without a struggle, the United States assumed a high degree of leverage considering the high level of Israeli dependence on U.S. aid. However, as the negotiations evolved, it became clear that should the United States use its leverage, that is, withhold the transfer of arms, it would weaken its own bargaining position as well as Israel's. Consequently, the United States had to negotiate long and hard, and many times had to follow the agenda and procedures established by Israel.

The year 1977 looked promising in terms of opening the channels of communication for a serious dialogue between Israel and Egypt. But it took more than a year and a half to translate Sadat's historic visit and the goodwill of the three leaders to a concrete peace treaty. During this time U.S. relations with Israel had been strained, but its relations with Egypt became closer than ever before.[5]

From Sadat's speech in Jerusalem and until the last days of Camp David, the gap between the Israeli and the Egyptian positions seemed irreconcilable. The major obstacle was the future of the West Bank. Begin refused to stop the settlements, negotiate the terms for an Israeli withdrawal from the West Bank, or consider Palestinian self-rule. Sadat and Carter, on the other hand, insisted on a link between an agreement on the Sinai and the West Bank. Moreover,

Sadat refused to allow Israeli settlements to remain in the Sinai after the with-drawal. He also rejected any suggestion that Israel would continue its use of the airfields for civilian purposes only. Begin and Sadat intransigence made the negotiations extremely difficult. It seemed that the peace negotiations had very little chance to bear fruit. It was only because the three leaders had such a strong interest in reaching an agreement that the Camp David Accords did materialize.

For personal and national reasons, Sadat was in the most need of an agreement. First, he felt a genuine need to fulfill a mission he believed that he was chosen to carry out. Second, he wished to terminate the war situation that was draining Egypt's ailing economy and straining its relations with the United States. Since the 1973 war, Sadat promised his people peace and a return of Egypt's lost lands. Lack of progress on the peace front could greatly weaken his leadership position. The Egyptian people expected Sadat to free the occupied Egyptian territories, that is, to achieve by peace what he could not achieve by war. Sadat was a unique figure—a combination of a media star and a statesman—and was very welcome in Washington as he became a personal friend of Kissinger and President Carter. In fact, throughout the negotiations Carter showed a clear pro-Sadat bias.[6] The combination of personal compatibility and shared political views made the American-Egyptian dialogue easier than the American-Israeli dialogue.

President Carter was convinced that the disengagement agreements left un-resolved issues that might be dangerous to the stability of the Middle East. Transition papers left by the Ford administration contained warnings that a new Israeli-Arab war might erupt if progress was not achieved. Carter hoped that with a new government in Israel, prospects for peace were greater. Hence, the combination of fear of war and a hope for peace gave rise to Carter's intense peace campaign. He hoped that Jordan would join the negotiations and that cooperation between Egypt, Jordan, Syria, and Saudi Arabia could be estab-lished. (The Washington team considered it highly unlikely that Egypt would agree to a bilateral accord, thus breaking ranks with other moderate Arab states.) The success of the disengagement agreements only two years earlier gave rise to these hopes.

Hence, on February 1977, months before Sadat's visit to Jerusalem and com-pletely without coordinating their actions, Carter created a Policy Review Com-mittee, headed by Secretary of State Cyrus Vance, to examine the situation in the Middle East, and especially the general strategy for promoting a renewal of Arab-Israeli negotiations.[7] The Policy Review Committee was considering two strategies: (1) to recommend an active U.S. intervention in the Middle East, and (2) to recommend minimum involvement, that is, a ''damage-Limiting'' ap-proach. Each approach could succeed or fail. The experts agreed that the major risk in the activist approach, favored by Carter, was unavoidable conflict with Israel, which was suspicious of any peace initiative. The decision was, however, to adopt the activist approach.

It is surprising that the participants in the Camp David negotiations under-estimated the conflicts of interests and the misperceptions involved. These were discernible long before September 1978, when the chief negotiators assembled in Camp David. Perhaps Carter's team of Middle East experts should have been more cautious and pursued more limited objectives. The assumption that Jordan, Syria, and Saudi Arabia would all come to the bargaining table was a gross overestimation. So also was the belief that a settlement on the Palestinian issue was feasible. Carter naively believed that he could tackle the most difficult issues head on. His advisers, although more skeptical, supported him in his efforts.[8]

President Carter, a man with strong religious and moral convictions, was heavily influenced by both. He felt an emotional, moral commitment to the Jewish people's right to resettle in their biblical homeland. But he also shared a moral commitment to the Palestinian rights as part of an overall commitment to human rights, a central tenet of his foreign policy.[9] Finally, he believed that the United States had a strategic interest in securing the stability of the Middle East and the flow of oil from the Persian Gulf. (This later became known as the Carter Doctrine.) It was probably the combination of the three causes that gave Carter the stamina, determination, and perseverance to continue his struggle for peace without which Camp David would have never become a reality.

In his efforts to achieve a comprehensive settlement, Carter misread (1) Begin's determination to maintain Israeli control over the West Bank and the Golan Heights, (2) the Soviet lack of leverage over their clients and their irrelevance to the negotiations, (3) Sadat's perception and definition of Egypt's national interest, (4) Hussein's reluctance to join the negotiations, and (5) the lack of American leverage over Israel. Under these circumstances it was clear that the negotiations would be difficult and unpredictable.

One of the most common and disturbing misperceptions was the meaning of peace. All three leaders talked about peace, but each defined it according to his own needs and interests. For Carter, peace meant a comprehensive settlement with benefits for all parties involved. Israel would gain security and recognition; Egypt, economic and political stability in addition to its lost lands. The Palestinians would gain their honor and lost homeland; Syria would trade off peace for territory; and Jordan would be secure in its East Bank. This plan was accepted by Sadat, but not by Israel. Hence, as the negotiations evolved, Israel found itself facing an American-Egyptian front.[10] Brzezinski, who suggested the strategy in a memo to Carter, argued that Sadat should come forth with a reasonable proposal, but would include one or two maximalist demands that the United States would subsequently publicly disown. The United States would later use these Egyptian concessions to pressure Israel to reciprocate.[11] This plan was supported by Vance, Carter advisers William Quandt and Hal Saunders, the State-NSC team, and the President. It seems that in its eagerness to capitalize on Sadat's visit to Jerusalem, the United States assumed leverage over Israel, enough to make it accept the Egyptian-American initiative. This was a major misperception. Consequently, the White House team seemed to have ignored previous developments, mainly the Ismailiya talks, which foreshadowed future negotiations and should have been studied more carefully. The two-day talks held in Egypt on December 25 and 26, 1977, were a complete failure. In contrast to the city's colorful decorations, the atmosphere inside the palace was gloomy. Begin and Sadat could agree on almost nothing and the negotiations went up a blind alley. The main problem was that both leaders believed that their own proposals were very generous, whereas the other side's proposals were unreasonable. The Ismailiya talks should have been an indicator to Washington of what was going to happen. Ignoring it was a major mistake.

A PEACEFUL SETTLEMENT: AN ISRAELI PERSPECTIVE

A settlement between Israel and its Arab neighbors required solutions to three major issues: (1) the Sinai peninsula, (2) the West Bank, Gaza, and Jerusalem, and (3) the Golan Heights. Strategically, Israel believed that a bilateral settlement with Egypt would best serve its interests, because it would buttress the status quo on the other two fronts. Moreover, Israel strongly believed that withdrawal from the Sinai in exchange for a *contractual peace* and full recognition of Israel was a very reasonable deal.

Indeed, Israel wanted to delay any settlement on the West Bank because the Begin government believed that within a few years the West Bank would be changed geopolitically to Israel's advantage. The settlements were to create a new reality that could not be ignored in future negotiations. Israel also believed that both Egypt and the United States, for different reasons, were very vulnerable and could be pressured to accept the Israeli position on a bilateral settlement.

Begin was right on all counts. Sadat's dramatic visit to Jerusalem put him in a very vulnerable position. It was clear that he needed to reach an agreement with Israel. In Washington, Carter needed a foreign policy achievement mainly for domestic reasons. But his eagerness to attain a settlement made him very vulnerable, too. Israel was the only party that had no immediate interest in changing the status quo. Its control over the Sinai, the West Bank, and the Golan Heights gave it a strong sense of security. This fact severely limited American leverage while enhancing Israel's.

Tensions between the United States and Israel grew as Washington opposed Israel's drive for a bilateral agreement with Egypt. Israel insisted that it would reduce the risk of war and would create new economic realities beneficial to all. The Suez Canal would reopen, the economic boycott would end, and trade between Israel and Egypt would flourish. Finally, an agreement would change Israel's political standing in the region by providing it recognition and legitimacy. Consequently, it would undermine the political position of the Arab rejectionist states and would support the moderate Arab states. Other Arab countries might then follow the footsteps of Sadat. But the most important achievement would be *peace* itself. The negotiations might create a momentum for peace that would perhaps change the state of mind of other Arab countries in the region from a psychology of war to a psychology of peace.[12]

In its efforts to translate its objectives into concrete peace proposals, Israel encountered opposition from both Sadat and Carter. Hence, Israel's proposals were revised and changed many times, as were the Egyptian and American proposals. However, all the various Israeli proposals did not include any concessions that were perceived by Israel to be detrimental to its national interest. Until the very last day of the negotiations, the United States pressured Israel to be more flexible. It was successful on the Sinai, but not on the West Bank. Sadat's expectations that the United States would be able to impose a settlement on Israel along the lines agreed between Egypt and the United States did not materialize, to Sadat's chagrin.

As early as December 1977, during the Ismailiya talks, it became clear that Israel and Egypt were far apart. Israel was not ready to make any concessions on the West Bank and the Palestinian issue, and insisted on dealing only with the future of the Sinai peninsula. Sadat, however, insisted on including these issues in any bilateral settlement. As Quandt noted, in Ismailiya Begin and Sadat were unable to agree to anything of substance.[13] Israel, however, believed that Sadat would ultimately agree to a bilateral agreement along the lines of the Israeli proposal. This belief was based on two interrelated factors.

First, Sadat was anxious to achieve a political victory, namely, a complete Israeli withdrawal from the Sinai. Second, he wished to fashion a new American-Egyptian relationship, even to displace Israel as America's closest ally in the region. He knew that a peace settlement was a prerequisite for this development. Begin gambled that Israel could resist U.S. pressures to an imposed compromise on the West Bank. Israel, therefore, maintained a strong and uncompromising position on the issues of the West Bank and the Palestinians.

Hence, the Israeli plan, as presented at the Ismailiya talks and reiterated later in the Jerusalem and Leeds talks, was tailored to achieve a separate peace with Egypt, while maintaining the status quo in the West Bank, Gaza, and the Golan Heights. Vance recalled that Carter, despite the emerging disagreements with the Israelis, continued the flow of aid, and the administration made no conscious decision not to intensify Israeli insecurity by using aid as a source of pressure.[14] This policy was opposed by National Security Adviser Brzezinski, who argued that Israel should be denied aid as a measure of coercion. The decision not to use leverage was based on Carter's feeling that any withholding of arms would be unsuccessful and probably lead to adverse consequences.

NEGOTIATING PEACE

In its initial proposal Israel did not agree to withdraw completely from the Sinai. It suggested that the settlements in Western Sinai and Sharm-el-Sheikh would remain under Israeli rule, an enclave within Egyptian territory. Moreover, Israel hoped that Sadat would permit a continued Israeli military presence both in the settlements and in the airfields. At first Israel and Washington did not know how determined Sadat was in his demand for a complete Israeli withdrawal and a dismantling of the settlements. It later became clear that Sadat refused to compromise on these questions, though Washington supported the Israeli request that the settlements would remain on Egyptian territory.[15]

Even more bothersome and difficult was the question of linkage, that is, the connection between the future of the Sinai and that of the West Bank and its inhabitants. Three questions were involved here: (1) territorial, namely, the final borders between Israel and Jordan, (2) security, namely, the security arrangement along the new borders, and (3) political, namely, the issue of sovereignty over the occupied territories before and during the Palestinian autonomy.

On all questions Israel and Egypt were at odds. Moreover, Sadat, both in his speech in Jerusalem and during the Ismailiya talks, rejected the notion of a bilateral peace with Israel and insisted on a comprehensive settlement including Jordan and the Palestinians. Israel knew that the United States supported this approach. However, it rightly assumed that Sadat's vital need for a settlement would lead him to ultimately agree to a bilateral agreement. The crucial question was whether Sadat would insist on the linkage principle in a bilateral agreement. If so, what should the Israeli position be?

It should not be assumed that the final borders and sovereignty of the Sinai did not demand long and difficult negotiations. However, Israel was flexible and more willing to compromise on this issue. It finally agreed to all of Sadat's demands including return of the airfields, demolition of the settlements, and withdrawal from Sharm-el-Sheik, all of which Israel had stated before that it would never do.

It has been suggested that Israel committed itself to a withdrawal from the Sinai *before* Sadat's visit to Jerusalem.[16] If so, Israel must have assumed that Sadat would not insist on a linkage, since Israel had never made any commitment on the West Bank or the Palestinian question. Begin, thus, greatly misread Sadat's policies. Moreover, he underestimated Sadat's fears of the Arab states' reaction to a bilateral agreement that would not include Israeli concessions on the West Bank and the question of the Palestinians.

Begin's misperceptions became evident during his visit to Washington on December 15–17, when he met with Carter and presented to him his famous "autonomy plan" for the West Bank and Gaza. Carter, according to his own account, was very impressed by Begin's plan for the Sinai, but considered the autonomy plan to be unacceptable.[17] Begin, on the other hand, believed that Carter liked his plan in its totality, that is, the autonomy plan as well as the plan for the future of the Sinai. Eli Rubinstein, a member of the Israeli delegation to Camp David, supported Begin's argument that it was Washington that shifted its position in March 1978 from support of Begin's December plan to opposition to it.[18] It seems that Begin misread Carter's reaction to his autonomy plan, a fact that resulted in many months of difficult negotiations.

Hence, Sadat's visit to Jerusalem produced impressive results in terms of an agreement on the Sinai, but no progress on the West Bank and the Palestinian question. The negotiations on the future of the Sinai and the Israeli-Egyptian border had no clear sailing either, and rough seas surrounded these talks, too.[19]

But Israel was willing to make far-reaching concessions on the settlements in the Sinai, the status of Sharm-el-Sheik, and the airfields. This fact enabled Sadat to agree to a contractual peace including exchange of ambassadors even before a complete Israeli withdrawal took place.

As the negotiations continued, two facts became evident. First, Sadat was willing to sign a bilateral peace treaty with Israel even if no other Arab state would join him. Washington, hoping that Jordan would join the negotiations, was surprised and very displeased. On this point Washington held a much harder line than Sadat. Carter, who made all the final decisions, believed that both Egypt and the United States should insist that Israel make the necessary concessions on the West Bank and the Palestinian issues, enabling Hussein to join the negotiations. Carter was disappointed to learn that Sadat was willing to defy the Arab states, to face condemnation, a possible cut of all Arab economic aid, and even physical threats, and go ahead with a bilateral treaty.[20] Israel, on the other hand, was pleased to learn that its plans materialized.

Sadat, however, insisted that a bilateral agreement would include Israeli withdrawals not only from the Sinai, but from all occupied territories. Throughout the negotiations Sadat adamantly adhered to a policy of linkage between an agreement on the Sinai and an agreement on the West Bank and the Palestinian issues. This position was strongly stressed at the Jerusalem talks, which followed the Ismailiya talks. In Jerusalem the Egyptian delegation, led by Foreign Minister Kamil, declared that it was not interested in vague statements. "It wanted an outright Israeli promise of withdrawal to the 1967 lines and Palestinian self-determination as the quid pro quo for Arab recognition and normal peaceful relations."[21] It was not surprising that the Jerusalem talks collapsed right after this statement.

The negotiation process, however, continued with the three main Israeli negotiators being Prime Minister Begin, Minister of Foreign Affairs Dayan, and Minister of Defense Ezer Weizman. They had different opinions vis-à-vis the Egyptian position, which enjoyed strong American support. Among the three, Begin and Dayan were the hard-liners. Weizman, who served as a British Air Force officer during World War II and was stationed in Egypt, was no stranger to the country. He knew Cairo inside out and even had family there, who settled in Egypt at the turn of the century. Whether this was the reason for the close relationships that had developed between "Ezra," as Sadat used to call him in a friendly way, or whether it was his openness to the Egyptian position, Defense Minister Weizman and Sadat had taken to each other when they first met in Jerusalem.[22]

But this friendship did not help to break the deadlock, which seemed final on March 1978. The major block was Begin's opposition to Sadat's linkage policy and his insistence on the autonomy plan. The American ambassador at large, Alfred Atherton, the American Ambassador in Tel Aviv, Samuel Lewis, and Secretary of State Vance, who traveled extensively and shuttled between the Middle East and Washington, were disappointed with the autonomy plan. Atherton complained that he felt frustrated and helpless trying in vain to bridge the gap between Sadat's linkage formula, designed to end the status quo on the West Bank, and Begin's autonomy plan, designed to perpetuate the status quo.[23]

DEADLOCK: BEGIN'S AUTONOMY PLAN

Dayan explained that the autonomy plan was born in Begin's mind as early as November 1977, after Sadat's speech in Jerusalem. He presented it to a small group of friends the night before he left for Washington. Dayan was the only person who saw the plan before that. When Begin presented his plan to Carter on December 16, it included twenty-six points and was entitled: "Home Rule, for Palestinian Arabs, Residents of Judea, Samaria and the Gaza District." The most controversial issue was the source of authority for the self-governing body on the West Bank. Begin suggested that this issue be left open. The inhabitants of the West Bank and Gaza would elect an administrative council with powers on domestic issues only. Israel would abolish the military government but would remain responsible for the security of the areas. Israelis would be allowed to settle in the West Bank, whereas as a reciprocal measure, Arabs, residents of the West Bank who would choose to become Israeli citizens, would be allowed to acquire land in Israel.

Carter's major reservation was that the autonomy plan did not specify any Israeli withdrawal; thus it completely ignored U.N. Resolution 242.[24] Carter assumed that a more flexible Israeli position might induce Hussein and the Palestinians to join the peace negotiations. He naively continued to believe that a tripronged settlement was possible. Carter's policy was heavily influenced by the Brookings Institute report, published in December 1975, which served as an intellectual basis for Carter's team.[25] The Brookings report took a comprehensive approach and stressed the need for a near complete Israeli withdrawal from all occupied territories. This was not the spirit of Begin's autonomy plan. However, at this time Carter still believed that the United States could convince Israel to make as far-reaching concessions on the West Bank as it was willing to make on the Sinai.

Sadat evaluated Israel's position more realistically and did not share Carter's view. He strove for a statement of commitment rather than real concessions. He understood that a comprehensive settlement was unattainable at that time, and that at best he could pressure Begin to include a statement on the West Bank and the Palestinian issue in a bilateral agreement. The difference between Sadat's plan and Begin's autonomy plan was that Sadat wanted a plan for a Palestinian self-government and not a plan for Palestinian home rule under Israeli occupation.

The negotiations, which began right after Sadat's visit to Jerusalem, were difficult and wary. The disagreements between Israel and Egypt were clearly summarized in a position paper published by the Israeli government in May 1980.[26] Israel wrongly assumed that the autonomy plan would satisfy the Arab desires for self-rule and they would forego their sworn intentions to destroy

Israel, which was how Israel defined the Palestinian drive for an independent state.

The Israeli autonomy plan was based on *functional principles*, that is, Palestinian governing powers and authority would be established on a functional, not a territorial basis. The Palestinian administrative council would be in charge of and have authority over functions, not over territory. Under the autonomy plan, Israel would not relinquish its occupation of the territories, because sovereignty would be vested in functions, not in territory. Begin believed that his approach, which invited the Palestinians to control all matters affecting their daily lives, was politically feasible.

The autonomy plan defined three categories of powers and responsibilities in various functional areas: powers to be transferred fully to the administrative council, such as the power to determine and administer budget (but not coin money), hire and fire personnel, enter into contracts, and so on; powers to be administered jointly with Israel, such as foreign trade, regional planning, and such; and powers to be reserved to Israel, such as defense and security, foreign affairs, and currency. Begin did not think that his plan would be an interim agreement of five years. He believed that this should be the final political arrangement. However, after much controversy, long negotiations, and even opposition from his own advisers,[27] he agreed to limit the autonomy to five years, but only after Israel was ensured a de facto veto power over the final agreement. Had Israel not been promised such a veto power, Israel would have never signed the Camp David Accords.

Begin's autonomy plan followed his interpretation of Resolution 242. He rejected the approach that it required a complete withdrawal from all or most territories conquered by Israel in 1967. He argued that international law distinguished between offensive wars, or wars of aggression, and wars of self-defense. Lands conquered by the attacked party during wars of self-defense rightly belonged to the winner. Begin's government, more than any previous Israeli leadership, was committed to the retention of the West Bank, not merely for security considerations, but for ideological reasons as well. Carter, on the other hand, was more willing than any previous president to include the PLO in the negotiations. This conflict of attitudes was looming over the negotiation process, especially after the collapse of the Jerusalem talks in January 1978.

The conflicts were three-sided: between Jerusalem and Washington, and between Jerusalem and Cairo. Following the Ismailiya talks and until the last days of Camp David, Sadat insisted that the parties should issue a declaration of principles including a clear statement of the Palestinians right for self-determination. This was unacceptable to Begin, who in turn suggested his autonomy plan, which was unacceptable to Sadat. Many mutual concessions were necessary to reconcile these differences. The question of how desperate Sadat was for a peace treaty determined his concessions. Israel hoped that his demands on the Palestinian issue were a mere "fig leaf," that is, a defense mechanism against attacks from various Arab states. Israel was only partially right.

Carter was very concerned about the deterioration in the Begin-Sadat relationship.[28] The feeling in Washington was that Begin not only obstructed all progress but was a source of embarrassment and frustration. In January 1978 the possibility of Camp David was first raised by Carter in a long talk with Brzezinski. The first thought was to invite Sadat alone for a weekend with the President at Camp David. Kissinger was also consulted and he made some important and realistic predictions about the situation. "Begin had no intention of giving up the West Bank," said Kissinger, "but the settlers in the Sinai would move out after an Israeli withdrawal was attained."[29] The President was encouraged and decided to eschew the issue of the West Bank. He decided to use Begin's autonomy plan as a framework and a basis for the negotiations, and to convince Sadat to be more flexible.

A new diplomatic campaign was launched. On January 4, Carter visited Egypt. On January 16–18 Secretary of State Vance was sent to Jerusalem. After the collapse of the Jerusalem talks, Vance met with Sadat in Cairo. The vigorous diplomatic campaign, however, produced very meager results. It seemed impossible to reconcile Begin's plan and Sadat's demand for an Israeli commitment to a complete withdrawal. Secretary Vance explained why the negotiations were deadlocked: "The Arabs wanted a return of all the occupied territories in exchange for merely an end to the legal state of war. Israel wanted full peace, normalization of relations, and security in exchange for only a partial withdrawal from the occupied territories."[30] Vance, more pessimistic than Carter's other advisers, informed the President that there was no prospect for the peace talks to succeed.[31]

Regardless of the gloomy predictions, Carter decided to do two things. First, he invited Sadat to visit Washington on February 3–4, 1978. Second, he developed an American plan and tried to "sell" it to Sadat and Begin.[32] The two-day talks revolved around the Ismailiya meeting. Sadat was surprised that Begin was so uncompromising about his autonomy plan. This became the major obstacle to any progress. At the Camp David meeting Sadat bitterly complained to Carter that he was convinced that Begin did not want peace.

Carter was less discouraged and tried to influence Sadat to take a more positive attitude.[33] Carter's plan was simple but brilliant. He suggested that Israel would be asked to reaffirm its commitment of 1970 to U.N. Resolution 242. Since the resolution implied a near complete Israeli withdrawal from all the occupied territories, a separate statement to that effect would not be necessary. In return, Carter suggested that Egypt would permit some of the Israeli settlements in the Sinai to stay under U.N. protection. Sadat rejected the idea but agreed to be more flexible on Jerusalem and state that it could remain undivided, as Israel demanded, with joint sovereignty over the religious sites.[34] At this point Carter believed that the meeting produced fruitful results and that Israel should be invited to give its reaction to the revised Egyptian proposal.

On February 16 Carter met in Washington with Moshe Dayan, and briefed him on his talks with Sadat. The main question that faced the Israeli government was Sadat's real intentions. Two main approaches evolved in Israel. The first argued that Sadat knew all along what Begin's position was on the West Bank. He knew that Begin would not agree to an Israeli withdrawal from the West Bank. His visit to Jerusalem, under these circumstances, implied that Sadat was prepared to conclude a separate peace treaty with Israel leaving the status quo in the West Bank, Gaza, and the Golan Heights. This approach assumed that Sadat's rhetoric was a mere "fig leaf," a defense against charges that he betrayed the Arab cause.

The other approach argued that Sadat genuinely meant what he said, and that his intransigent demand for an Israeli withdrawal was serious.[35] Not only Israel was puzzled by Sadat's behavior; Washington, too, was confused and uncertain. Sadat gave mixed signals and it was difficult, if not impossible, to predict his actions and reactions.[36]

On the one hand, his bold, unilateral diplomatic offensive, which began with his courageous visit to Jerusalem, indicated that he was not seeking a cautious and safe policy. On the other hand, he was uncompromising about his linkage policy, insisting on an Israeli commitment to withdraw from all occupied territories in exchange for peace. During February and March of 1978 it seemed that he was even ready to risk the collapse of the peace process. Israel believed that Sadat's intransigence on the settlements in the Sinai and the question of the West Bank meant that he capitulated to the hard-liners on his team who exhibited open dissatisfaction with his previous position.[37] Consequently, negotiations in Jerusalem, Cairo, Ismailiya, and Washington were deadlocked. Both Begin and Sadat hardened their positions, and by March 1978 it seemed that the peace process was over.

Israel reacted by hardening its position further. In early 1978 it announced an expansion of the settlements in the Sinai, as a direct pressure on Sadat and Washington. This controversial policy was viewed by some not as a reaction but as a provocation.[38] The question, however, of what had happened first, Sadat hardening his position or Israel hardening its position, became irrelevant in March. It can be argued that both Sadat and Begin, misreading and mistrusting each other, decided simultaneously to harden their positions as bargaining chips. It seemed that in this power game no one really scored major gains.

LEVERAGE: MYTH AND REALITY

It became clear that the three men who controlled the peace agenda, Sadat, Begin, and Carter, had to change course or admit failure. None of them wanted to risk the political repercussions that might have ensued. Carter and the American team, after evaluating the situation, decided to underwrite a substantive change, that is, to write off Syria and the PLO but not yet Jordan, who they thought showed some interest in joining the negotiations. It was surprising that after all these months of fruitless negotiations that Washington still hoped Begin would make meaningful concessions on the West Bank. In a meeting with King Hussein in Teheran in January 1978, Carter said that he believed that some progress was made. It seemed that Carter ignored two facts. First, without an unequivocal commitment from Begin to withdraw from the West Bank, or from most of it, King Hussein could not join the negotiations. Second, Carter wrongly assumed that the United States could coerce Israel to accept its interpretation of Resolution 242, which implied an Israeli withdrawal from most of the West Bank.

American leverage was sought mainly through the withholding of arms, which coincided with Carter's general doctrine of self-imposed restraint in American arms sales. On May 19, 1977 Carter announced a new policy; henceforth all arms transfers were to be viewed as an "exceptional foreign policy implement, to be used only [when] it . . . clearly . . . contributes to our national security interests."[39] While imposing restrictions on all arms sales, Carter acknowledged the fact that Israel presented a unique problem. Without mentioning his aspirations for a peace treaty and the problem that an arms embargo at this sensitive moment might create, he made statements reiterating the historic U.S. commitment to assure the security of Israel. It was clear that Carter wished to restrain arms shipments to Israel but was aware of the fact that any change in the strategic balance of power in the region at this point might be detrimental to the peace process. The long-standing political dilemmas again restricted U.S. policy.

The long-standing political dilemmas were demonstrated by the fact that two years earlier, with the signing of the Sinai II agreement, Kissinger had promised Israel a handsome package of sophisticated arms, including F–15's, Lance missiles, and advanced electronic warfare devices. It was difficult for Carter to suspend the agreement, although midlevel State Department and Pentagon bureaus suggested that he withhold all arms shipments including supplies in the pipeline. Among the items not approved for sale to Israel were CBU–72 cluster bombs. However, other important Israeli requests, including FLIR night-fighting infrared equipment, were approved. The sale of Cobra helicopter gunships was postponed, and Israel's request for the coproduction of the F–16 was denied. Israel was prevented from exporting the Kfir fighter aircraft to Ecuador on the grounds that it contained a General Electric engine and was therefore subject to U.S. restrictions on arms transfers. This hurt Israel's economic and technological growth, but was neither threatening or detrimental to its security. Leverage, therefore, was not achieved. Finally, Carter's incoherent arms sale policy gave Israel mixed signals and hardly helped the peace process.

Sadat, who expected the United States to exert meaningful leverage on Israel, was very disappointed. He expressed deep frustrations and anger in his meetings with Carter.[40] He believed that Egypt's willingness to make peace with Israel and defy all the Arab League resolutions should have satisfied Israeli demands. Israel should not have additional demands. He felt betrayed by Begin and complained "the nature of peace which Israel today says she wants to secure is nothing in effect but a new attempt to thwart the establishment of peace."[41] Sadat was ready to suspend all talks with Israel and break up the military committee in Cairo, but finally agreed to allow Carter some more time to continue the negotiations. He left Washington on February 5, 1978, disappointed but hoping that Carter would be successful in coercing Israel to accept the American-supported Egyptian proposal.

The same day that Sadat left Washington, Foreign Minister Dayan arrived in New York. He met with Carter on February 16, and the main theme of their talk was Carter's belief that King Hussein should and would join the negotiations and perhaps get the peace process out of the quagmire. Dayan argued that this was not plausible. Moreover, Israel was not prepared to follow the American-Egyptian guidelines vis-à-vis the West Bank. Indeed, Israel's interpretation of Resolution 242 was that it did not necessarily apply to the West Bank at all! Dayan explained that the Israeli proposal is based on Begin's autonomy plan and the understanding that the final arrangements be delayed for five years. Interestingly, Carter did not dismiss the Israeli autonomy plan. He believed that although it was flawed and needed revisions, it was a promising point of departure for an interim agreement. Two questions bothered Dayan, and Carter could not answer them. First, would Sadat insist that Syria join the negotiations before any treaty was signed? Second, would Sadat sign a treaty with Israel if an agreement was reached on the Sinai but not on the West Bank? Carter sent the questions to Sadat, but received no concrete answers.[42]

The hope that 1978 would be the year of peace was slowly fading away. Egypt and Israel were hardening their positions and expecting the United States to pressure the other side to make concessions. Carter decided to assume a more active role by drafting an American peace proposal and convincing both Egypt and Israel to accept it with minor revisions. The American proposal shared many of the Egyptian proposals. Quandt goes as far as to argue that Carter and Sadat tried to conspire against Israel, using a coordinated strategy. The plan was to put forward an Egyptian proposal calling for far-reaching Israeli concessions on the West Bank, which would be rejected by Begin. Meanwhile, Carter would keep the heat on Begin to accept U.N. Resolution 242. At an appropriate time, after it was clear that a deadlock had been reached, the United States would put forward an American compromise proposal built around Begin's autonomy plan, which would be followed by an agreement based on Resolution 242, including an Israeli withdrawal after a transitional period. This would look like a major Egyptian concession and Israel would have to reciprocate by making counter concessions. The problem with this plan was that the two parties could not adhere to the agreed strategy. "This stratagem was probably a bit too Machiavellian and could have placed Sadat in an awkward position if Israel had failed to make comparable concessions."[43]

Others on the American team echoed Quandt's account of the events, although in a less conspiratorial way. Brzezinki suggested that Sadat would make a strong statement that U.N. Resolution 242 applied to all territories. The United States would support him. Begin would reject Sadat's statement, allowing the United States to suggest its own compromise formula.[44] Vance suggested that Atherton would then return to the Middle East to negotiate a compromise based on the new U.S. proposal. The plan, however, did not materialize because, according to Brzezinski, the two sides did not reach an understanding vis-à-vis the substance of the American proposal.

Only after this scheme collapsed did the United States realize the urgency of the situation and embarked on a new plan, which helped to put the peace process on the right track again. By early 1978 U.S. policy toward the Middle East had become less ambitious and more focused. "We resigned to the fact that a comprehensive settlement was years away at best. Instead, we were determined to make certain that Sadat's peace initiative was translated into a tangible accommodation between Egypt and Israel, one that would generate progress on the . . . much sensitive Palestinian issue."[45]

THE PEACE PROCESS: AN AMERICAN PERSPECTIVE

The United States made no secret of the fact that its approach to peace and its interpretation of U.N. Resolution 242 approximated the Egyptian approach. Hence, the American peace proposal provoked a harsh and negative Israeli reaction. Moreover, Israel knew that on some issues the United States was less compromising than Sadat. For example, the United States opposed a bilateral agreement, whereas Sadat was willing to accept it. The second and more difficult question facing the American team was to link or not to link. Should the United States accept and support Sadat's demand to link any agreement on the Sinai to Israeli concessions on the West Bank?

The third issue was the role of Jordan. The rather naive view that Jordan could and should join the negotiations was a long-standing American position. However, after tiring months of unfruitful negotiations, Carter had to accept the disappointing fact that Israel would not commit itself to major territorial concessions on the West Bank. Moreover, the United States had to formulate a proposal that would not seem to lead to the creation of a Palestinian state. Carter had learned that Begin was extremely firm on this issue. It took the United States many painful months to realize what the Egyptian and the Israeli priorities were and to revise its policy accordingly.

As the year 1978 progressed, it became clear to all the participants that if any agreement was to be reached, two conditions must exist. First, it had to be a bilateral agreement, with the Soviet Union excluded. Second, some linkage had to be established with the issues of the West Bank and the future of the Palestinians. These were difficult conditions for both Israel and Egypt. Begin had to agree to a linkage and to a complete withdrawal from the Sinai, including a dismantling of all existing settlements. An additional Egyptian demand was that Israel give up the strategic airfields in the Sinai. On his side, Sadat had to face the Arab world as the only Arab leader who agreed to sign a peace treaty with Israel before the Palestinian issue had been resolved. It took many months of political maneuvers to reach such an agreement. The month of March was perhaps, the most difficult one, but also the turning point of the peace process.

March 1978 began with a severe blow to that process. On Saturday, March 11, a group of Palestinian terrorists launched a bloody attack on an Israeli bus, killing more than thirty passengers and Senator Abraham Ribicoff's niece, whom they encountered on the beach where they landed. Israel reacted by attacking Palestinian bases in Lebanon in a swift, small-scale invasion known as the Litani Operation. The timing of the PLO attack could have been a calculated assault on the peace process. If so, it did have partial success. It greatly embarrassed the United States, which in February issued the most far-reaching statement supporting the Palestinian cause. The statement said that "Resolution 242 is applicable to all fronts of the conflict," and that "Israeli settlements in occupied territory are contrary to international law." The White House also repeated in full the Aswan statement (issued on January 4, 1978 during Carter's visit to Egypt) on the legitimate rights of the Palestinians.[46]

The terrorists' attack and the Israeli counterattack required an American reaction. The United States was considering major arms transfers to the region, first recommended by Secretary of State Vance to the President in February. The deal included fifty F–5s to Egypt, sixty F–15s to Saudi Arabia, and seventy-five F–16s and fifteen F–15s to Israel. The main objective of this package deal—one of the most controversial arms sales to this day—was to induce the main participants in the peace process to cooperate with each other and the United States. Saudi Arabia was included in the package, assuming that its cooperation was crucial. The hostilities that broke out in March enraged Carter. He was angry with the PLO, as well as with the Israeli response, which he considered excessive.

Another question concerned the Egyptian reaction. Although Israel informed and briefed Egypt on the operation five minutes after the first Israeli tank crossed the Lebanese border, Israel expected an extremely harsh reaction and a possible termination of all the negotiations. To Israel's surprise, the Egyptian reaction was very mild. In a short cable, Sadat acknowledged receiving the Israeli message. "Sadat's reaction immediately received a political interpretation. It was at this moment that Israel began to believe that Sadat wholeheartedly wanted peace."[47] The United States, Israel, and Egypt wished to resolve the strain created by the PLO attack and continue with the peace process. The solution was found by the creation of UNIFIL, a U.N. patrol force that was to take up positions in southern Lebanon after a complete Israeli pullout. Once again a U.N. peace-keeping force played an important role in keeping the peace process going.

On April 28 Carter sent to Congress an arms package of $4.8 billion, the largest of its kind, to Saudi Arabia, Israel, and Egypt.[48] The arms package (the "plane" package) was apparently expected to yield political leverage. Israel reacted with much anger to these tactics of inducement and coercion. It realized that it had lost its exclusivity in arms supplies, and it became extremely anxious about the use of arms as leverage. Moreover, arms for the Arabs was interpreted in Israel as an erosion of U.S.-Israel relations. "The image was of an either/or relationship, a zero-sum game, with little willingness to accept the creation of a new Arab-American relationship side-by-side with a continuing U.S.-Israeli one.''[49] Israel felt deceived because its share of seventy-five F–16s was part of the Sinai II agreement of 1975, which was given in writing and was not conditioned upon any further concessions.

Israel's strong reaction showed that the United States could perhaps achieve more leverage by supplying arms to the friendly Arab states than by denying arms to Israel. The arms sales proposal followed a series of unsuccessful meetings with Israeli leaders, including a meeting between Carter and Begin on March 21. Although Carter assured Begin that the United States would support his autonomy plan with some revisions, Begin refused to show any flexibility. He would not stop the settlements, would not agree to a political withdrawal from the West Bank, would not dismantle the settlements in the Sinai, and he refused to recognize that Resolution 242 applied to all fronts. Regardless of the grim prospects, Carter was not ready to declare the peace process dead. He appointed Alfred L. Atherton, Jr., as Ambassador at Large for the Middle East peace negotiations and Harold H. Saunders as Assistant Secretary of State for Near East and South Asian Affairs. He continued to hope that the arms package would induce or coerce cooperation. His policy was, however, only partially successful.

One of the prevalent American misperceptions concerned the role of Saudi Arabia in the peace process. Washington assumed that Sadat would not be able to conclude a peace treaty without the support of the Arab world, particularly of Saudi Arabia.[50] The sale of U.S. advanced planes to Saudi Arabia was seen as a necessary step in the right direction. Carter was disappointed that Israel's strong reaction to the arms sale did not, however, translate into political concessions. Minister of Defense Weizman made it clear when he said, ''None of the parties in Israel . . . will agree to a withdrawal from Judea and Samaria. . . . Consequently, the United States cannot expect it.''[51]

It was naive to expect immediate Israeli concessions as a result of the plane package because the package did not have immediate military implications for Israel. Israel did not face any immediate shortage of arms. Moreover, it was privately reassured that more F–16 planes would be supplied on a later date. The seventy-five planes included in the package were promised as a first installment on a long-term arms-sale commitment.[52] Hence, it is difficult to see how the plane package could affect Israel's negotiating position. It could perceivably have resulted in the hardening of Israel's position, or could have no real effect at all. In fact, between March and June, Israel refused to make any concessions regarding the West Bank and insisted on keeping the settlements in the Sinai under U.N. or Egyptian control. Egypt's position was diametrically opposed to that. Tensions between the United States and Israel continued with no prospects for a breakthrough in sight. The plane package came to a final vote in the Senate on May 17, 1978, but it did not result in the expected leverage.

The United States had to reassess its position and make some important decisions. A new planning group was formed, headed by Secretary of State Vance. The two major issues were how to coerce Israel to accept the principle of "territories for peace" as expressed in Resolution 242, and how to induce Egypt to be more flexible on the West Bank and a Palestinian self-rule that implies an independent Palestinian state. Finally, the United States had to abandon its hope to bring Syria and Jordan to the bargaining table.

Israel's position on the West Bank was firm. On June 18 Israel sent a formal letter to Carter suggesting a plan for a five-year Palestinian autonomy that would not lead to an independent Palestinian state. The final status of the West Bank and the Gaza Strip would be decided following further negotiations. Israel did not mention Resolution 242 or the role of Egypt and Jordan in the negotiations. Israel's letter included the condition that the autonomy plan would become effective only after peace treaties with Egypt and Jordan had been signed. Israel clearly was not ready to consider a complete or a near complete withdrawal. However, it agreed to a complete withdrawal from the Sinai in exchange for a formal, contractual peace with Egypt. Carter continued his mediation efforts regardless of the tremendous difficulties. He assumed that the three leaders would agree on an overall settlement as a first step toward resolving all the differences including the unpopular details. Carter shared Begin's opposition to an independent Palestinian state. He agreed to a functional approach to the issue of Jerusalem, accepted some border adjustments, and preferred, like Israel, a federation between Jordan and the Palestinians.

On the other hand, Carter shared Sadat's view that an agreement on the Sinai should be linked to the West Bank. He demanded more Israeli concessions there, including a halt of new settlements. He accepted Sadat's demand for a complete Israeli withdrawal from the Sinai, but rejected Sadat's suggestion of June 1978 that Gaza would be returned to Egypt and the West Bank to Jordan. Carter preferred to leave the question of the final status of the West Bank and Gaza open, to be determined after the five-year interim period.

During May, June, and July, extensive negotiations were taking place. Vice President Mondale met with Sadat in Alexandria, Vance met with Dayan in London, Weizman with Sadat in Vienna, and there was a meeting between Sadat and Israel's opposition leader Peres in Vienna. At this point Secretary Vance suggested a formal meeting in London between the Israeli and Egyptian foreign ministers. For security reasons the two-day discussions took place on July 18 and 19 at Leeds Castle in Kent. Although no concrete agreement was reached, the negotiations were of critical importance. All the participants agreed that Leeds signified a breakthrough that opened the road to Camp David.

The main issue on the agenda was the future of the West Bank. At Leeds Egypt presented its first detailed proposal entitled: "A Plan for an Israeli Withdrawal from the West Bank and Gaza, and Security Arrangements." The proposal specified the particular arrangements necessary for securing the legitimate rights of the Palestinian people. It required a complete Israeli withdrawal from all territories including Jerusalem, and suggested that Jordan and Egypt assume responsibilities during the five-year interim period. At the end of the five years, talks would be held between the Palestinians, Jordan, and Egypt to determine the final status of the territories. Security arrangements would be concluded before the Israeli withdrawal and would include some U.N. peacekeeping forces.

Israel's reaction was predictable. Dayan summarized it in three points. First, Israel rejected any proposal based on a complete or a near complete Israeli withdrawal to pre–1967 borders. Second, Israel would only consider a proposal that suggested territorial compromises. Third, if Israel's autonomy plan was accepted, Israel would agree to discuss the issue of sovereignty after the interim period.[53] Although the gap between the two sides remained large, the atmosphere was positive. The Egyptians and Israelis were negotiating, genuinely trying to reach an agreement. It seemed that if Egypt would accept the Israeli proposal that the final status of the West Bank and Gaza would be determined *after* the five-year interim period and not *before*, the major road block would be eliminated. Israel agreed to replace its West Bank military authority with a civilian authority as part of the autonomy plan. Not surprisingly, the most important move toward an agreement was achieved with no pressure, leverage, or coercion.

Sadat, perhaps more than Begin, could not risk termination of the negotiations. He had no interest in perpetuating the Israeli-Egyptian conflict. Israel never threatened the survival of Egypt. Second, the return of the Sinai was essential to Sadat's rule. Finally, the termination of the state of war was extremely appealing to Sadat because of the severe economic problems that plagued the Egyptian economy.[54] The American assessment that an agreement was feasible was sound and valid. Hence, on July 20 Carter told his negotiating team that he was considering a summit meeting between Begin and Sadat. Simultaneously, the American team began to finalize a new American proposal on the West Bank and Gaza.

The revised proposal was based on the Leeds talks and included ideas from previous American proposals, Begin's autonomy plan, and Sadat's Ismailiya proposal. On August 6 a team of American negotiators headed by Secretary Vance flew to the Middle East for preliminary talks about the latest American initiative. Vance told Begin that the United States did not support his intransigent position on the West Bank and that his autonomy plan was a point of departure only. Vance also extended to Begin an invitation to come to Camp David for a summit meeting with Sadat and Carter.[55]

According to this own account, Carter felt that he had reached the end of the round. "I finally decided it would be best, win or lose, to go all out. . . . As dismal . . . as the prospects seemed—I would try to bring Sadat and Begin together for an extensive negotiating session with me."[56] Carter wished to ensure the cooperation of Begin on the sensitive issue of the West Bank. This could have been attained either by coercion or by inducement. The American team disagreed on the tactics. Quandt advocated the second approach, arguing that Carter should move away from the confrontational approach toward Begin, which was part of the American strategy in early 1978.[57] Others, especially Brzezinski, advocated a harder line and the use of pressure. As a result of his attitude, Brzezinski had been portrayed in Israeli circles as the "evil spirit of the White

House, the 'eminance grise' behind the administration's vigorously anti-Israeli actions."[58]

The American team recognized that "Begin would never relinquish Israel's claim to the West Bank without a fight. Gentle persuasion would not do." Hence, the United States would have to use leverage but be very careful not to alienate Israeli people or the American Jews.[59] Washington again resorted to suspending Israel's long-term military modernization plan. The United States decided not to withhold any immediate arms shipments but to hold in abeyance new sales requests. In addition, restrictions were put on arms coproduction and technology transfers, crucial for Israel's own defense industry. The United States was also delaying negotiations on loans and grants to finance the purchase of arms.[60] These were typical tactics used by the United States to exert leverage. However, as the negotiations progressed it became clear that these tactics yielded very little leverage.

It could be argued that American pressure did produce some Israeli concessions. Begin's autonomy plan and Dayan's proposal for Palestinian representation in the Geneva talks could serve as examples. Israel, however, rejected this theory arguing that the autonomy plan represented Israel's concept of a just solution to the Palestinian question. Indeed, it was difficult for the United States to pressure Israel for two reasons. First, Israel's arms inventories enabled it to sustain a short-term arms embargo. Second, a long-term arms embargo would have changed the region's strategic balance of power, jeopardizing U.S. interests. Harold Saunders expressed the American dilemma when he told Congress: "Governments do not sell their futures and their policies for 300 tanks or 100 airplanes. ... You do not trade tanks for negotiations."[61] Hence, it seemed that on the eve of Camp David both Israel and Egypt were almost completely free to pursue the course of action of their choice.

CAMP DAVID: MISSION IMPOSSIBLE

Although both Sadat and Begin reacted with enthusiasm to Carter's proposal for a summit meeting, there was very little to be enthusiastic about. Ten months of intense negotiations produced very little results. Carter felt that his political fortunes were slipping. Both Begin and Sadat were difficult partners, and each expected the United States to pressure the other for concessions. Both conveyed contradictory messages and refused to compromise on the West Bank.

It is unclear what expectations the three leaders had at this crucial moment. It is equally unclear what concessions they were ready to make before they went to Camp David. Sadat probably expected more meaningful autonomy for the West Bank than "garbage collecting." Begin probably expected Sadat to make some concessions in the Sinai and was determined not to sign any agreement that might lead to the establishment of a Palestinian state. However, Carter correctly assumed that both Begin and Sadat would eventually reach an agreement.

The thirteen days of Camp David were turbulent and tense. The negotiators seemed to be less flexible than was expected. On September 6 the three leaders met for the first time, at Carter's cabin. Begin was appalled by Sadat's eleven-page proposal. He considered it a retreat from the Egyptian Leeds proposal, which Israel had rejected. In essence the Egyptian proposal demanded a complete withdrawal from all the territories and a return to the international borders with Egypt and Syria as they were during the British mandate. On the West Bank Israel would withdraw to the 1949 cease-fire line with Jordan. Israel would evacuate all military and civilian settlements in the Sinai. Security arrangements would protect Israel's sovereignty and existence. U.N. peacekeeping forces would be deployed along the new borders. Israel would enjoy freedom of navigation in the canal and other waterways. With the signing of a peace treaty, Israel would relinquish its governing authority to Egypt and Jordan, who would rule the territories for the interim period of five years. The Palestinians would participate in the process through their elected representatives. Six months before the end of the interim period, the Palestinians would establish a permanent government and become a sovereign political entity, preferably in association with Jordan. Last but not least, on the question of Jerusalem, Sadat offered a combination of an Israeli withdrawal with a joint administrative authority to govern the city after an Israeli withdrawal from the old city.

All the members of the Israeli delegation agreed that Israel could not accept the Egyptian proposal. They decided not to present an Israeli proposal before they explained to Sadat why his proposal was rejected. Begin's first point was reasserting his opposition to any agreement that would lead to the establishment of a Palestinian state. Sadat replied that he, too, preferred a federation with Jordan, but this decision had to be made by the Palestinian people. On the issue of Jerusalem, there would be no Arab sovereignty nor an Israeli withdrawal. The discussion shifted from one issue to another in a disorganized manner. The meeting ended with the request that the United States prepare its proposal to be discussed on September 10.

Begin came to the negotiations with an advantage over Carter and Sadat. He could walk out at any time and it would not weaken his power position at home. On the contrary, he could even make some political gains, blaming the failure on Egyptian intransigence and American clumsiness.[62] Sadat, on the other hand, needed concessions, not only on the Sinai but also on the West Bank. The American proposal was, therefore, a compromise between Begin's autonomy plan and Sadat's plan for Palestinian self-rule. After an interim period of five years, negotiations among all the parties involved, including the Palestinians, would determine the final status of the West Bank in accordance with U.N. Resolution 242.

Before submitting the American proposal to the Israeli and Egyptian delegations, Carter held a crucial meeting with Begin on Friday, September 8. Both leaders were anxious and worried. During the meeting Begin adamantly rejected any proposal that would weaken Israel's claim to the West Bank. "The Israeli strategy was to hold off making any concessions on the things important to Sadat, such as settlements in Sinai, until he had agreed to drop most of his unacceptable demands on the West Bank and Gaza.''[63] After the meeting, Harold Saunders began to revise the American proposal again. A total of twenty-three drafts were prepared before the last version, a document of seventeen typed pages, was submitted to the two delegations, on Sunday, September 10.

The schedule for September 10 included a tour of Gettysburg in the morning and a working session in the afternoon. The working session, which began at 3 P.M., continued until 3 A.M. the next morning, with no fruitful results. The only issue on the agenda was the American proposal, which was rejected by Begin. It suggested four steps, on all of which the United States and Israel were in disagreement. First, a freeze on all settlements on the West Bank for the duration of the interim period. Second, establish now the procedure by which the final status of the West Bank would be determined at the end of the five years. Third, determine now the source of sovereignty during and after the interim period, and fourth, create a formula that would ensure the execution of an Israeli withdrawal from territories in accordance with Resolution 242.

The Israeli delegation's reaction to the American proposal was divided. Dayan and Weizman were more flexible because they believed that this was a historic opportunity that should not be missed.[64] Begin, adamantly rejected any proposal that would weaken Israel's claim to the West Bank. The Israeli delegation was in agreement that a distinction should be established between a complete withdrawal from the Sinai and no withdrawal from the West Bank. On the issues of the settlements and the source of sovereignty, Begin refused to compromise. Dayan and Weizman were more forthcoming. The meeting ended with harsh tones and no results. The American delegation agreed to revise its proposal again, but made clear that it was running out of patience. The Israelis were no less nervous. Dayan was convinced that hidden microphones were installed in all the rooms and that the Americans were tapping the phones. He could not otherwise explain how the Americans knew every word that was said in the Israeli private discussions.[65] At this point it was unclear how the disagreements would be resolved.

Monday, September 11, was the day dedicated to a Carter-Sadat meeting. Carter informed Sadat of his meeting with the Israeli delegation the previous day. Begin promised to submit to Carter his written proposal before this meeting. The Israeli delegation worked on the proposal between 3 A.M. and 10 A.M. the next morning. The revised proposal insisted that Israel was neither prepared to dismantle the settlements in the Sinai, nor to withdraw from the West Bank. Israel, however, showed some flexibility on a withdrawal from the Sinai and a freeze on settlements in the West Bank. The account of the Egyptian reaction to the Israeli proposal gained conflicting interpretations. Israeli journalists reported that Sadat was appalled and said: ''If this is the Israeli proposal, we might as well call the whole thing off and go home.''[66] Quandt recalled that ''Sadat's initial reaction was positive . . . he asked for some time to consult with his colleagues before giving his final comments."[67]

The following days were long, tense, and demanding. It was clear that if the issue of Palestinian autonomy was resolved, an agreement could be signed. The problem was that Egypt saw autonomy as a first step toward Palestinian self-determination, whereas Israel saw autonomy as a final status, providing the Palestinians a limited form of administrative self-government while Israel retained its political and military control over the West Bank. The question was how much leverage Carter had to coerce or induce the two leaders to make reciprocal concessions.

As a first step, the American team decided to press Begin to go as far as he could in accepting the application of the general principles of Resolution 242 to all fronts. On the other hand, Egypt had to be pressed to accept a Palestinian self-rule that would not imply a Palestinian state. Part of the plan was to exert pressure on Begin from within, that is, mobilize members of the Israeli team to support the American proposal. On Monday evening Carter invited Minister of Defense Weizman and General Tamir, his adviser, to a private, informal talk. Carter made it clear that he supported Sadat's demand for more autonomy for the Palestinians than suggested by Begin. Using subtle threat, Carter intimated that if Camp David ended in a failure the United States would go along with an Egyptian request for a bilateral memorandum of understanding between the United States and Egypt. Carter knew that Israel was extremely sensitive to such a possibility. Other Israeli guests on Carter's list were Minister of Foreign Affairs Dayan and the legal adviser, Barak. The talks did create a sense of urgency in the Israeli delegation, but not enough to bring about a compromise.

Israel's reaction was especially harsh because Egypt submitted that morning a proposal rejecting Begin's autonomy plan, although it was willing to agree in principle to an interim period for a transition of power. Egypt continued to insist on an Israeli withdrawal from Jerusalem. Finally, Egypt did not feel committed to an exchange of ambassadors as part of a peace treaty.

Dayan was perhaps the most pessimistic. During a brief encounter with Ambassador Lewis on Tuesday morning, he said: "The talks are deadlocked and I want to go back tomorrow."[68] Lewis reported Dayan's remark immediately to the American team, which decided, in face of the strong Israeli reaction, to again revise its proposal. A discussion session between the American and the Israeli teams, which was scheduled for that evening, was postponed to the next day, and Carter accepted Begin's request to hold a private meeting with him that evening.

The Tuesday evening meeting focused on the principle of nonacquisition of territories by war. Begin said that he would never sign an agreement that would impose this principle on Israel. Moreover, he threatened to leave and make a public statement explaining his version of the failure of Camp David. He added that "Israel was ready to continue the negotiations anytime, anywhere."[69] Carter was defensive, trying to explain to Begin that neither he nor Sadat wanted such an outcome. "It was a heated discussion, unpleasant and repetitive. I . . . accused him of being willing to give up peace . . . undivided Jerusalem, permanent security for Israel . . . just to keep a few illegal settlers on Egyptian land."[70] The next day Carter summoned the American team and asked them to revise the American proposal to save the negotiations.

Two main problems had to be resolved. Israel agreed to withdraw from the Sinai but insisted that the settlements and the two airfields remain under Israeli jurisdiction. Egypt adamantly rejected this proposal. On the other hand, Egypt demanded a meaningful autonomy for the West Bank, which Israel adamantly rejected. Sadat was losing his patience. He was irritated by Begin's haggling over minutiae. On Thursday, September 14, the situation seemed hopeless. Egypt and Israel were in disagreement over the autonomy plan and no agreement could be found for the settlements in Sinai. The mood in the American team was gloomy. Carter felt that a full agreement was beyond reach.[71] Even a special meeting between Sadat and Weizman produced no results. Weizman, enraged and frustrated, felt that peace was being given up in exchange for the settlements in the Sinai. He told Begin "we must evacuate the settlements in the Sinai if peace is to be attained." Begin answered angrily, "I heard you."[72]

As a last resort, Sadat decided to invite Dayan for an informal talk. Carter felt that this might save the negotiations.[73] They met on Thursday afternoon, alone. Sadat went right to the point. "I invited you here," he said, "because it doesn't seem as if a compromise is going to be reached and I would like to hear your opinion." Dayan answered: "No one in Israel will approve the dismantling of the settlements in the Sinai." Sadat concluded: "There is no sense in staying here if you cannot commit Israel to that."[74] Tired and frustrated, Sadat was ready to give up and leave. Friday morning he called Vance and informed him that he was preparing to leave that day. Simultaneously, Dayan reported to Begin: "This was the end." Dayan went to his room and started to pack.

Begin invited Vance for a last meeting with the Israeli delegation. Dayan recalled that Vance, unlike himself, was angry and vocal. He waved his hands, raised his voice, and said that the United States had tried everything possible to satisfy the demands of both sides; it even compromised on issues it never thought it would, but to no avail. Begin tried to explain that all Israel objected to was a Palestinian state. The meeting was cut off when Vance was asked to meet Carter. Before he left he suggested that no one leave and that the negotiations continue with the three parties revising their proposals again.[75]

Carter, afraid that Sadat might leave, went to his cabin for a private talk. According to Brzezinski and Quandt, Carter was very rough on Sadat. He warned him of the grave results if he departed. Not only would it mean an end to all peace efforts, but it would also mean the end of the special relationships between the two nations and the two leaders.[76] Sadat, shaken by Carter's assertiveness, agreed to continue the negotiations. Carter promised to try and convince Begin to give up the settlements and the airfields in the Sinai, whereas Sadat would give up his adamant demands for Palestinian self-rule.

That weekend was the most crucial in all the peace process. The three leaders lacked the power to coerce each other to make concessions. But they were ready to compromise because they all needed an agreement. This belief probably kept the peace process going. The breakthrough occurred when Begin, who was the least willing to compromise and the least vulnerable of the three, decided that Israel's vital interest in a peace treaty justified the sacrifice of the settlements and the airfields in the Sinai. This decision opened the door to reciprocal concessions from Sadat on the West Bank.

Dayan and Weizman, who believed that peace with Egypt justified this price, had greater influence on Begin than any American threats to withhold arms.[77] During the weekend Weizman and Dayan began to explore the possibility of alternative airfields in the Negev (the southern region of Israel), whereas the American negotiators discussed with Dayan security arrangements including a U.S.–Israeli security pact. Friday evening seemed like a breakthrough on the Sinai. Saturday was dedicated to a search for a compromise on the West Bank.

THE BATTLE OVER THE WEST BANK AND JERUSALEM

Barak, the Israeli legal adviser, became the focus of the negotiations. On into Saturday the participants grew more optimistic. Israel agreed to evacuate the settlements and the airfields in the Sinai, subject to a vote of confidence in the parliament. As for the West Bank, Begin shocked everyone when he agreed to include a statement recognizing the legitimate rights of the Palestinian people. He explained to his surprised team: "The Palestinians have some rights, and every right is legitimate."[78] Israel, however, demanded the separation of future Jordanian-Israeli negotiations on peace from the four-party talks on the final status of the West Bank and Gaza. Its goal was to avoid applying Resolution 242 to the West Bank. Barak argued that since there were only twenty-four hours left to negotiate, the final formula for the West Bank and Gaza should be put in as broad and vague terms as possible. "The formula would have to fuzz over the issue rather than resolve it."[79]

The final formula, which was developed by Barak and Vance, established two sets of negotiations, one between Israel and Jordan, the other between Israel and the representative of the Palestinians. Following Israel's demand, Resolution 242 was applied to the negotiations only, without explaining what this meant in concrete terms. This vague formula allowed each side to create its own interpretation. More specifically, it allowed Israel to accept Resolution 242 without committing itself to a withdrawal from the West Bank and Gaza. This was clearly a fig leaf for Sadat; it was not a substantive formula for resolving the Palestinian question. But Sadat was willing to make this concession and leave the final status of the West Bank and Gaza on hold, saying only that the end results should be in accordance with all the principles of Resolution 242. The draft also included a statement about the legitimate rights of the Palestinian people. Ambiguity was the key factor in the success of Camp David.

Camp David had, however, to survive yet another major crisis. On the last day, Sunday, September 17, after nearly all the points were agreed upon, the issue of Jerusalem was raised. During lunch, Vice President Walter Mondale showed Begin and the Israeli ambassador to the United States, Simcha Dinitz, the American draft letter to Sadat reiterating the American position that East Jerusalem should be considered part of the West Bank; thus, its final status should be subject to future negotiations. Upon reading the proposal, Begin exploded: "I will never sign this. Never in my life! Come, we are going home."[80] The historical opportunity to bring peace to the Middle East again seemed to have slipped away. Begin felt betrayed and tried to resist the pressure of the shortage of time and the urgency of the moment. He insisted that he would rather see the peace process fail than give up Jerusalem. Several hours of intense negotiations followed, involving everybody on both the American and the Israeli teams. The crisis was resolved at four in the afternoon, after it had been agreed not to include the issue of Jerusalem in the final Accords. Carter, Sadat, and Begin were to attach to the Accords letters expressing their position on the issue. The letters carried the same date as the Camp David Accord, September 17, 1978.

Sadat's letter reaffirmed the Egyptian position that Arab Jerusalem was an integral part of the West Bank and should, therefore, be under Arab sovereignty. Begin's letter stated that Jerusalem was one city, indivisible, and the capital of the State of Israel. Carter's letter reaffirmed the American position as stated by Ambassadors Goldberg (1967) and Yost (1969) in the United Nations.[81] Since the letters were not an integral part of the Accords, they did not have any operative meaning. The question of Jerusalem was left open, to be negotiated among the four parties after the interim period ended.

The settlements on the West Bank were another unresolved issue. In the Camp David Accords, no clear-cut commitment was made by Israel on this matter. Carter asked Begin to write him a letter committing Israel to refrain from establishing new settlements during the negotiation period. Begin wrote the letter on September 27, but he promised only a three-month freeze. The argument evolved over the interpretation of "the negotiation period," which Carter argued was the whole five-year interim, whereas Begin argued that it was limited to the three-month Israeli-Egyptian peace negotiations. However, in the late afternoon of September 17, all were optimistic. In Begin's cabin, Israeli and Egyptian leaders were toasting the new agreement. Begin presented Sadat with a small gift, a peace medallion, created by the Israeli artist Yaacov Agam. The Camp David Accords became a reality. The official signing ceremony took place in Washington at 10:30 P.M. that evening.

OVERVIEW

The peace process, which began in mid–1977, ended on March 26, 1979, with the formal signing of the peace treaty between Egypt and Israel. Conflicts of interests, a legacy of mistrust, misperceptions, and matters such as national pride, personal prestige, and individual ambitions made an agreement almost impossible. Still unresolved is the question of how much, if at all, U.S. coercion or inducement played a role in the bargaining process.

Neither Israeli nor American officials have acknowledged the fact that leverage was used. Brzezinski suggested that the United States was mistaken in not using its leverage by denying Israel military aid. He complained that, although Israel showed no willingness to compromise on the West Bank and insisted on maintaining the status quo in complete defiance of U.S. policy, the United States nonetheless continued to preserve for Israel a privileged status. "American aid continued to flow . . . not to intensify Israel's insecurity by using aid as a source of pressure on Israel."[82] Brzezinski expressed the American dilemma very clearly: a denial of arms could undermine Israel's strategic superiority, which in turn would undermine the U.S. power position in the region. He argued that Israel manipulated the situation to America's disadvantage. It created an image of an important ally. "Whenever possible, the words 'ally,' 'special relationships,' or 'strategic asset' were proposed for inclusion in Presidential statements, in order to reinforce in the public's mind the special links binding America and Israel."[83] The United States should have resisted these tactics, argued Brzezinski, and should have punished Israel whenever that was needed. Weizman, on the other hand, argued that the United States did not, and could not have used leverage because Israel had already received military aid in stunning proportions. It was, therefore, impossible to pressure Israel by a withholding of arms.[84]

Carter and Mondale denied that conflicts over arms supplies derived from political causes, or that military aid was used for political pressure.[85] Carter's denial of a license to coproduce the F–16 in Israel, his refusal to allow Israel to sell the Kfir jet fighters to Ecuador, and some restrictions on the export of other weapon systems to Israel, such as cluster bombs and Cobra helicopter gunships (approved by the end of 1977), could not be seen in the context of leverage. It was part of Carter's global policy of reducing the U.S. role as the number one supplier of arms in the world. But his "plane package" in 1978, to sell airplanes to Israel, Egypt, and Saudi Arabia, could be defined as a covert act of coercion/ inducement. The "plane package" was clearly a means of pressure, since the United States included in it the F–16s promised to Israel by Kissinger as part of the 1975 disengagement agreement. The timing of the package was also significant in that it was announced in February 1978, when the Israeli-Egyptian talks seemed to have collapsed following the Ismailiya talks.

During the negotiations other measures of limited leverage were taken by Washington. These included delays rather than direct withholding of arms. The longstanding tactics of restricting military credits, or the threat to do so, were also used. For example, in October 1978, when Israel refused to freeze the settlements on the West Bank and disputed Carter's interpretation of the Camp David Accords on this issue, the Department of State delayed submission of Israeli arms procurements to Congress saying that they were "still under review." On the other hand, as a measure of inducement, Israel was promised to be handsomely rewarded for helping the peace process to come to a happy ending. During the "plane package" negotiations Israel was promised additional F–16s, as well as shipments of cluster bombs and FLIR infrared weapon systems. Before, during, and after the Camp David negotiations, Israel was unofficially told that punishment and reward would follow its behavior. The accent was on the reward side, implying that Israel would be assured alternative airfields, and arms supplies would be upgraded and speeded up.

Following the signing of the peace treaty, the administration submitted to Congress a request for a "supplemental 1979 Middle East Aid Package for Israel and Egypt,"[86] The package included $3.3 billion in military aid to Israel, of which $800 million was a grant to build two new airfields in the Negev. The rest was used for the purchase of new weapons systems to make up for security hazards necessitated by the treaty. The United States also signed a memorandum of understanding, long sought by Israel, promising U.S.–Israeli cooperation on R&D projects. Another provision was a promise by the United States to take steps against third party transfers of American arms if those posed a threat to Israel. Finally, the United States agreed to advance by a full year delivery of the F–16s. (These planes were actually scheduled for Iran but were halted after the revolution.)

The United States used a combination of promises to supply arms, threats to deny them, and economic pressure concerning grants and loans to finance these large amounts of arms sales. These tactics produced much less leverage than was expected. Interestingly, the most effective pressure was Israel's desire to avoid a severe conflict with the United States. Long-term political considerations played a much more important role than short-term tactics of withholding arms. During the difficult moments of Camp David, the members of the Israeli team felt pressured, not by overt or covert American threats, but by the understanding that a collapse of the peace process might have long-term effects on U.S.–Israeli relations. Indeed, American friendship was much more important to Israel than the United States had realized.

The success of the Camp David negotiations led to euphoria in Washington, Cairo, and Jerusalem. Carter hoped that similar agreements with Jordan, Syria, and Saudi Arabia would follow. King Hassan of Morocco agreed to continue his efforts. King Hussein met with Saudi officials, and Vance flew to Damascus to hold talks with Assad. The disappointments proved that "progress toward an Israeli-Arab peace depends first on convincing human beings—individually and then collectively—that peace is possible."[87]

Camp David demonstrated that peace was a process, not an individual act. Perceptions of national interest were more important than tactics of coercion and inducement. The struggle for peace meant reconciling the irreconcilable. It was of extreme importance for all, especially for the United States. Neither Israel nor Egypt could risk a schism in their relations with the United States. But most of all, neither wished to be responsible for destroying the best chance peace had ever had in the Middle East. Although the Camp David Accords did not settle all the Israeli-Arab conflicts, they did create peace between Egypt, the largest Arab country, and Israel. Throughout the negotiations leverage played a minimal role. Understanding and defining national interests, focusing on long-term relationships, and developing alliances based on mutual benefits yielded more results than coercion or inducement.

NOTES

1. For a detailed account, see Aitan Haber, Ehud Yaari, and Zeev Schiff, *The Year of the Dove* (Hebrew) (Tel Aviv: Zmora, Bitan, Modan Publishers, 1980), Chapters 1–4.

2. The Herut party's ideology claims that Eretz Israel, the land of Israel, includes both the East and the West Banks of the Jordan River. Its anthem says: "Shtei gadot La'Yarden, zo shelanu, zo gam ken." Translated: the Jordan River has two banks; both are ours.

3. "Carter took the lead in articulating a new position . . . on the Palestinian question, calling for the creation of a 'homeland' for the refugees. . . . [H]is preference was a link between a Palestinian homeland and Jordan." William B. Quandt, *Camp David* (Washington, DC: Brookings Institute, 1986), p. 60.

4. President Carter believed that the agreement had better chances with the cooperation of the U.S.S.R. Thus he negotiated a joint American-Soviet statement, issued on October 1, 1977 and calling for a Geneva forum that would open multilateral negotiations including Syria, the PLO, and Jordan, all of which rejected the direct negotiations approach with Israel.

5. For President Carter, negotiations with Prime Minister Begin were always difficult and many times annoying; see Quandt, *Camp David*, p. 83.

6. The American team was fond of Sadat. Begin and Dayan, on the other hand, were considered hard to deal with.

7. Cyrus Vance, *Hard Choices* (New York: Simon and Schuster, 1983), pp. 164–165; also Quandt, *Camp David*, p. 38.

8. Interview with Alfred R. Atherton, September 1986.

9. Jimmy Carter, *Keeping Faith* (New York: Bantam Books, 1982), p. 277.

10. Quandt, who took part in the negotiations, describes it as almost an Egyptian-American conspiracy.

11. See discussion in Zbigniew Brzezinski, *Power and Principle* (New York: Farrar, Straus, and Giroux, 1983), pp. 240–242.

12. Former Prime Minister Rabin in a symposium, Tel-Aviv, June 1986.

13. Quandt, *Camp David*, p. 159.

14. Vance, *Hard Choices*, p. 236.

15. Eliyakim Rubinstein, former adviser to Minister of Defense Dayan, in an interview, September 1986.

16. See discussion by David Pollock, *The Politics of Pressure* (Westport, CT: Greenwood Press, 1982), p. 223.

17. Carter, *Keeping Faith*, p. 299.

18. Eliyakim Rubinstein, "The Peace Negotiations: Some Road Marks," Israel's Information Center Bulletin, September 1980, p. 6.

19. For example, the issue of the Israeli resort area at Taba has yet to be resolved.

20. Atherton interview.

21. Quandt, *Camp David*, p. 164.

22. Ezer Weizman, *The Battle for Peace* (New York: Bantam Books, 1981), p. 86.

23. Atherton interview.

24. Moshe Dayan, *Shall the Sword Devour Forever?* (Jerusalem: Edanim Publishing, 1981), pp. 93–94; Carter, *Keeping Faith*, pp. 298–299.

25. President Carter appointed three members of the Brookings Institution group to high posts: Brzezinski, Quandt, and Robert Bowie. A fourth, Philip Klutznick, was appointed Secretary of Commerce.

26. *Autonomy—the Wisdom of Camp David* (Washington, DC: Embassy of Israel, Israel, 1980.

27. Interviews with Ezer Weizman and General Tamir (ret.), June 1986.

28. Carter, *Keeping Faith*, pp. 304–305.

29. Ibid., p. 306.

30. Vance, *Hard Choices*, p. 167.

31. Carter, *Keeping Faith*, p. 305.

32. Quandt, *Camp David*, pp. 170–171.

33. Carter, *Keeping Faith*, p. 308.

34. Ibid.

35. Saadia Touval, *The Peace Brokers* (Princeton, NJ: Princeton University Press, 1982), p. 290.

36. Atherton interview.

37. Weizman interview.

38. Pollock, *Politics of Pressure*, p. 224.

39. Andrew Pierre, *The Global Politics of Arms Sales* (Princeton, NJ: Princeton University Press, 1982), p. 52.

40. Carter, *Keeping Faith*, p. 307.

41. Anwar el-Sadat, *In Search for Identity* (New York: Harper & Row, 1978), p. 299.

42. Carter, *Keeping Faith*, p. 310.

43. Quandt, *Camp David*, pp. 175–176.

44. Brzezinski, *Power and Principle*, p. 244.

45. Ibid., p. 235.

46. Quandt, *Camp David*, p. 179.

47. Haber et al., *Year of the Dove*, p. 255.

48. The package included sixty F–15 Eagle aircraft, the most advanced fighter in the U.S. inventory, for Saudi Arabia; fifty F–5 Es for Egypt; fifteen F–15s additional to the twenty-five already sold and seventy-five F–16s for Israel. Israel received twenty additional F–15s later.

49. Pierre, ''Beyond the Plane Package: Arms and Politics in the Middle East,'' *International Security* (Summer 1978), p. 149.

50. Secretary of Defense Harold Brown, in a meeting with Weizman; quoted in Weizman, *Battle for Peace*, p. 242.

51. Ibid.

52. Weizman interview; also *Boston Globe*, April 28, 1978.

53. Dayan, *Shall the Sword Devour Forever?*, p. 124.

54. Under Nasser, over 60 percent of Egypt's products were exported to the Eastern bloc, whereas they supplied less than 50 percent of Egypt's imports. Thus Egypt was short of hard currency. It was essential to change this situation. Only trade with the West

could provide Egypt with the capital and technology so desperately needed. See Salim Mansur, "The Egypt-Israel Relationship: An Anatomy of Wasted Decades," in *Peace-Making in the Middle East* (Totowa, NJ: Barnes & Noble, 1985), pp. 15–46.

55. Secretary Vance carried in his pocket two identical sealed envelopes to Begin and Sadat, inviting them to Camp David.

56. Carter, *Keeping Faith*, p. 316.

57. Quandt, *Camp David*, p. 203.

58. Weizman, *Battle for Peace*, p. 259.

59. Quandt, *Camp David*, p. 203.

60. Weizman and Tamir interviews.

61. House hearing "Proposed Arms Sales," Harold Saunders testimony, 1979 (conversation with Saunders).

62. See, for example, Quandt's discussion, *Camp David*, p. 208.

63. Ibid., p. 225.

64. Weizman interview.

65. Dayan, *Shall the Sword Devour Forever?*, p. 146.

66. Haber et al., *Year of the Dove*, p. 131.

67. Quandt, *Camp David*, p. 230.

68. Haber et al., *Year of the Dove*, p. 333.

69. Ibid., p. 334.

70. Carter, *Keeping Faith*, pp. 386–387.

71. Quandt, *Camp David*, p. 233.

72. Haber et al., *Year of the Dove*, p. 340.

73. Quandt, *Camp David*, p. 234.

74. Haber et al., *Year of the Dove*, p. 341.

75. Dayan, *Shall the Sword Devour Forever?*, pp. 146–147.

76. Quandt, *Camp David*, p. 239.

77. Weizman said that he and Dayan threatened to leave Camp David and to go public with what happened there. Weizman argued that Begin was greatly influenced by this act.

78. Haber et al., *Year of the Dove*, p. 346.

79. Quandt, *Camp David*, p. 244.

80. Haber et al., *Year of the Dove*, p. 347.

81. The American letter confirmed that the official U.S. position was that Jerusalem should be considered part of the West Bank, subject to provisions of the Geneva convention of 1949, and its final status should be resolved by negotiations among the parties. Begin rejected this approach.

82. Brzezinski, *Power and Principle*, p. 236.

83. Ibid.

84. Weizman interview.

85. See *Department of State Bulletin*, July 11, 1977.

86. The supplemental aid to Egypt and Israel was debated in the 96th Congress, 1st session, during April and May of 1979.

87. Harold Saunders, *The Other Walls* (Washington, DC: American Enterprise Institute, 1985), p. 1.

5

The Lebanese Crisis (1982–84)

In the annals of the Reagan administration, the Lebanese crisis will not be recorded as a success story. Following the Israeli invasion of June 1982, the United States became intensely involved in the crisis and within three months sent 1,800 Marines and a 33-ship armada to Lebanon. From that time and until the marines were pulled out in February of 1984, U.S. foreign policy suffered a succession of frustrations and failures.

The most frustrating feature was the U.S. lack of leverage and its total inability to influence the policies of either its friends or its foes. At a time when leverage was most needed, it was nonexistent. This lack ultimately caused the United States to withdraw from the Lebanese scene and to admit that its policy was a failure.

The Lebanese crisis looked very different from the American and the Israeli perspectives. Moreover, it involved regional actors as well as the Soviet Union. The data suggest that if the United States had studied these variables thoroughly, it probably would have adopted a different approach to the situation. Consequently, the outcome could have been more advantageous to the United States.

The Lebanese crisis was preceded by certain major events that drastically changed the political map of the region, challenged the American power position, and threatened the stability and status quo of the Middle East. The energy crises of 1973 and 1978, the demise of the shah, the Soviet invasion of Afghanistan, and the Iran–Iraq war were new realities that demanded an assertive American reaction. The Israeli invasion of Lebanon was an additional complication to the already chaotic situation. Reagan followed the Truman and Eisenhower doctrines and declared the Middle East to be a region of vital importance to the United States and that, if needed, American force would be used to protect it.[1]

Under the new circumstances it was essential for the United States to gain and maintain leverage over both Israel and the friendly Arab states. Leverage would enable the United States to protect and promote its two most vital interests: to reinforce containment, block Soviet influence in the region, and control upheavals that threaten the flow of oil. Leverage was exercised through the delivery or suspension of arms. Since all the friendly nations of the Middle East enjoyed generous transfers of American arms, the withholding tactic was used to express displeasure with the client state's behavior.[2] The regional and global dilemmas, however, exacerbated the region's political complexities and often rendered American leverage ineffective, albeit the use of disciplinary measures.

Even before the fragile status quo was shattered by the Israeli invasion, the United States felt an urgent need to resolve or at least control the instabilities in the Middle East. The best means was revitalizing the stalemated peace process, bringing Hussein to the bargaining table, and finding a solution to the Palestinian problem. Syria, being a Soviet satellite, has always been a difficult issue. The United States hoped that Saudi Arabia, as Syria's main provider of aid, would have leverage there when the time came. Former Secretary Haig envisioned a policy based on a "strategic consensus." Haig aspired to create a mini NATO in the Middle East, a collective security alliance that would include the "Gang of Four"—Israel, Egypt, Jordan, and Saudi Arabia, all states friendly to the United States. The alliance was expected to serve as an arm of the United States and protect its interests in the region. The "strategic consensus" idea was basically a military, not a political concept, and it led the United States to (1) military cooperation with Egypt, (2) large arms sales to Saudi Arabia, including the sale of sixty F–15s and five AWACS planes, (3) strategic cooperation with Jordan, including a plan to establish a Jordanian Rapid Deployment Force, armed and trained by the United States at a total cost of $220 million (this force was expected to counter revolutions or upheavals in the Persian Gulf countries, mainly Saudi Arabia), and (4) strategic cooperation with Israel. The "strategic consensus" never materialized, although it was never completely shelved. It failed because it underestimated the strong antagonisms that existed among the prospective members of the alliance.[3] Another policy option that the United States had been pursuing was establishing bilateral relationships with each of the four countries, with a special emphasis on Saudi Arabia's role as a regional power broker. To America's chagrin, however, this option did not yield the expected results either. Saudi Arabia's influence over the other Arab states proved to be no more than a myth.

In fact, U.S. policy in the Middle East before the Israeli invasion was very ambiguous.[4] Former Secretary Haig made a number of statements indicating that the United States wished the PLO and Syrian power to diminish.[5] On the other hand, the United States negotiated, on July 1981, a cease-fire agreement between the PLO and Israel, which froze the status quo and gave Syria and the PLO control over the northern border.[6] Israel, which signed the agreement very reluctantly, was soon angered by U.S. acceptance of the Saudi Fahd Peace Plan, introduced in August 1981. It clearly suggested the creation of a Palestinian state, which the United States promised Israel not to support. The inconsistent U.S. policy was an effort to reconcile its need to maintain friendly relations with both Israel and the moderate Arab states. Consequently, the Reagan administration continued to provide both sides with sophisticated weapons. Washington courted King Hussein and offered him generous arms deals as an inducement to join the peace process. The United States even tried to leave the door open for Syria to return to the Western camp, a hope that Assad liked to nurture.

Israel, however, enjoyed the status of the most favored client in the region. It was perceived as a Western democracy, liberal, and capitalistic; hence, the United States felt special affinity with Israel. Moreover, the United States had a moral obligation to protect Israel, the land of the survivors of the Holocaust, and assure them that such a tragedy would never reoccur. However, the most important factor in the U.S.-Israel friendship was the strategic interest. Israel's existence as a pro-Western regional power has been vital to American strategic interests. After the revolution in Iran and the instability of the region ever since, the United States needed a strong and reliable ally there. Israel fulfilled both requirements. Its strength was enhanced by the peace treaty with Egypt and by the massive American military aid. The improved Israeli military and political capabilities made it a very valuable American ally.[7]

U.S.-Israel cooperation has been based on overlapping, long-term foreign policy goals: first, to curb Soviet influence, which was against both the U.S. and Israel interests; second, to secure U.S. control over the petroleum riches of the region, and third, to maintain the status quo and the stability of the area. However, Begin's rise to power threatened the future of the partnership.

Begin, the extreme idealist, was a man of strong principles who very rarely compromised. Consequently, during the Lebanese crisis of 1982, the United States and Israel had major disagreements concerning the definitions of their respective national interests. The origin of this conflict has been subject to two major interpretations.

The first approach argues that Washington and Jerusalem adhere to conflicting political doctrines because their vital interests are in conflict.[8] The United States has a vital interest in peace to secure the flow of oil, which is threatened in times of war. Peace enables the United States to maintain friendly relations with both Israel and the Arab states. War obliges the United States to choose between the support of one side or the other. Peace also helps to curb Soviet influence. The U.S.S.R. has been exploiting the Israeli-Arab conflict by playing the "Arabs against the Jews," and gaining influence through the transfer of arms and defense technology. Peace would terminate this practice.

From the Israeli perspective, however, the picture looks different. Israel's most vital interest is its security. Controlling strategic positions in the West Bank and the Golan Heights is more vital to Israel than peace. Hence, a situation of "no peace no war" is preferred over a withdrawal from all or most territories. (Israel claims that it cannot trust the Palestinians' commitment to peace after an Israeli withdrawal.) The conflict is, therefore, between the U.S. position of "peace in exchange for territories," and the "Israeli stance of no peace but territories and security."

The second approach is based on a different assumption. It argues that both nations rank peace as their highest priority.[9] Israel is, perhaps, more interested in peace than the United States. Peace will relieve Israel of the permanent threat to its existence. Peace will enable Israel to devote its scarce resources to its desperately needed economic recovery.[10] Peace will gain Israel much-awaited Arab recognition. Israel's economy could gain tremendously from the opening up of Arab and African markets. It could become a technological center, leading the Middle East into the twenty-first century. Hence, Washington and Jerusalem both want peace. The disagreements are not conceptual. They involve disputes over the strategies and tactics that would best serve the cause of peace, that is, how, when, and in exchange for what should Israel withdraw.

Both approaches can be validly defended. The advocates of the first approach are usually those who are critical of Israel's policies.[11] The advocates of the second approach are usually supporters of Israel's policies. They argue that Israel has accepted U.N. Resolution 242; consequently, it agreed to the principle of "territories for peace."[12]

The theoretical controversy has yet to be resolved. However, during the Lebanese crisis it became clear to both the United States and Israel that major policy disagreements existed between the two allies. The issue of leverage either to deter Israel from pursuing policies that were opposed by the U.S. government, or coerce Israel to comply with desired American policies became crucial. When sought, it has at best been very limited.[13] Interestingly, the Soviet Union, for the same reasons, has found it equally difficult to exert leverage over its client state, Syria, especially during 1983–84.[14] It was not the first time that the Soviet Union experienced a lack of leverage in the Middle East. In 1972 President Sadat unilaterally terminated fifteen years of Soviet-Egyptian cooperation, and the Soviet Union continued to support him during the October 1973 war.

In 1982, on the eve of the Israeli invasion of Lebanon, the United States and Israel experienced growing friction concerning long-term policies, which was aggravated by serious disagreements on short-term policies. First, Israel rejected the U.S. position on the West Bank settlements. Second, the United States opposed Israel's intervention in the Lebanese civil war. The war involved Syria and the PLO, both major recipients of Saudi aid. The United States hoped that with Saudi Arabia's mediation and Special Envoy Philip Habib's diplomatic efforts, a settlement could be reached. The United States was wrong on all counts. The invasion became inevitable when Syria refused to pull out its SA missiles from the Bequ'a valley. Israel decided to invade, and all the diplomatic efforts to resolve the severe conflicts among Israel, Syria, and the PLO failed.

THE ISRAELI INVASION OF LEBANON

The Israeli invasion of Lebanon was launched on June 6, 1982, but it was planned and coordinated with the leaders of the Lebanese Christian Phalangist movement a few years earlier. According to the Israeli writers Schiff and Ya'ari, the first plans to invade Lebanon were conceived as early as April 1981, as a response to the deployment of SA–6 missiles in the Bequ'a valley by Syria, and the growing military strength of the PLO in Lebanon.[15] Begin believed that the United States would support an invasion following remarks by then Secretary of State Haig, who visited Israel in 1981 and expressed concerns about PLO and Syrian aggression. A Syrian attack in 1981 on the Christian city of Zahla led the Phalangists to contact Israel and ask for its direct military intervention. The ties between the Lebanese Christians and Israel were beginning to take the form of a military alliance.

In its planning stages as well as its early days, the invasion was presented as a limited, local affair aimed at destroying PLO bases in southern Lebanon. On Sunday, June 6, 1982, Israeli forces crossed Israel's northern border, and Prime Minister Begin announced: "The Israeli army has been ordered to push the PLO forces northward to a distance of 25 miles from the Israeli border to place their artillery beyond the range of Israeli territory."[16]

The invasion, named Peace for Galilee, was a response to changes that took place in Lebanon during 1981–82. The PLO created a state within a state, threatening the security of the Israeli civilian population living in range of its guns. Both the PLO and Syrian forces in Lebanon upgraded their military capabilities. Syria entered Lebanon in 1976 as a "peacekeeping force," but in 1981 it was fighting alongside the PLO and other extreme Muslim groups against the Christian militias. Israel feared that the very existence of the Christian community in Lebanon, with whom it had strong relations for a number of years, was in danger. Cooperation between the Christian Phalangists and Israel began on March 12, 1976, when a high-ranking Phalangist officer went to Israel by boat from Beirut and established direct communications between the Phalangists and the Israeli government. Since that time strong, regular ties existed between the two. The Phalangists appealed to Israel for help, maintaining that "without protection from air attacks they faced slaughter and possible annihilation." The Israeli Air Force was ordered to lend support to the Christians to prevent the danger of a holocaust.[17]

However, Israel's primary goal in the invasion was to destroy the political, military, and spiritual bases of the PLO in Lebanon. Israel viewed with alarm the fact that Lebanon had become a privileged sanctuary from which the PLO could launch effective attacks with impunity. The armed truce on Israel's northern border did not put an end to the dreaded war of attrition that weakened Israel's bargaining power over the West Bank.

The United States shared Israel's anxiety over the militarization of the PLO in Lebanon. A cease-fire agreement negotiated by Philip Habib, with Saudi Arabia's mediation, and signed on July 24, 1981, did not answer Israel's security problems. Moreover, Syria continued to refuse to pull out its Soviet-made SA missile batteries from the Bequ'a valley. These missiles hampered the routine reconnaissance flights that Israel was conducting over Lebanese territory. (Until that time these flights were tacitly tolerated by Syria.) The missiles were deployed in spring 1981 during the battle on the Christian city of Zahla, which was provoked by Bashir Gemayel. Phalangist control of the city, which is located near the Bequ'a valley and almost on the Beirut-Damascus highway, could have threatened the Syrian positions. Using the excuse of self-defense, Syria deployed the missiles and scored a major political and strategic victory over the Phalangists and Israel.

Syria assumed that if the deployment of the missiles would lead to a localized clash, provided that it would not develop into a full-scale war, it would help end Syria's isolation in the Arab world (Syria sides with Iran against all Arab states), and it might erode the normalization of the Egyptian-Israeli relations, a long-standing Syrian objective. Hence, Syria scored a much-needed, substantial political victory.[18]

The American diplomacy headed off the impending confrontation, but not for long. Habib's shuttle between Damascus, Jerusalem, Beirut, and Riyadh created a new modus vivendi. The Syrians retained their missiles, and thus claimed a political victory while refraining from launching them against manned Israeli aircraft, thus permitting the IAF (Israel Air Force) to continue its reconnaissance flights and ground attacks against PLO military objectives. Israel, however, never accepted the new status quo and believed that only the destruction of the PLO bases in Lebanon would secure its northern border. It also linked tensions in the West Bank and the Gaza Strip, which had become a severe domestic problem, to PLO propaganda.

Hence, the invasion came in answer to pressing security and political problems. Defense Minister Sharon, who initiated the invasion, argued that it was the only way to end the dangerous status quo. He wished to change the political map of the Middle East so that it would serve Israel's interests.[19] Sharon's supporters included Prime Minister Begin, who saw in Arafat a follower of Hitler; Minister of Foreign Affairs Itzhak Shamir, who became Begin's successor; and Israel's Chief of Staff Refael Eitan.

Before approving the "Sharon invasion plan," the Israeli government had to consider how it would affect its relations with the United States. Israel decided to withhold information about the invasion on June 6, because it assumed that the United States would oppose a large-scale military action. First, the United States could not risk a conflict with its Arab friends, which support of the invasion might have incurred. Second, any Israeli confrontation with Syria might have developed into an American-Soviet confrontation. Israel could not ignore the fact that Syria was a Soviet client and the U.S.S.R. could have reacted strongly to a Syrian military defeat. Israel wished to avoid any global crisis that could instigate a strong Soviet reaction that could lead to a crisis in U.S.-Israeli relations. On the other hand, Israel believed that it was possible to carry out a large-scale invasion and avoid American punitive action, although Israel assumed that the United States would oppose the act. Finally, Israel gambled that U.S.

leverage would be very limited, given the domestic and global constraints, and it could be thwarted easily.

When planning the invasion, Israel had to consider important regional factors, especially a possible strong reaction from Syria, which was expected to resist any act that might diminish its power position in Lebanon. Syria had aspirations not only to become the major Arab power in the Middle East, but to become the leader of the pan-Arabism movement, which was without a leader since the death, in 1970, of the Egyptian ruler Nasser. Second, Assad had an interest to continue hostile relationships with both Israel and the United States, mainly for domestic reasons.

Syria's intervention in Lebanon began in the third week of November 1976, when it deployed thousands of troops to the three major cities of Beirut, Sydon, and Tripoli. Syria took over the radio and TV stations, the airports, main roads, and the military camps. Between the fall of 1976 and the Israeli invasion of June 1982, Lebanon was controlled by Syria, which had 50,000 troops deployed, occupying half of the country. The rest was divided among the PLO, the Christians, and the Shi'ites. President Assad wanted complete domination over any Lebanese government. There were no reasonable concessions that the Americans or Lebanese could offer Assad. He was not ready to negotiate a settlement of the Golan Heights. Washington argued that all he wanted was to stay in power. "The best way for him to do that is to maintain a state of confrontation with the Israelis and the Americans and thus justify the militarization of the Syrian society which he needs to protect his regime from a coup attempt. Washington believes that the way to get concessions from Mr. Assad is not by offering him things but by threatening his power base."[20]

The Egyptian reaction to an Israeli invasion was another issue that Israel had to consider. A large-scale invasion could threaten the very fragile peace treaty between the two nations. Egypt, which was condemned by every Arab state for signing a peace treaty before the Palestinian issue was resolved, was expected to take a firm stand against the invasion. President Mubarak could have suspended or even terminated the peace treaty. The only regional support that Israel could count on was that of the Lebanese Christian militia, with whom Israel had coordinated the invasion.[21]

However, the United States was the main consideration. Israel had to decide whether the United States would resort to disciplinary measures in order to impose compliance. Israel remembered that on previous occasions American reaction had been rather harsh. In June 1981, after Israel had bombed the Iraqi nuclear reactor, Reagan immediately suspended the shipment of F–15 jet planes, as well as shipments of other weapons. Later that year, after Israel announced the annexation of the Golan Heights, Washington angrily announced the cancellation of the memorandum of understanding, a strategic agreement signed with Israel two weeks earlier. The memorandum was of special importance to Israel because it counterbalanced the sale of five AWACS planes to Saudi Arabia. President

Reagan also suspended $300 million in potential economic benefits by cancelling import contracts with the Israeli defense industry.[22]

Although Israel rightly assumed that the invasion of Lebanon would find a better understanding in Washington, it needed more information about the possible U.S. reaction before it crossed the Lebanese border. Secretary Haig described the first time he heard about the invasion plan. It was in October 1981, the day after Sadat's funeral, when Haig met with Prime Minister Begin at the Hyatt Prince Hotel in Nasser City. At the meeting Begin told Haig that Israel had begun planning a move into Lebanon that would not draw Syria into the conflict. This was the first time Begin or any other Israeli had been quite so specific. "If you move, you move alone," reacted Haig. "Unless there is a major international recognized provocation, the United States will not support such an action." Begin answered that Israel's goal was only to push the PLO back from the border area and then go to the United Nations and ask for a guarantee that the PLO would not be back." "Does that make sense to you, Al?" Begin asked. "I repeated that while it might make sense from the Israeli point of view, Israel will be alone if it carries out such a plan."[23]

Two months later, on December 5, 1981, former Defense Minister Sharon met in Jerusalem with special envoy Philip Habib and Bill Brown, U.S. Deputy Ambassador in Tel-Aviv. Sharon briefed them about Israel's plan to invade southern Lebanon. He explained that if the PLO continued to violate the cease-fire agreement, Israel would completely destroy all PLO bases in Lebanon. Philip Habib said: "this is the 20th century, you cannot just invade a sovereign country, besides you will instigate a war with Syria and the whole Middle East will go up in flames." Sharon answered: "the Syrian army can keep out of it. We can free Lebanon of the presence of the PLO without any confrontation with Syria." Sharon then introduced a detailed map of southern Lebanon on which PLO bases were marked as the targets for a possible invasion. Habib and Brown informed Washington of the meeting. This was the first time that Israel presented a detailed invasion plan to Washington.[24]

Israel's plan to invade Lebanon did not encounter strong American opposition, although Haig in his memoirs tries to depict his reaction as being unequivocally harsh. According to Israeli writers Schiff and Ya'ari, U.S. reaction to the Sharon-Habib meeting was rather mild because State Department officials believed that the plan would never be approved by the Israeli Cabinet.[25]

Encouraged by the American inaction, Israel decided to test once more the American attitude toward a large-scale invasion. On February 3, 1982, Begin sent General Yehoshua Saguy, the director of Israel's military intelligence, to Washington to meet with Haig. General Saguy had formally informed Haig that Israel had made the decision to move into Lebanon if the PLO continued to attack Israel's northern border. During the six months that the cease-fire with the PLO was in effect, 17 Israelis were killed and 288 were wounded in PLO violations of the cease-fire. Israel would attack, Saguy said, if these incidents continued. He explained: "A large-scale force would advance from the Israeli border to the southern suburbs of Beirut. Its target would be the PLO infrastructure; the Syrians would be avoided if possible."[26] General Saguy stressed the limited nature of the planned invasion and assured former Secretary Haig that its aim was not Syria but the PLO.

Indeed, the United States was well informed about the 1982 invasion. In addition to information communicated by Israel, a flow of information came from the Christian Phalangists. On April 8, 1982, John Chancellor of NBC-TV presented detailed maps of the planned Israeli military operation. He told viewers that the Israelis would move in three forces: one would move along the coastal road into the refugee camps of Sydon and Tahir, the second would bypass the UNIFIL forces in the direction of Damour, and the third would advance toward the Bequ'a valley in an effort to reach the Beirut-Damascus highway. Chancellor explained that as many as 1,200 Israeli tanks would take part in this large-scale military operation, and that the Israelis were even considering an attack on Beirut.[27] This was basically the Israeli plan, which was leaked to Chancellor from Phalangist sources. It is hard to believe that what was known to John Chancellor was unknown to the CIA. However, Washington did not consider these "rumors" to be of real concern! Washington assumed that strong warnings communicated to Israel on several occasions would be enough to deter it from carrying out its invasion plan.

In a classical case of misperception, Israel believed that it had made its concerns and plans very clear. Israel repeatedly stated that it would retaliate against PLO attacks on its civilian population. The U.S. position, however, even after General Saguy's visit to Washington, was anything but clear.[28] Accepting former Defense Minister Sharon's opinion that Haig would support the invasion, Begin decided to go ahead with the plan. Ready to invade, Begin decided once again to discuss it with Washington. Late in May 1982, Defense Minister Sharon was dispatched to present to Haig and other high-ranking State Department officials two contingency plans. The first plan was limited only to pacifying southern Lebanon. The second plan was more daring and was aimed at reaching Beirut and changing the political map of the region. Sharon presented detailed maps and arrows were drawn to show force movements. One arrow was missing from the maps: the arrow in the direction of the Bequ'a valley. No arrow reached Beirut.[29] The attentive people in the audience were appalled. Haig's reaction was strong and clear: the United States would never approve of such an action unless it was in reaction to an internationally recognized PLO or Syrian provocation. Following the meeting, Haig sent a letter to Begin repeating what he had said to Sharon.

Haig wanted to leave no ambiguity on the extent of U.S. concern about possible future Israeli military action in Lebanon. He asked Begin to continue to exercise complete restraint and refrain from any action that would further damage the understanding underlying the cessation of hostilities. Haig sent a second message to Sharon saying that only an internationally recognized provocation could warrant an Israeli retaliation. Sharon's reply was that no one has the right to tell Israel what decision it should take in defense of its people.[30]

Haig's message was ineffectual because his other statements, that is, his attacks on the Soviet Union and its surrogates, Syria and the PLO, and his assertions that their power and influence ought to be diminished, were taken more seriously in Israel. In fact, Israel hoped that the United States would accept its argument that the PLO guerrilla activities were a legitimate casus belli.

Shortly before the invasion, in April 1982, Haig warned that the U.S.S.R. had emerged as a global military power "increasingly bold in the use of its power and might to promote violence in areas. . . . The U.S.S.R. uses satellite states as instruments of Soviet purpose." He suggested that in this power competition the United States developed and sustained a relationship with the U.S.S.R. that recognized that the competition would proceed but that the use or threat of force be constrained.[31]

Israel believed that Haig implied that Syria, which was considered the "Cuba of the Middle East," was spreading anti-American feelings and trying to destabilize the region. In this context, Israel assumed that a military operation that would reduce the power of Syria would be welcomed.

President Reagan was unaware of the political dynamics of the Israeli-Arab conflict. Although considering the Middle East a vital U.S. interest, Reagan failed to make it his top priority. Unlike Carter, the Reagan administration did not think that a resolution of the Arab-Israeli conflict was a prerequisite for stability in the region. Hence, it did not plan to launch any new peace initiative. Israel misread the American lack of interest in the Middle East to be support for its legitimate security anxieties, although it knew that the United States could not overtly help Israel. On the regional level, such a support would alienate America's Arab friends, whereas on the global level, it might instigate an aggressive Soviet reaction.

Former Secretary Haig, who claims to be the only one in the Reagan administration to be alarmed by Israel's plans, attempted in vain to communicate his concerns to the President and his national security adviser, William Clark. He believed that war was near. "Our duty to attempt to prevent it was obvious; our ability to do so, questionable." He informed the President of the meeting with Saguy and asked Ambassador Lewis to contact Begin and tell him that an Israeli operation would not be tolerated in the current circumstances.[32]

Washington did not listen to Haig's policy proposals. He suggested to internationalize the Lebanese conflict and to call an emergency conference, which would be composed of the European countries participating in the U.N. forces in Lebanon (France, Ireland, the Netherlands, and Norway), Saudi Arabia and Kuwait as the gulf state representatives, Syria, and the United States. The U.S.S.R. and Israel would not be invited. Reagan did not accept the idea and instead invited Prime Minister Begin to Washington on an official visit on June 21, 1982, to discuss U.S.-Israeli relations. Encouraged and influenced by Defense Minister Sharon's strong arguments that Israel would enjoy Haig's support, Begin decided to go ahead with the invasion plans. The Israeli Army was ordered to start preparing a large-scale invasion.[33]

THE COLLAPSE OF AMERICAN POLICY IN LEBANON

U.S. foreign policy in the Middle East inevitably led to unplanned growing American involvement in the region's politics. Unwillingly, the United States was becoming increasingly involved in the crisis until at the height of it, America completely dispensed with the use of surrogates and acted directly. It is unclear whether the United States could have headed off the impending catastrophe had its policy been more clear and consistent. Indeed, while Israel was planning the invasion and misreading the U.S. position, Reagan was caught in his own misperceptions, assuming that Israel would never carry out its plan. Reagan wrongly assumed that he had the situation under control by (1) warning Israel against excessive military acts in Lebanon, (2) establishing a cease-fire between Israel and the PLO through Habib in July of 1981, and (3) supporting the Saudi peace initiative of August 1981 (the Fahd plan). Indeed, the role of Saudi Arabia was highly exaggerated because it was providing Syria with massive economic aid. For example, when Saudi Arabia was asked by the United States to influence Syria to pull out its missiles from the Bequ'a valley, it was incapable of doing it.

Israel continued its invasion plans. On March 8 an important "invasion game" took place. In the game the Phalangists played a major role. They were supposed to take over territories cleared by the IDF (Israel Defense Forces) of PLO and Syrian forces and reinstate their control over Lebanon. Chief of Staff Refael Eitan was the main architect of this cooperation, whereas many Israeli military officials opposed it, claiming that the Phalangist militia was unreliable, that it used Israel as a tool to achieve its parochial goals, and that Israel should not get involved in the ethnic politics of Lebanon. These arguments, which proved later to be true, had no influence on Begin, Sharon, and Eitan. The decision was made and the invasion goals were clear: to destroy the Syrian and PLO bases in Lebanon, after which a Christian-controlled government, with whom Israel could reach a peace treaty, would be established.

Israel, however, could not carry out its plan before April 1982, the date set for the completion of the evacuation of the Sinai. Israel could not risk the fragile peace treaty with Egypt, which was of vital interest to both the United States and Israel. However, any provocation after this date would be used as a casus belli. This happened when the Israeli ambassador to London was shot and seriously wounded by PLO guerrillas.

On April 27, 1982, Haig made a foreign policy speech, stressing the need for urgent diplomatic action to end the civil war in Lebanon and prevent an Israeli invasion; however, to no avail.[34] The issue of the invasion was discussed in the Israeli Cabinet many times. Not once did Sharon mention the fact that the plan included Beirut or the takeover of the Beirut-Damascus highway. In an important Cabinet meeting on May 10, Sharon portrayed the U.S. attitude as supportive and the invasion goals as limited.[35] In April Begin revealed the plans to the leaders of the opposition party, the Labor Alignment, presenting the invasion as a limited military operation. Two former generals, Chaim Barlev and Itzhak Rabin, and Labor leader Shimon Peres participated in the meeting and strongly opposed the invasion. Cabinet member (Likud) General Tzipori argued that a war with Syria would be inevitable. The criticism did not change either Begin's or Sharon's plans. On May 13, when the invasion plans were completed and only the date was not yet set, the Israeli chiefs of staff held a meeting in which General Saguy expressed strong opinions against the invasion. He predicted a war with Syria, claiming that the goal of the invasion was really political and not military, and questioned the reliability of the Phalangists as strategic allies and political friends. Saguy's most important criticism, however, concerned U.S. and the U.S.S.R. reactions.

The most vital interest of the United States was stability in the region; hence, it could not support the invasion. Saguy predicted that the U.S.S.R. would keep a low profile since it, too, had no interest in upheavals in the area. "After the war, the issue would be reestablishing Lebanese sovereignty, and this would become the major problem with which Israel would not be capable of dealing."[36]

Begin and Sharon did not share Saguy's opinion. Moreover, Sharon's visit to Washington in late May 1982, in which he introduced the invasion plans, convinced Begin that the invasion would enjoy U.S. support. The only fear was that if the invasion lead to a Syrian defeat, the Soviet Union would intervene in support of their client state. Israel assumed that the United States would lend Israel tacit support not to alienate its Arab friends. Israel's misperception was based on long-standing mutual interests—containment and protection of the U.S. power position in the region. However, Israel ignored the vital U.S. interest to maintain the status quo and avoid any possible upheaval that might threaten the flow of oil. Conditions were set for the large-scale invasion to begin.

OPERATION PEACE FOR GALILEE

On Friday, June 3, 1982, Shlomo Argov, the Israeli Ambassador to England, was shot and critically wounded by terrorists. An emergency Cabinet meeting was called to approve extended airraids on PLO bases in and around Beirut. Chief of Staff Eitan represented Sharon, who was on a secret visit to Rumania. The next evening, Saturday, June 5, Begin summoned the Cabinet to his home, asking the members to approve a limited invasion of Lebanon aimed at destroying PLO bases within a twenty-five-mile zone, titled Peace for Galilee. Defense Minister Sharon, now back from Rumania, explained that the IDF planned a limited invasion without engaging the Syrians.[37] While the issue was debated, Israeli forces were already at their posts, ready to move. Throughout the military campaign, Sharon was acting on his own, often without Israeli Cabinet approval and sometimes even without the knowledge of the Prime Minister.[38]

After Cabinet approval of a limited military operation that would last no more than twenty-four to forty-eight hours, the navy, army, and air force crossed the Lebanese border in a coordinated effort, not only to destroy PLO bases in southern Lebanon, but also to destroy the Syrian SA missile batteries, to reach the Beirut-Damascus highway, to cut off the Syrian forces in Beirut from their bases in the Bequ'a valley, and to trap about 10,000 PLO members in Beirut. Sharon never intended to limit the operation to a twenty-five-mile zone. Forces advanced simultaneously in three spearheads, while landing boats took paratroopers behind enemy lines north of Sidon, as support forces to tank divisions and army forces that were advancing from the south. The Cabinet members were not informed during their daily meetings about the extended goals of the invasion. Even Chief of Staff Eitan complained that he was not consulted.[39] Sharon hoped to engage the Syrians and to defeat them swiftly. In his script, Syria would either fight and suffer a humiliating defeat, or order a retreat to Damascus. Since a humiliating defeat might cause an upheaval or even a coup in Syria, Sharon assumed that Assad would choose to pull out all Syrian forces from the Bequ'a valley, which would give Israel a victory without fighting a war. Sharon could not have been more wrong! Assad neither ordered a retreat nor pulled out. Syria's power position in Lebanon never diminished, in spite of its military defeat. Israel clearly won the battle, but Syria won the war.

The invasion was conducted in phases: (1) June 6 to June 11, the major battles, (2) June 11, a first cease-fire, (3) June 12 to June 24, a slow movement (the "salami tactic") of Israeli forces toward Beirut and the Beirut-Damascus highway, and (4) June 25, a second cease-fire.[40] In early July the United States launched a diplomatic campaign to reach a PLO and Syrian evacuation from Beirut. Israel used the last weeks of July and the first week of August for a slow advancement of IDF forces into the suburbs of West Beirut. By the end of August, Beirut was a city under Israeli siege. Israel used its strategic advantage and shelled West Beirut heavily and regularly in order to coerce the Syrians and the PLO to evacuate the city.[41]

Israel's siege of the city, combined with the daily heavy shellings, was successful. In late August the PLO and Syrian forces evacuated Beirut under the supervision of 800 American marines, who returned home by the end of August after their mission was completed. Reagan, believing that all was going well, made public, on September 1, his comprehensive peace plan. In the same week Bashir Gemayel, the pro-American Christian leader, was elected President of Lebanon. However, on September 14, Bashir Gemayel was assassinated, and on September 15, Israel moved into West Beirut. On September 16, to avenge the death of their leader, the Phalangists took over two refugee camps—Sabra and Shatila—and for two days massacred hundreds of Palestinian refugees. On September 26, under heavy domestic and American pressure, the Israeli forces evacuated West Beirut. A multinational force consisting of 1,800 American marines, British, French, and Italian forces, took positions in West Beirut.[42] Very soon the American peacemaking mission changed to an active involvement in the hostilities. The United States came very close to a dangerous military confrontation with the Soviet client, Syria, and experienced major conflicts with its own client state. U.S. leverage over its allies or its foes was practically nonexistent.

When Israel crossed the Lebanese border on Sunday, June 6, Reagan was attending a seven-nation summit meeting in France. He was completely taken by surprise when he was informed of the invasion. From Reagan's point of view, the timing could not have been worse.

Reagan's European tour was a succession of embarrassments. The allies rejected his proposal to put sanctions on the trans-Siberian pipeline, conflicts developed over U.S. economic policies, the situation in Poland was troubling, and the United States was unable to negotiate a settlement in the Falklands war. The Israeli invasion of Lebanon was the last mishap in Reagan's frustrating tour, which was supposed to build up his position as a world leader. The invasion shattered the fragile status quo that existed in Lebanon among Israel, Syria, and the PLO, and the United States felt that it had to honor its commitment to protect the stability of the region even by force if necessary. The United States learned, after two frustrating years, that this mission was impossible. The Reagan plan to use the termination of the status quo to negotiate a settlement of the Israeli-Arab war was short-lived. No progress was achieved in solving the Palestinian problem either.

President Reagan, who did not give the Middle East a top priority before the invasion, was faced with the urgent need to develop both long-term and short-term policies concerning the crisis. First, he had to stop the hostilities and confine them to southern Lebanon. Second, he had to prevent any superpower confrontation that might result from an Israeli-Syrian war. Reagan's peace initiative of September 1, 1982 was the intended U.S. long-term policy. On the immediate level the United States harshly condemned the invasion and demanded an immediate cease-fire and a withdrawal of all foreign forces from Lebanon. Reagan and the seven European nations interrupted their economic summit and warned Israel of the "disastrous consequences" of continued violence in the Middle East.

Reagan broke away from the meeting and conferred with Philip Habib who arrived from London earlier that day. Secretary Haig, who was with Reagan in Versailles, said that the United States was extremely concerned that the violence would broaden to a possible war between Israel and Syria.[43] At the United Nations, a Security Council resolution demanded an immediate pull out of Israel's invading forces. At the demand of the United States, however, the resolution called upon both Israel and the PLO to halt all military actions "within Lebanon and across the Lebanese-Israeli border."[44]

Israel was not worried about Reagan's initial harsh response. Indeed, it was unaware of the fact that the President felt deceived and manipulated and that the risk of an Israeli-Syrian war was unacceptable to the United States. Hence, on June 7, Begin reported to the Cabinet that American reaction was more favorable than expected. He assured Habib during several meetings that Israel would not engage the Syrians and asked Habib to carry this message to Assad. Haig confirmed receiving the messages from Habib.[45] The Syrian issue was very controversial in Israel and while the invasion was in progress, high-ranking military officials were arguing for and against a limited war. Defense Minister Sharon advocated a confrontation with Syria, believing that it would be severely beaten. However, most high-ranking Israeli military officials opposed a fight.[46]

During the first stage of the invasion, that is, between June 6 and June 11, when the first cease-fire took effect, the United States strongly opposed the invasion and hoped that Begin would keep his promise not to advance beyond the twenty-five-mile zone. Habib was used as a "go between," promising Assad that Israel was only fighting the PLO. While still in Europe, Haig told reporters that the United States "did" not want Israel to go in in the first place. We have been very very clear about it for an extended "period."[47]

In this statement Haig referred to his talks with General Saguy and Defense Minister Sharon in which he stressed his objection to a large-scale invasion without proper provocation. Israel, however, gambled that this opposition would not be translated to actual punitive actions, that is, the withholding of arms. The sudden death of the Saudi Arabian king helped Israel's power positions.[48] Israel assumed that the United States more than ever needed a strong friend in the Middle East. Hence, the United States could hardly pressure Israel by using withholding of arms. Meanwhile, the Israeli forces were advancing in the direction of Beirut, without the knowledge and approval of the Cabinet. The Israeli government was equally surprised when Begin revealed his political plan for peace with Lebanon and a return to the preinvasion ante with Syria. Begin discussed his policy in a speech to the Knesset and in a message to Habib.[49] Syria reacted by adding 16,000 troops to its forces in Lebanon, bringing the total to nearly 40,000. The Israelis continued to send messages that they did not wish to engage the Syrians, but at the same time their columns continued to advance straight up to the Beirut-Damascus highway. The objective was to link up with the Phalange that would cut the main body of Syria off from their contingent in the capital.[50]

On June 9, while Reagan was in England trying to cope with the Falklands crisis, the situation in Poland, the Siberian gas pipeline, and his disagreements with European allies, he was notified that the Israelis had moved closer to a war with Syria by destroying the SA–6 missile sites and downing twenty-three Syrian MIGs. At the same time Israeli forces were advancing rapidly toward the Beirut-Damascus highway. It is clear that the Israeli Cabinet was never informed or asked to approve the "Greater Ceder" plan. In order to prevent a harsh domestic reaction to the attack on Syrian forces, the fight was presented as an Israeli reaction to a Syrian provocation.[51] One of Sharon's objectives was to reach the Beirut-Damascus highway. This was Syria's first strategic aim when its forces entered Lebanon in 1976. The isolation of Beirut from Damascus was considered essential.[52]

A serious conflict of interests developed between the United States and Israel. The growing power of the PLO in Lebanon was a major concern to Israel but not to the United States. Also, Israel believed that the status quo benefited the PLO and Syria and should therefore be changed. The United States feared that the intense crisis might lead to a conflict in U.S.-Soviet relations.[53] In addition, Israel wished to reach a bilateral peace with Lebanon after a Christian government was installed there. The United States believed that Jordan was the key to any peace settlement. Israel preferred to keep Jordan out, since it did not wish to make concessions on the West Bank.

Israel not only ignored these conflicts, but misperceived an overlap of interests between the United States and Israel based on overlapping long-term interests, that is, to curb Soviet influence, to establish American hegemony in the region, and to secure the flow of oil. Israel wrongly believed that the invasion was advancing these goals, whereas the United States feared that the invasion was endangering these interests.[54]

However, the United States could hardly pressure Israel to stop its advancement toward Beirut and the Bequ'a valley. The Reagan administration's immediate goal was a cease-fire. The fighting between Israel and Syria was unexpectedly heavy. The Sharon plan of an easy Israeli victory did not materialize. Syria received an immediate resupply of weapons from the U.S.S.R. for everything that was destroyed or captured by the Israeli forces. Fighting fiercely, Syria refused to retreat and moved 16,000 more fighters from the Golan Heights and Syria into Lebanon. Israel finally accepted the U.S. demand for a cease-fire, repeating the famous tactic it used during the October 1973 war, that is, Israel accepted the cease-fire formally while continuing its military campaign informally. In the cease-fire negotiations, the United States used its traditional measure of coercion, namely, the withholding of seventy-five F-16 jets, promised for delivery after the complete evacuation of the Sinai, which occurred only two weeks before the Lebanese invasion.

The formal procedure of military aid required the President, after concluding the deal with Israel, to send Congress a thirty-day notification, explaining the request and asking for approval. Following the invasion, the President immediately suspended the notification to Congress. The correlation between the suspension of the F-16 and Israel's acceptance of the cease-fire was, however, doubtful. The cease-fire of June 11 was accepted because it served Israel's own interests. In fact, two previous suspensions of arms (carried out in 1981) were ineffective, too, and did not change Israel's policies concerning the Golan Heights and the settlements in the West Bank. Moreover, the continued withholding of arms during 1982–83, did not result in Israel's compliance with American policies either. In all the mentioned cases Israel continued to pursue its policies regardless of U.S. withholding of arms.

Many Israeli military experts believe, however, that the cease-fire of June 11 was a grave mistake. Israel ceased fire short of reaching both the Beirut-Damascus highway and the Bequ'a valley. The argument was that had Israel achieved these strategic goals before June 11—Israel reached the Beirut-Damascus highway later—the Lebanese crisis would have taken a completely different course. The cease-fire agreement of June 11 was mediated by the United States who hoped that it would soon lead to a broader agreement on a mutual withdrawal of all Israeli and Syrian forces from Lebanon. In fact, however, the cease-fire helped Syria to regain its military strength with the aid of massive shipments of Soviet arms paid for by Saudi Arabia, while Israel's strategic and political positions were deteriorating rapidly.

The Lebanese crisis created major dilemmas resulting in political difficulties that the United States could neither predict nor control. The United States found itself constantly surprised and unprepared. Consequently, its policy led to a succession of ad hoc, inconsistent reactions to the changing environment. Indeed, American policy lurched from opposition to support of the invasion. At least four conflicting approaches can be identified between June 1982 and February 1984.

(1) During the first two weeks, the United States strongly opposed the invasion, defining it an "excessive use of force," and demanding an immediate cease-fire followed by an Israeli withdrawal. (2) Following the PLO and Syrian heavy losses, which led to their evacuation from Beirut, the United States reversed its policy. Now supportive of the invasion, Washington adopted an optimistic view that an era of new opportunities for peace had begun. (3) Disillusioned by the Israeli battle and takeover of West Beirut and the assassination of Bashir Gemayel, and frustrated by Israel's rejection of the Reagan peace plan, Washington reversed its policy again. Now Israel was viewed as the major obstacle to the resolution of the Lebanese crisis. This new attitude, however, did not last long either. (4) The May 17 agreement signed between Israel and Lebanon, followed by Syria's intransigence and refusal to cooperate in any way, resulted in another policy reversal. A U.S.-Israeli rapprochement, culminating in the signing of a new strategic cooperation agreement on November 1983, took place.

It is not surprising that initial U.S. reaction to the invasion was negative. However, as Israel expected, the sharp, open criticism was followed by very little action. In fact, the only significant U.S. reaction was the withholding of the notification of the sale of F–16s, and it had no immediate effect on Israel's military power. On a similar occasion, when the United States was unhappy with Israeli military action, that is, the bombing of the Iraqi nuclear reactor in June 1981, its reaction was much stronger. Neither actions had any affect on Israel's capability to defy U.S. policy guidelines.

The mild American reaction angered many people, especially Israel's opponents in Congress, who expected the administration not only to demand a cease-fire and a pull out, but also to use its leverage and suspend all shipments of arms to Israel. Especially critical were Congressmen Oakar (D-OH), Miller (R-OH), and Roth (R-WI).[55] When asked about the possibility of withholding arms shipments to Israel, Haig said that "the issue of continuing arms shipment was under review, but the immediate emphasis was on containing the conflict and that arms cutoff now may not serve that purpose."[56]

Moreover, on June 10, the United States vetoed U.N. Security Council Resolution 508 condemning Israel's failure to withdraw from Lebanon and calling for an end to hostilities in six hours. Indeed, after the initial surprise effect faded, Washington began to believe that the invasion might lead to a positive change, heralding a new era, and creating new peace opportunities. This opinion was not shared by Israel's critics who argued that Israel's policies conflict with U.S. interests and should, therefore, be changed even by coercion, if necessary.

The argument was that the United States was embarrassed by the Israeli invasion, which also hurt Reagan's personal prestige. Senior Representatives in Congress, midlevel State Department officials, and influential political leaders advised the President to use the law forbidding Israel to employ U.S. arms except in "legitimate" self-defense as coercion. The administration's reluctance to use leverage was compared with the action that President Carter took in 1978 during the Litani campaign, when Israeli troops crossed the Lebanese border and destroyed PLO bases in southern Lebanon. "Carter sent Begin a short, stern note warning that U.S. weapons flow would stop immediately if the tanks were not pulled out. Begin complained, but did what Carter demanded." Reagan was advised to follow in Carter's footsteps and threaten to stop all shipments of arms to Israel until Israel complied.[57] Reagan's misperception that the invasion might promote the peace process probably influenced his decision not to use leverage. In fact, only when Israel began the battle of West Beirut did the United States try to exert leverage, and these efforts were not very successful.

The second phase of U.S. policy in Lebanon had begun after the first cease-fire was declared. Washington wrongly assumed that with the destruction of the PLO, the strengthening of the Lebanese Christians, and the Syrian defeat, a era of new opportunities had opened up in the Middle East.[58] The invasion was assumed to promote major American foreign policy goals: (1) to establish the United States as an exclusive powerbroker friendly to both Israel and the Arab states, (2) to reinstate a sovereign government in Lebanon free of pro-Soviet, Syrian influence, and (3) with the role of the PLO diminished, Hussein would be willing to join the peace process. Reagan imagined a possible end to the Israeli-Arab conflict under his leadership. This vision was based on the shared U.S.-Israeli misperception that after its defeat, Syria would be willing to accept a withdrawal agreement that would include Israel, Syria, and the PLO.

Israel's involvement in Lebanon entered its second phase after the cease-fire of June 11, which Israel accepted with mixed feelings. It soon became clear that the cease-fire benefited Syria at Israel's expense. Angry and frustrated, Israel decided to pressure Syria by using the "salami tactic," that is, advancing carefully toward the Beirut-Damascus highway and cutting off Syrian and PLO forces in Beirut from their bases in the Bequ'a valley and Damascus. The advanced

Israeli forces would threaten Damascus from positions only twenty-five miles away from the capital. The plan included shelling Beirut systematically and a takeover of the city after a complete Syrian and PLO evacuation. This plan was expected to yield the political gains that the June 5 invasion failed to do. On June 23 the Israeli forces reached the Beirut-Damascus highway and took positions twenty-five miles from Damascus. The Syrian and PLO forces in Beirut were trapped in the sieged city that was heavily bombed. Israel's strategy was successful.[59] Syria and the PLO were ready to evacuate Beirut. Israel, however, wanted more. In addition to a complete Syrian evacuation from Lebanon, Israel demanded a peace treaty with a Christian-controlled government.

The United States fiercely opposed Israel's policies. For the first time Washington seriously considered sanctions against Israel. Not surprisingly, U.S. leverage proved very limited. When the Reagan administration realized that Israel was determined to advance beyond the twenty-five-mile zone, the President considered canceling his meeting with Prime Minister Begin, planned for June 21. In addition, he mentioned the possibility of suspending the sale of F–16 jets.[60] Reagan feared that additional pressure on Syria, which already lost billions in military equipment and was being resupplied by the Soviet Union, might create a superpower confrontation. Washington demanded a clear Israeli commitment to stop all military activities immediately, not to enter West Beirut, and to work out a withdrawal plan. On June 17, and after Begin assured Washington that he would comply with these demands, Reagan announced that Begin's visit to Washington would take place as planned.

Israel, however, never gave up its plan to take over West Beirut. Sharon was convinced that only a final blow to the PLO and Syrian forces there would enable Israel to change the political map of the region. Israel assumed that Washington would lack the power to deter Israel from carrying out its plan. Moreover, Begin believed that Washington would ultimately understand that the destruction of Beirut was the only way to bring Syria to the bargaining table.[61] Indeed, in late August 1982 Washington found itself in the awkward position of having to accept Israel's strategy as a fait accompli, while lacking the leverage to change it. Shultz expressed the U.S. dilemma, saying that the United States was completely committed to the support of Israel and that the relationships between the two nations remain strong.[62]

It was a clear case of reversed patron-client relationship. The United States accepted the heavy shelling and the six-week siege of Beirut. Israel's military campaign ended with a negotiated settlement for the evacuation of the PLO and Syrian forces from Beirut under the supervision of a multinational force including 800 U.S. Marines. French, British, and Italian forces also participated in this force. The marines arrived in Beirut on August 25; the other forces a week earlier. The multinational force's mission was completed and the marines returned to their bases on September 10, 1982, only to come back several days later to cope with a much more serious situation.

THE REAGAN PEACE PLAN

The last week of August and the first two weeks of September were days of great hope in Washington and Jerusalem. All believed that with the PLO crushed and the Syrian war machine destroyed, Hussein would gladly join the peace process to get his share of the bargain. Reagan decided that the time was ripe for a far-reaching peace initiative.

On September 1 Reagan announced that the war, tragic as it was, opened new opportunities for peace in the Middle East. "So tonight," he said, "I am calling for a fresh start. This is the moment for all those directly concerned to get involved—or lend their support—to a workable basis for peace."[63] Reagan's optimism was strengthened by the low profile of the Soviet Union. He assumed that the U.S.S.R. had a vital interest in preventing any additional humiliation of Syria. It would, therefore, support a peace plan. It was also assumed that the U.S.S.R. would wish to avoid any unnecessary adventures that might lead to superpower tensions. Finally, Reagan hoped that both Assad and Hussein would join the bargaining table, which until then they had refused to do.

Secretary of Defense Weinberger later confirmed that at that time the United States received assurances from Israel, Syria, and the PLO that they were ready to negotiate a complete force withdrawal as a first step toward a broader agreement. Syria told Washington that it was ready to withdraw; Israeli statements had been that they wanted to withdraw. The PLO, when it was still a force, said that the important thing was to pursue those objectives. Hence, Weinberger expected the different governments to do exactly what they said.[64]

After a year-and-a-half of a low priority, the Middle East became a vital component of U.S. foreign policy. Ignoring the approaching disaster in Lebanon, Reagan embarked upon an ambitious peace initiative. Jordan and Saudi Arabia were the major components of the plan. Jordan and the Palestinians were expected to work out a plan for the West Bank and the Gaza Strip that would give the Palestinians self-government in association with Jordan.

The plan rejected the idea of an independent Palestinian state in exchange for an Israeli commitment to freeze the settlements and renounce any claim to permanent control over these territories. Jordan, therefore, became the linchpin of Reagan's peace initiative.

The first blow to the peace plan came when Israel rejected it. Begin could not accept the plan because it required a return of most of the territories to Jordan and a freeze of the settlements. He called for an urgent Cabinet meeting and stated that "this peace plan died at birth." The timing of the new peace initiative could not have been worse. Israel, still in the midst of a military campaign, lacked the political framework and the peace of mind needed to respond to the peace initiative. The doves could not mobilize enough support; the hawks successfully blocked any favorable decision.

King Hussein, who welcomed the American peace initiative, was frustrated over the U.S. lack of leverage. After giving the plan a qualified endorsement,

Hussein met with Arafat and began to work out a common approach \
tiations about the West Bank. In effect, such an approach would have r
the Rabat decision of 1974, which gave the PLO the exclusive right to re\
the Palestinians in any peace negotiations.[65] Hussein remembered Re\
promise of December 1982, when he visited Washington, that if he joined and
revived the autonomy talks, the United States would insist that Israel freeze the
settlements. Reagan also offered Hussein a generous arms deal, including F–16
jets, and the establishment of a Jordanian Rapid Deployment Force financed and
trained by American military personnel.

Hopes faded quickly with Israel's intransigence. Syria's shadow was also
clouding the future of the Reagan peace initiative. The Soviet Union was replenishing Syria's devastated military arsenal, supplying Assad with an estimated
$2.5 billion worth of arms, roughly double what was lost during the war. The
bill, as usual, was picked up by Saudi Arabia. No development in the Lebanese
crisis was so dramatic and so unpredictable as Syria's resurgence as a political
and military force in Lebanon. In fact, Syria became the linchpin in the Lebanese
political scene. As its military capabilities grew, it could fulfill its old objective,
to gain a de facto veto power over the situation in Lebanon. In January 1983
Syria could successfully announce that no agreement could be carried out without
its consent.[66]

Saudi Arabia, which was expected to play a major role in the peace process
because it was financing Syria's arms purchases, proved to be a major disap-
pointment. Reagan expected the Saudis to influence Syria and the PLO to join
King Hussein in the negotiations. In fact, the Saudis could not even influence
Syria to reciprocate and pull out of Lebanon after an Israeli withdrawal. As 1983
progressed, it became clear that Syria's decision to withdraw would not be
influenced by Saudi pressures or even by Soviet leverage. Moreover, Assad was
furious that Saudi Arabia could not prevent the Lebanese government from
signing the May 17 agreement with Israel. "The Lebanese were upset that the
Saudis did not pressure Assad to withdraw, Iraq blamed Saudi Arabia for not
forcing Syria to reopen a pipeline that would enable Iraq to export enough oil
to fund its war with Iran. The Reagan administration was disappointed that the
Saudis did not press the PLO to approve Hussein's entrance into the peace
process. Nor can Washington understand why Riyadh does not use its leverage
to obtain a Syrian withdrawal. Above all the entire Arab world is frustrated that
the Saudis cannot deliver the U.S.—cannot force it to recognize the PLO and
press Israel to withdraw from the West Bank."[67]

The final blow to Reagan's peace plan was the assassination of Bashir Gemayel, the President-elect of Lebanon, on September 14, 1982. With the char-
ismatic Christian leader dead, Reagan's plan evaporated into mirages. Everything
that could go wrong actually did, and only several hours after Gemayel's assassination, all hell broke loose in Lebanon.

The death of Bashir Gemayel, Israel's closest friend in Lebanon, destroyed
six years of preparations and planning for a political settlement between Israel

and its northern neighbor. Shocked and frustrated, Israel decided to use the chaos and carry out its old plan to move into West Beirut. Only a few hours after the assassination, Israeli forces took over West Beirut, violating all previous promises to the contrary. The United States was furious but lacked the leverage to deter Israel. The traditional tactic of withholding of arms could temporarily have delayed the delivery of the F–16s. But this would not have bothered Israel, which did not expect delivery before 1986. The situation was best explained by the British *Daily Telegraph* and the *Guardian*.

"The Reagan administration . . . is not in a real sense, able to control Israel since the only effective measure would have to be so drastic that it would imperil Israel's existence. Cuts here and there in arms or aid make no difference."[68] Moreover, "Mr. Begin has no world strategy to carry out, no foreign rulers to appease, no rival superpowers to outflank . . . with the PLO fighting machine defeated, with the Soviet Union disinclined to get involved, and with a staunch electoral behind him, he has aces to Mr. Reagan's nines."[69]

According to Israeli sources, a joint takeover of West Beirut was planned for mid-June with Gemayel.[70] Sharon's original plan was to help Gemayel's forces take over West Beirut after the evacuation of PLO and Syrian forces, while Israel provided artillery support. The Cabinet and even Begin were not completely informed about the various secret agreements. The plans, however, had to be changed when it became clear that the Phalangists were unable to carry them out. Sharon suggested to Begin that Israel move into Beirut unilaterally, pulling out only after a peace treaty was signed. The majority of the Israeli Cabinet rejected Sharon's plan. The plan, however, was never abandoned and was executed when a power vacuum was created following the assassination of Gemayel.

Indeed, during the two first weeks of September the political climate in the Israeli Cabinet was tense. Members were suspicious of each other, information was only partially available, and Sharon's exclusive control of the decision-making process was resented by most members. Reagan's peace initiative took everyone by surprise. It was hardly the right time to develop long-term peace plans.

Hence, the United States and Israel were entering the third phase of the Lebanese crisis, the phase of friction and conflict. It is important to mention in this context that the resignation of Secretary of State Haig only a few weeks after the invasion was launched was undoubtedly to Israel's disadvantage.[71] Haig was one of the staunchest supporters of Israel in general and of the invasion (although after the fact) in particular.

During the early days of Secretary of State Shultz, Washington wrongly believed that Syria would be willing to negotiate an all-out force withdrawal if Israel would reciprocate. Washington's hope was based on the Syrian pullout from Beirut two weeks earlier, and on Syrian statements. Washington greatly underestimated Syria's gains resulting from its stay in Lebanon and ignored Syria's losses resulting from pulling out. Although Syria's political and strategic reasons for not withdrawing from Lebanon were very clear, Washington lacked the insight to perceive them.

Syria's position in Lebanon was greatly influenced by the three critical days of June 9 to 11. During that time of heavy fighting, the future of the Bequ'a valley, and consequently the Syrian position in Lebanon, was determined. The first cease-fire that began on June 11 allowed the Syrians to catch their breath and restore their military and political positions. The assassination of Gemayal further enhanced Syria's position.[72] Syria was becoming more and more confident with its bargaining power in Lebanon.

MILITARY AID AS LEVERAGE

Washington wrongly assumed that Israel's hard-line position was the main obstacle to the resolution of the Lebanese crisis. Moreover, Washington expected Syria to cooperate in a step-by-step withdrawal with no major difficulties. Israel did not share this theory and insisted on taking special measures to ensure a withdrawal. Tensions between Washington and Jerusalem were escalating to a full-scale crisis. Israel believed that only a joint American-Israeli pressure would bring Syria to make concessions. The United States underestimated the importance of Lebanon to Syrian politics and believed that Syria would voluntarily accept a diminished role in Lebanon. Indeed, it might be glad to have a way out of the prolonged, unresolved, costly civil war. The United States did not realize until much later that a strong, sovereign government in Lebanon was against the Syrian national interest, especially if this government was Christian and pro-Israeli.

At the time of the invasion, Syria had 25,000 men in Lebanon as a "peace-keeping force" (the Arab Deterrent Force). In addition Syria had along the Syrian-Lebanese frontier a defense force of one brigade (about 10,000 men) and seven to eleven commando units. The major Syrian force of four armored divisions and two machinized infantry divisions was stationed in the Golan Heights. Israel claimed that these divisions were the best-armed and the best-led Arab forces in the Middle East. The Syrian Army was equipped with the most sophisticated Soviet arms, including T–72 tanks, MIG–25 and MIG–25R (Foxbat) jets, SA–342 Gazelle attack helicopters, SA–5, SA–6, SA–9, SA–7, and SA–8 (mobile) missiles, SCUD-B and SCUD-C SS missiles and rockets, and the most advanced SS–21 missiles, which can carry nuclear warheads. (Syria is the first-known country to receive these missiles outside of the U.S.S.R.[73]) Israel argued that the United States was very naive to believe that Syria would be willing to withdraw its forces and lose its control over Lebanon. Hence, Israel considered Syria to be the major obstacle to any agreement, whereas the United States considered Israel to be the hindering factor. The growing conflict between the two allies gained headlines in September 1982. The *New York Times* revealed that the Israeli government, angered by the U.S. peace initiative and the with-

holding of the sale of the F–16 jets, decided to use its leverage by refusing to share military intelligence information with the United States.

In a meeting in Washington, Sharon told the Secretary of Defense Casper Weinberger that Israel would not share military intelligence from the war in Lebanon until the Reagan administration removed a variety of sanctions against Israel. One of the sanctions was Reagan's refusal to inform Congress of the sale of the fighter-bombers long promised to Israel. The *New York Times* reported that American military officers and CIA officials attached great importance to Israel's sharing of military intelligence. The United States was especially interested in ECM's developed in Israel and used to destroy Syria's missile sites. Israel, in turn, requested the delivery of the promised F–16s to maintain its air superiority over increasingly capable Arab air forces. "The bargaining process over intelligence sharing and F–16 deliveries served as a backdrop to the larger dispute that Israeli and American officials say they expect over Mr. Reagan's new Middle East peace plan."[74] Although Washington insisted that there was no connection between the continued delay in F–16 shipments and Israel's rejection of the peace plan, and that approval was "only a matter of timing," the two were probably connected. Moreover, it was never denied that the F–16s could become part of the bargaining over sharing intelligence information.

Israel's rejection of the Reagan peace plan was another painful issue. Israel argued that the plan could ultimately lead to the establishment of a Palestinian state, which would pose a serious danger to its security. It was clear that without coercion, Israel would never accept the U.S. peace plan. However, the withholding of the sale of the jets was a very questionable coercion measure. Washington decided to openly discuss its differences with Israel, in order to embarrass Israel and show its Arab allies, who supported the peace initiative (although with some reservations), that it exerted pressure on Israel to withdraw from Lebanon and accept the peace initiative. In answer to reporters' questions, Secretary Shultz explained the American concept of leverage in terms of delivery or withholding of arms to Israel.

Q: The Israeli Cabinet has . . . formally rejected the President's peace proposals. . . . What is he going to do? Is he going to put pressure on the Israelis?

Q: Is there any chance that the State Department, the President, will try to use American aid to pressure them, specifically the sending eventually of the F–16 fighters? And secondly, are the Israelis trying to bargain with you over that by withholding military intelligence information in exchange for F–16s?

A: Our emphasis will be on the importance of peace. . . . I think this is a tremendous pressure. "Pressure" isn't the right word.

Q: Are you saying that you wouldn't deny that you might use the withholding of aid?

A: We do not have any plans to try to maneuver people in peace negotiations by talking about aid.

Q: So you are ruling it out, the use of—

A: I am saying that the objective of peace is so important that when this is fully realized—and . . . if King Hussein and other Arabs respond favorably to the President's initiative—then the prospects of peace with neighbors becomes much more real.[75]

Indeed, Israel was not coerced by Washington, although the United States strongly objected to Israel's takeover of West Beirut (Israel's control, however, lasted only a few days). It was the tragic massacre at the refugee camps, which shocked the Israeli society and threatened the future of the Begin government, that led Begin to pull out from Beirut on September 26, 1982. Two days later President Reagan told reporters that the U.S.-Israeli conflict was being resolved to U.S. satisfaction.

Q: Shortly before the Israeli invasion of Lebanon, the administration informally notified Congress that it was planning to send more F–16s to Israel. There's been no formal notification since then. Is the delay linked to difficulties in relations with Israel? When do you think formal notification will go up and under what conditions?

A: They're still on tap, and we haven't sent the formal notification up. And, very frankly . . . in the climate of things . . . we did not think it was the time to do it. However, there has been no interruption of those things that are in the pipeline.[76]

The withholding of arms tactic had a very questionable effect, since Israel continued to reject the Reagan peace plan and insisted on achieving all its political goals in Lebanon before considering any concessions. First, Israel demanded a bilateral peace treaty with Lebanon. Second, the negotiations were to take place alternately in Beirut and Jerusalem, giving Jerusalem a political recognition. Third, no negotiations concerning the future of the West Bank with the PLO. Fourth, no freeze of the settlements. Fifth, a simultaneous withdrawal of all Syrian, PLO, and Israeli forces from all of Lebanon. Finally, security arrangements along the Israeli-Lebanese border should include Israeli patrol forces. These demands were vital interests to Israel. However, the United States considered them "excessive." Israel was prepared to resist U.S. pressures, namely to ignore the tactic of withholding of arms and to survive a "long, cold winter" on the political front. The Israelis were preparing for a long stay in Lebanon. While American diplomacy was trying to bring about a withdrawal of both Syrian and Israeli forces that were facing each other in the seventy-five-mile-long Bequ'a valley, there were no signs that either force intended to pull out.[77]

By the end of 1982 U.S.-Israeli relations reached a new low. Reagan acknowledged the fact that the United States was using, although with very limited success, tactics of withholding of arms. Israel had no immediate plan to pull out from Lebanon and it refused to support the Reagan peace plan. U.S. efforts failed, however, not only with Israel. Syria and Jordan were no less intransigent. Senior administration officials reported an increased concern over U.S. failure to initiate negotiations for the withdrawal of Israeli, Syrian, and Palestinian forces from Lebanon. The administration tried in vain to use its leverage by asking Congress to reject an amendment that would have significantly increased the amount of foreign aid to Israel. Not surprisingly, Israel reacted with great anger and said that it was astonished by this act.

Washington's frustrations grew and it feared that the historical opportunity for a new beginning was slowly fading away. Habib and Draper, the American negotiators, were holding Israel primarily responsible for the lack of progress.[78] The feeling was that Washington could not influence either Israel or Syria to pull out. Each demanded that the other satisfy its conditions as a prerequisite for negotiations. Israel insisted on a bilateral peace agreement with the Amin Gemayel government, and refused to include Syria in the negotiations or the agreement itself. Syria, on the other hand, refused to give up its power position and influence in Lebanon and demanded to be included in any agreement with the Lebanese government. Washington apparently overlooked the fact that both Israel and Syria had leverage over the United States. Moreover, U.S. hopes that Saudi Arabia would be able to influence Syria's policies, and that Israel could intimidate Syria by its military superiority, did not materialize. Both Saudi Arabia and Israel failed to induce or coerce Assad to be more flexible. Reagan was extremely disappointed to see his peace initiative withering away. In an effort to use leverage, Reagan again asked Congress to reduce aid appropriations to Israel for fiscal year 1983. Apparently, neither Reagan nor Congress considered these threats to be realistic. Congress did not consider the issue and the President did not pursue it.

Throughout the crisis Congress was neither instrumental nor influential in initiating or implementing U.S. policy in Lebanon. During 1982–83 Congress sent Reagan conflicting messages concerning U.S. policy in Lebanon. Many members of Congress expressed strong objections to the invasion and demanded a strong American reaction. On the other hand, many legislators expressed support for Israel's policies. For example, Congressman Charles Schumer (D-NY) argued that Israel had a legitimate casus belli. It was an act of self-defense against the continued violence and terrorist activities against its citizens. The massive Soviet support of the PLO and Syria threatened Israel's security and warranted the invasion.[79] Congressman Kemp (R-NY) explained how U.S. global and regional interests were served by the invasion. It brought an opportunity to restore sovereignty in Lebanon and to assure the security of America's vital ally, Israel. No withdrawal should take place before an effective reassertion of Lebanon central government control over the country. Moreover, an Israeli withdrawal must be contingent upon a Syrian withdrawal from Lebanon. On the global level, Kemp said that the Soviet Union had suffered a major setback in its quest to expand its influence through Syria and the PLO. "The PLO, the Cuba of the Middle East . . . are a threat to free people worldwide." Syria, which occupied nearly two-thirds of Lebanon's territory, had to accept the fact that its aspirations for a greater Syria could not materialize. "Clearly the status quo ante in Lebanon was intolerable from the standpoint of the Israelis who lived in the range of PLO artillery, intolerable for Lebanese who have been denied their country, and intolerable for the U.S. and the Western world who seek stability and freedom from terrorism.'' Kemp sent a cable to Reagan saying that ''Israel has given the U.S. the opportunity to set back Soviet/Syrian advances in the Middle East, to destroy international terrorism's most fertile base of operation, to restore the rights of the Lebanese and reinvigorate the Camp David process.''[80]

Indeed, no consensus existed in Congress either for or against the invasion, and Congress could not reach a consensus to ''punish'' Israel by withholding of arms. The division between Israel's supporters and opponents was not along party lines. This situation made it very difficult, if not impossible, for Congress and the President to coordinate their policies. Congress, a poorly organized political institution, was too divided to play a major role in formulating or even influencing U.S. policy in the Middle East. Moreover, Reagan was not consistent in his policies during the crisis, and no coherent plan that Congress could approve of, or object to, existed. Congress dealt mainly with aid appropriations to Israel, and throughout 1982–83 fulfilled the President's aid requests. When the 1983 aid appropriation bill was under consideration, Washington experienced its worst conflict with Israel. This, however, did not affect the level of aid appropriated. Congress approved the same level of aid as was requested before the invasion: $785 million in economic aid and $1.7 billion in military aid. The total aid approved for 1983 was $2.485 billion, signed into law by the President on December 21, 1982.

The most controversial issue in 1983 was the May 17 agreement. The U.S. position concerning it was not clear. During the winter of 1983, the U.S. vehemently opposed the idea of a peace treaty between Israel and Lebanon, whereas Israel absolutely refused to give it up. Unlike Israel, the United States maintained that the treaty would create additional, unnecessary difficulties with Syria. Washington's second concern was that the fragile government of Amin Gemayel would not survive such an act, and chaos would again reign in Lebanon.[81] Because of its lack of leverage, Washington had to capitulate again to Israel and give its after-the-fact blessing to the May 17 agreement, which was signed after much Israeli pressure. America's concerns, however, did materialize. The treaty, which never took effect, was soon abrogated under heavy Syrian pressure.

The May 17 agreement marked the beginning of the fourth phase of U.S. policy in Lebanon and the renewal of the cooperation between Israel and the U.S., which culminated with the signing of the strategic cooperation agreement in November 1983. The tragic death of 241 marines on October 23, 1983, by a terrorist bomb only accelerated the antagonism between the United States and Syria, and enhanced the cooperation between the United States and Israel. The new approach was outlined in a highly classified White House paper, ''National Security Decision Directive 111,'' signed by the President on October 29, 1983. The document, which was the result of a two-week debate within the National Security Council, had set forth priority goals for the entire Middle East. Its most important section dealt with the need to improve relations and repair the strained ties with Israel. Two days after N.S.D.D. 111 was signed by the President, Lawrence S. Eagleburger, then the State Department's Under Secretary for Political Affairs, was sent to Jerusalem to discuss the matter with Prime Minister Shamir. The agreement on strategic cooperation between Jerusalem and Washington, which was announced during Shamir's visit to the U.S. on November 29, 1983, was probably the result of this new approach.

The American-Israeli rapprochement was attributed to the political losses that the two allies suffered. "Both burned by the war in Lebanon, badly need each other. There remain underlying tensions about how to reconcile the two countries' interests in the Middle East."[82] It seemed that the only real point of contention at that time was over how many new concessions the *United States will offer Israel* as part of a revived "strategic cooperation" agreement.

On October 24, 1983, a day after the brutal bomb attack on the marine barracks, Shultz expressed the vital need for U.S.-Israeli cooperation. Such a cooperation was considered a prerequisite for any peace agreement. Shultz announced that because this important region had become an arena of competition between the United States and the Soviet Union, Americans "have a deep commitment to Israel and in strengthening the trends of moderation in the Arab world, and because our role of leadership in the Middle East is a reflection of America's responsibility as a world leader."[83] These ambitious goals could not be achieved without the strong cooperation of Israel.

The new approach was a reaction to the fact that Syria had emerged as the most important power on the Lebanese scene. This was detrimental to U.S. policy, which assumed a Syrian withdrawal from Lebanon soon after its humiliating military defeat. The American support of the May 17 agreement angered Syria and increased tensions between the two nations, which deteriorated even more with the new rapprochement between the United States and Israel.

During 1983 U.S. involvement in Lebanon intensified. Between October 23 and December 31, the United States had an armada of thirty-three ships, including battleships and aircraft carriers, off the Lebanese coast, and marines engaged in exchanges of fire with Syrian forces in Lebanon. The battleship *New Jersey* used its five-inch and sixteen-inch guns a few times during that period to shell Syrian positions that were firing at U.S. positions. Two Tomcat jets (F–14s) were shot down on December 4, 1983; one aviator was killed, the other, Lieutenant Robert Goodman, was taken prisoner by the Syrians.

Reagan knew that a failure in Lebanon would be a great liability to his reelection campaign. He needed a quick, major breakthrough in Lebanon. The thrust now was to achieve a political progress at any cost. The new approach held Syria responsible for the deadlock, and the thrust was to find ways to coerce Syria to soften its tone and to start negotiating a bilateral troop withdrawal agreement with Israel. In implementing its new policy, the United States was using the "stick and carrot" tactic. The "stick" was the strategic cooperation agreement with Israel, expected to threaten Syria's security by exhibiting a strong U.S. commitment to protect Israel in case of war with Syria. Washington hoped that it would influence Syria to reconsider its refusal to come to the bargaining table. The "carrot" was Saudi Arabia's economic aid to Syria. Saudi Arabia was expected to induce Syria by offering a generous aid package in exchange for political concessions. In 1983, Saudi Arabia gave Syria a whopping *$2 billion* to replace arms, another *$4 billion* to help construct the Soviet-made SS–21 missile batteries, and an estimated $500 million to make up for damaged military equipment.[84]

Israel's expected role as a "stick" was very correctly described by Flora Lewis. She argued that the reversal of U.S.-Israeli relations had developed in late 1983 and could have long-term implications for both countries. The United States was trying to engage Israel as the active protector of what were seen as America's interests. The cost of this policy was that Washington had to yield to Israel's policies. A year earlier "Washington was pressing for Israeli withdrawal from Lebanon and trying to promote Jordanian-Palestinian talks with Israel under the Reagan initiative. Now the United States wants Israel to take the lead in 'checkmating' Syria's President Hafez-al-Assad.''[85]

The strategic cooperation agreement, which was announced during the visit of Prime Minister Shamir to Washington in November 1983, conferred many benefits upon Israel. First, the agreement created a joint political-military planning team, which held its first meeting in January 1984, and set guidelines for the future cooperation between the two nations. Consequently, the United States capitulated to Israel's pressure and declared Israel the most important U.S. strategic ally in the Middle East. Reagan did not mention his previous demands for an Israeli withdrawal, Israeli acceptance of his peace plan, or his demand for a freeze of settlements in the West Bank. Moreover, Reagan expressed deep understanding of Israel's hard line, saying that it could not be expected to pull out its forces as long as Syria refused to reciprocate. The agreement took not only the Pentagon by surprise but the Department of State as well. In addition to the joint planning committee, the agreement included a variety of measures to aid Israel economically as well as militarily.[86] Reagan also announced the lifting of the ban he had put on shipments of cluster bombs, which was in effect since the summer of 1982. Another major American concession to Israel was Washington's approval of the use of U.S. aid funds to finance weapon procurements in Israel. For years Israel requested permission to use aid funds for the development and production of the Israeli fighter-jet, the Lavie, as well as other major Israeli-made weapon systems. This was the first time in thirty-four years that such permission was granted. Not everyone was happy with the new U.S.-Israeli deal. For example, Brzezinski, the National Security Adviser to President Carter, expressed a very critical view of the administration's policy.

In an article in the *New York Times'* op-ed page, he lamented the administration's policy, arguing that "our Middle Eastern policy is in shambles." The United States has no strategy, he said, and has been reacting to events tactically. Moreover, it has been reduced to playing a subordinate role. "Militarily, America is acting as an auxiliary to the Lebanese Army and, politically, as a proxy of Israeli foreign policy." Ignoring Vietnam and Central America, Brzezinski went to the extreme, saying that "most tragically, perhaps for the first time ever, uniformed Americans have been dying neither in defense of American national interest nor on behalf of any genuine American policy objectives.'' He developed a conspiracy theory and argued that ''Begin and Ariel Sharon quite deliberately sought to preoccupy the United States with Lebanon. Diverting United States diplomatic efforts into Lebanon and involving the United States in a protracted diversionary crisis was the most effective way of derailing the Reagan Plan for a Jordanian-West Bank confederation.''[87]

Brezezinski's ''conspiracy theory'' did not seem valid, since the invasion took place three months before Reagan launched his peace plan. Hence, chronologically, the invasion came first and Reagan's peace plan, offering a Jordanian-Palestinian coalition, came second. It was impossible to suggest before the destruction of the PLO bases in Lebanon.

The renewed cooperation between the United States and Israel on the executive level was received with great reservations on Capitol Hill. More and more members of Congress became unhappy with the situation and demanded a disentanglement from Lebanon. Until the end of 1983 Congress did not play an active role in the Lebanese crisis. Even when it invoked the War Powers Act in September 1983, it provided the President with as much time as he wanted to keep the marines there. But now Congress became a little nervous. On Capitol Hill a consensus was building for a pullout from Lebanon. This was primarily the result of the Legislators' concern with the coming 1984 elections. ''Concern over Lebanon has grown in my district,'' said Bill Richardson (D-NM). ''I sense that the President is losing support.''[88] Other representatives, among them previous supporters of Reagan's policy like Les Aspin (D-WI) and Lee Hamilton (D-IN), warned that Americans were unlikely to support a continued marine presence in Lebanon in the absence of progress toward peace. House minority leader Robert Michel suggested: ''should we not consider removing American marines from Lebanon, keeping our fleet offshore and leaving it to Israel, our strategic partner, to work out in ways it might choose, a solution to the Lebanese problem?''[89]

A major factor influencing the critical view, which many legislators had adopted by the end of 1983, was the Defense Department Committee Report, which was presented to the President in December 1983. Admiral Long's report criticized not only the security arrangements and the increased peril to the U.S. Marines, but also the political aspects of America's role in Lebanon. The commission expressed a critical opinion concerning the role of the marines as a ''peacemaking force'' and the expectation that it would help bring about a Lebanese national reconciliation. More and more people adopted the view that Israel and Syria, the two rivals, should be left alone to resolve the Lebanese conflict between themselves. The public became more and more frustrated with the situation, and the death of the 241 marines raised fears of a ''new Vietnam.'' Reagan and his advisors were aware of and worried by the shift in the public mood.[90]

Reagan began to realize that the combination of Saudi inducement and Israeli coercion, in which he put great hopes, did not yield the desired results that were so critical to his public image in an election year. The strategic cooperation agreement angered Syria, but it resulted in adverse consequences, making negotiations with Syria even more difficult. Moreover, it frustrated many Arab states, among them Saudi Arabia. The agreement failed to threaten Syria because of its unique position. On the one hand, Syria was protected by the Soviet Union, which supplied it with sophisticated weapons in the billions. On the other hand, Syria was supported by the Saudis who were picking up the bill. As a result, Syria became militarily stronger and politically more influential. The Jesse Jackson-Syrian affair showed that Syria was very sophisticated and shrewd in conducting its political affairs.

On the Israeli front, the United States did not have much success either. Israel refused to make any concessions in Lebanon, or even freeze the settlements, which angered Hussein. Reagan realized that America's leverage over Israel, its client state, or Syria, the Soviet Union's client state, was nonexistent. The United States was facing a political deadend, and the only way out was an American pullout.

In evaluating the situation in Lebanon, Washington realized to its chagrin that from September 1982, when 1,800 marines were deployed in Lebanon, until February 1984, when the marines were pulled out, the U.S. heavy involvement resulted in neither the resolution of the conflict nor the amelioration of its consequences. After Amin Gemayel took his brother's place as President of Lebanon, the United States found itself heavily involved and highly committed, not only to the support of Israel, but also to the support of the fragile Gemayel government. However, the year and a half of intense military and political involvement had cost the United States more than 260 lives, and the situation was only getting worse.

With the November elections at the door, Reagan decided to pull out the marines and to look for a scapegoat who could be blamed for the failure in Lebanon. There was not much more that he could do.

OVERVIEW

The Lebanese crisis in the study of U.S. leverage as a political tool is especially challenging. Both superpowers strive to gain leverage because achieving compliance through leverage is preferable to achieving compliance through the use of brute force, especially in the Middle East, which is both complex and dangerous. For decades, intense unresolved conflicts among different religious and ethnic groups, including the Israeli-Arab conflict, have plagued the region. The complex reality of the Middle East has made analysis based on traditional concepts of patron-client relationship dubious, since the theories have left out or ignored the crucial systemic variables and have underestimated the regional variables.

In the case of Lebanon, the regional and global dilemmas that dominate the politics of the Middle East were the major causes for the lack of U.S. leverage over either the actors or the events. The traditional analysis, however, misperceives this lack of leverage to be the result of (1) tactics of coercion or inducement used by the patron state to attain leverage, and (2) domestic pressures, that is, Congress and lobby pressures. These misperceptions led to the wrong foreign policy decisions in Lebanon. The United States became intensely involved because it believed that it should directly protect its interests in the region if and when they were threatened. However, the President failed to reduce tensions in the region *before* Israel invaded Lebanon. On the other hand, once the invasion began, the United States, unlike the Soviet Union, chose to become intensely involved. Moreover, at some point Washington decided that the Lebanese crisis, unfortunate as it might be, could help promote U.S. long-term policy goals: (1) to promote a comprehensive settlement of the Israeli-Arab conflict, (2) re-establish the Lebanese government's sovereignty over its territory, (3) reduce the power and influence of the Soviet Union and its surrogates, Syria and the PLO, and (4) establish the American power position and hegemony in the region by being the "powerbroker" and the dominant political force in the Middle East. However, because U.S. policy was based on misperceptions, it did not achieve any of these goals. Moreover, the pullout of the marines ordered in February 1984 came after many political embarrassments both in the international scene and at home. The Reagan peace plan, which was announced with much fanfare on September 1, 1982, was quietly buried only a short time later, after all involved rejected it as unacceptable to them.

The United States experienced conflicts with its allies as well as with its foes. Israel, Jordan, and Saudi Arabia pursued independent foreign policies that many times conflicted with U.S. policies. Syria was especially noncooperative, refusing at times even to talk to American officials. The United States was faced with the embarrassing fact that it had no leverage over any of the nations involved in the crisis. Israel and Syria were able to manipulate the global and regional environments and to pursue their respective political goals with impunity. No serious coercive measures were taken by Washington during the crisis, and even the suspension of the F-16s was eventually lifted. Faced with a fait accompli, the United States, albeit reluctantly, accepted most of Israel's military actions. The United States could not stop arms shipments to Israel as long as the U.S.S.R. was supplying Syria with quality and quantity of arms. Washington's leverage was also hampered at crucial times by the failure of the Reagan administration to make timely policy decisions and convey them to Israel clearly, firmly, and unambiguously.

Hence, the United States faced in Lebanon a "no win" situation. Leverage was nonexistent, and with no leverage Washington could not have any influence over the course of events. With no influence, Washington could only stand still and wait for progress to happen as a result of local interaction. Unfortunately, the situation went from bad to worse. The Soviet Union, faced with the same problem, wisely decided at the early stages of the crisis to keep a low profile and let the local actors fight out their differences in their own way. Captive of the traditional concept of leverage, Washington failed to see the obvious paradox in its patron-client relationship with Israel. Consequently, Washington underestimated Israel's leverage over its patron state.

In fact, there was not much that the United States could do to help resolve the Lebanese crisis. Washington should have done less, that is, adopt a low profile and try to promote its foreign policy goals in a more subtle manner. Reagan should have avoided both the intense military involvement and the political fanfare that accompanied his initiatives. Finally, Washington should have assumed lack of leverage and should have constructed its policies accordingly. Wishful thinking and assumed leverage should not become the guidelines of foreign policy. Realistically, only major changes in the international and regional environments could restore American leverage in the Middle East.

NOTES

1. Leonard Binder, "U.S. Policy in the Middle East: Exploiting New Opportunities," *Current History* (January 1983), pp. 1–4, 37–40.

2. For example, after the bombing of the Iraqi nuclear reactor on June 8, 1981, the U.S. suspended all arms shipments and imposed an embargo on the supply of uranium to power Israel's small American-made research reactor; see details in Steven Weissman and Herbert Krosney, *The Islamic Bomb* (New York: New York Times Books), 1981.

3. For a detailed analysis of the strategic consensus concept, see Amos Perlmutter, "Reagan's Middle East Policy: A Year One Assessment," *Orbis* (Spring 1984), p. 26.

4. Alfred R. Atherton, "Arabs, Israelis, and Americans: A Reconsideration," pp. 1194–1209.

5. Former Secretary Haig, April 27, 1982, before the U.S. Chamber of Commerce, *Department of State Bulletin* (June 1982), pp. 40–44.

6. Israel opposed the agreement because it did not stop the PLO attacks on villages in northern Israel. ABC-TV "Nightline," June 7, 1982.

7. See discussion by Shoshana Bryen, "Advancing U.S.-Israel Strategic Cooperation," *Middle East Review* (February 1984); also Steven Spiegel, "Israel as a Strategic Asset," *Commentary* (June 1983), pp. 51–55.

8. Seth Tillman makes this argument in *The United States in the Middle East* (Bloomington: Indiana University Press, 1982).

9. See Abba Eban, *An Autobiography* (New York: Random House, 1977); also Yitzhak Rabin, *The Rabin Memoirs* (Boston: Little, Brown, 1979).

10. At that time Israel's annual inflation rate was exceeding 400 percent and it was spending over 30 percent of its GNP on defense.

11. See Sean MacBride, *Israel in Lebanon* (London: Ithaca Press, 1983), pp. 1–19; also interview with King Hussein, *New York Times*, March 14, 1984.

12. In 1970 and as a result of this decision, the Likud party resigned from the coalition and the Israeli government dissolved.

13. For example, the United States used withholding of arms twice in 1981, as a

reaction to the bombing of the Iraqi nuclear reactor and after Israel annexed the Golan Heights.

14. See Klaus Knorr, *The Power of Nations* (New York: Basic Books, 1975), pp. 185–189.

15. Zeev Schiff and Ehud Ya'ari, *War of Deception* (Hebrew) (Jerusalem: Schocken Publishing, 1984), pp. 185–189.

16. *New York Times*, June 7, 1982.

17. Chaim Herzog, *The Arab-Israeli Wars* (New York: Random House, 1982), p. 339.

18. Mark Heller (ed.), *The Middle East Military Balance, 1983* (Tel Aviv: Jaffee Center for Strategic Studies, 1983), p. 8.

19. Schiff and Ya'ari argue that General Sharon began to prepare the invasion immediately after he became minister of defense in August 1981.

20. Reuven Avi-Ran, *Syrian Involvement in Lebanon: 1975–1985* (Hebrew) (Tel Aviv: Ma'arachot Press, 1986), pp. 86–87; also *US News & World Report* (January 9, 1984).

21. Schiff and Ya'ari give an excellent account of the Israeli-Phalangists relations; see *War of Deception*, pp. 40–76.

22. Alexander M. Haig, *Caveat* (New York: Macmillan, 1984), p. 328.

23. Ibid., p. 326.

24. Schiff and Ya'ari, *War of Deception*, p. 81.

25. Ibid., p. 82; the information was confirmed by Israeli military officials in interviews.

26. Haig, *Caveat*, p. 332.

27. John Chancellor, NBC-TV Evening News, April 8, 1982.

28. Atherton, "Arabs, Israelis, and Americans," p. 1194.

29. General Sharon also omitted the map of his planned operation "Large Ceder," which included a joint Israeli-Phalangist takeover of Beirut.

30. Haig, *Caveat*, pp. 330–333; also Schiff and Ya'ari, *War of Deception*, pp. 87–90.

31. Former Secretary Haig in address before the U.S. Chamber of Commerce, Washington, DC, April 27, 1982.

32. Haig, *Caveat*, p. 333.

33. Schiff and Ya'ari, *War of Deception*, p. 124.

34. See Secretary Haig's statement on the Middle East, *Department of State Bulletin* (October 1982), p. 11.

35. Arye Naor, *Cabinet at War* (Hebrew) (Tel Aviv: Lahav Press, 1986), pp. 39–41.

36. Schiff and Ya'ari, *War of Deception*, pp. 120–122; General Saguy's criticism was shared by many high-ranking Israeli military officers.

37. Naor, *Cabinet at War*, pp. 47–48.

38. Steven L. Spiegel, *The Other Arab-Israeli Conflict* (Chicago: University of Chicago Press, 1985), p. 415.

39. Naor, *Cabinet at War*, p. 56.

40. Publications of *Israel Defense Forces Spokesman*, 1982–1984.

41. Although the Soviet Union kept a relatively low profile, it expressed strong verbal opposition to the invasion. For example, during July 26, 27, and 28, 1982, it even threatened to react. President Reagan addressed these threats in a news conference, July 28, when he demanded withdrawal of all PLO and Syrian forces from Beirut; *New York Times*, July 29, 1982.

42. *New York Times*, September 27, 1982.

43. Ibid., June 7, 1982.

44. Ibid., June 8, 1982.

45. Haig, *Caveat*, p. 337; also Naor, *Cabinet at War*, pp. 58–60.

46. Interviews with Israeli military officials.

47. *New York Times*, June 7, 1982.

48. On June 13, 1982, Saudi Arabia's King Khalid, ruler since 1975, died of a heart attack at age sixty-nine. The unexpected crisis was resolved when Crown Prince Fahd became king.

49. Naor, *Cabinet at War*, pp. 60–62.

50. Ibid., p. 16; see also Avi-Ran, *Syrian Involvement*, pp. 150–151.

51. Naor, *Cabinet at War*, p. 67.

52. Herzog, *Israeli-Arab Wars*, p. 345.

53. On various occasions during June, July, and August 1982, the Reagan Administration expressed concern over a possible confrontation with the Soviets. See Haig's meeting with Gromyko on June 18, 1982. Washington officials were concerned that "Israel military moves might encourage the Russians to send forces to the area in response." *New York Times*, June 21; also remarks by President Reagan in news conferences, July 1 and 29, 1982.

54. See, for example, President Reagan's strong message to Prime Minister Begin, June 6. He urged him to stop the invasion and pull out immediately. Reagan threatened to cancel Begin's visit to Washington and ordered the immediate withholding of the promised F–16 jets. These orders were reversed later.

55. *Congressional Records*, Vol. 128, June 1982.

56. *New York Times*, June 8, 1982.

57. Evans and Novak, *Washington Post*, June 9, 1982.

58. See, for example, Secretary Shultz's news conference of July 12, 1982; also Reagan's peace initiative of September 1, 1982.

59. MacBride, *Israel in Lebanon*, pp. 143–169; also *Palestinian Studies*, No. 85, p. 197.

60. Congress was also displeased with Israel's policies. On June 22 Prime Minister Begin met with a group of Senators who strongly criticized him. The *New York Times* reported on June 23 that the meeting on the Hill was a highly emotional confrontation. Indeed, the President continued to hold in abeyance the decision to sell Israel the promised F–16 jets.

61. Secretary Haig shared this opinion and said that only a total military defeat of the PLO and Syria could bring about a withdrawal of all the foreign forces from Lebanon; see Haig, *Caveat*, p. 318.

62. Shultz's news conference, August 20, 1982, *Department of State Bulletin*, September 1982, p. 8.

63. *New York Times*, September 2, 1982.

64. NBC-TV, "Meet the Press," February 12, 1984.

65. Larry L. Fabian, "The Middle East: War Dangers and Receding Peace Prospects," *Foreign Affairs* (January 1984), p. 637; also Naor, *Cabinet at War*, pp. 146–147. (Estimated cost of the Jordanian Rapid Deployment Force, $220 million.)

66. Fabian, "The Middle East," p. 647.

67. Jacob Goldberg, *New York Times*, June 20, 1983.

68. *Daily Telegraph*, September 3, 1982.

69. *British Guardian*, September 3, 1982.

70. The first detailed account of the invasion was published in *Kadour Sheleg* (Hebrew) by Shimon Scheiffer (Tel Aviv: Edanim Press, 1983).

71. Haig's resignation was announced on June 26, 1982.

72. Avi-Ran, *Syrian Involvement in Lebanon*, pp. 163–164.

73. Mark Heller et al., *The Middle East Military Balance* (Boulder, CO: Westview), 1983.

74. *New York Times*, September 5, 1982.

75. Shultz, CBS-TV, "Face the Nation," September 5, 1983, *Department of State Bulletin*, October 1982.

76. News conference, September 28, 1982, *Department of State Bulletin* (November 1982).

77. *New York Times*, December 1, 1982.

78. Ibid., December 6, 1982.

79. *Congressional Records*, June 10, 1982, Vol. 128, p. 2745.

80. Ibid., June 10, 1982.

81. See reports on a U.S.-Israeli rift, *New York Times*, December 7, 11; also Weinberger's statement on NBC-TV news program "Today," March 1, 1983. The threat of a Soviet action following their deployment of the advanced SA–5 missiles in Syria manned by Soviet personnel was discussed in the *New York Times*, March 2, 1983.

82. *Wall Street Journal*, November 30, 1983.

83. Shultz's statement to the Senate Foreign Relations Committee, October 24, 1983, *Department of State Bulletin*, October 1983.

84. The estimates gathered from various sources, among them the *New York Times* and Israeli sources in interviews.

85. Flora Lewis, *New York Times*, October 31, 1983.

86. See Shoshana Bryen, "Advancing U.S.-Israel Strategic Cooperation," *Middle East Review*, February 1984.

87. Zbigniew Brzezinski, "America's Mideast Policy in Shambles," *New York Times*, October 9, 1983.

88. *U.S. News and World Report*, January 9, 1984.

89. Ibid.

90. President Reagan dispatched Habib and Draper on December 1, 1983, to help alleviate Israel's anxiety and end the deadlock. He believed that the major problem was Israel's insistence on direct negotiations and a peace treaty with Lebanon. On December 17 he sent a message to Prime Minister Begin urging him to step up the pullout. Reagan still hoped that Hussein would join the peace process. During Hussein's visit to Washington on December 20, 1983, Reagan promised him military aid and the creation of a Jordanian Rapid Deployment Force in exchange for his cooperation.

6

The Peace Process in the 1980s: New Games, Old Rules

The decade of the 1980s has been, perhaps, the most violent in the history of the Middle East since the end of World War II. The civil war in Lebanon, which began in 1975, has not yet been settled; the Iran-Iraq war had spread to the Persian Gulf and threatens the free flow of oil; the U.S. massive military presence there has had very little effect on the almost decade-old war. The Israeli-Arab conflict has entered a new era with the uprisings in the West Bank and the Gaza Strip, which began in December 1987, but the many divisions and conflicts in the Arab world make the negotiation process very difficult. Domestic scandals in the United States, such as the Iran-Contra affair and the Iraqi pipeline project, created a sense of urgency and a feeling that the issues should be addressed differently. Terrorist acts, including the kidnapping of American officials, add to the confusion. Surprisingly, President Reagan decided to launch a new peace initiative in 1988, albeit it being an election year. The prospects of this new peace initiative to succeed were, however, very dim.

Just a decade earlier, Kissinger had successfully negotiated a disengagement agreement between Israel and its arch enemy Syria, whereas in 1979 Egypt took a gigantic step and signed a peace treaty with Israel. The hopes of the late 1970s that the peace process would gain momentum and spill over to Jordan and the Palestinians did not materialize, to the chagrin of all. No end is seen to the cruel power struggle between the Shi'ites, Sunni, Druse, Palestinians, and Christians in Lebanon. The presence of 1,500–2,000 Iranian soldiers in the Ba'al Beck region in Lebanon, who provide logistical support to the Hozballah extremist group, radicalized the conflict. Syria played a strange role, helping the Iranians (by allowing them to use their embassy in Damascus to supply money, weapons, and ideological leadership to the Hozballah in Lebanon), the Shi'ites, the Druz, and some Palestinian groups. Because Syria has been the major Soviet client in the Middle East, Soviet participation in the peace process became inevitable. Indeed, Egypt, Jordan, and Saudi Arabia, all moderate Arab countries, insisted that the peace process begin with an international peace conference, with the U.S.S.R. an equal partner.

U.S. hopes of the early 1980s that Lebanon would provide a constructive context for a renewed U.S.-Israeli-Syrian dialogue withered away quickly. The informal, tacit Israel-Syrian agreement of the early seventies that divided Lebanon between them—Syria controlled the North and Israel maintained a sphere of influence in the South, whereas both contained the PLO—ended with the 1982 invasion.

U.S. hopes that this arrangement, unusual as it was, would promote the peace process as well as help to move the Syrians away from their Soviet patron proved unrealistic. Indeed, U.S. involvement in Lebanon was a frustrating chapter in American foreign policy. Israel's hopes did not materialize either. The United States pulled the marines out of Lebanon in February 1984, only to return to the region in 1987 to protect Kuwaiti oil tankers in the Persian Gulf. The policy has been highly criticized by members of Congress and the general public.

The confusion and uncertainties grew with the 1987 uprisings in the West Bank and the Gaza Strip. The United States and Israel agreed that the Palestinian issue could no longer be ignored. They, however, disagreed on the tactics and strategies that would best promote a settlement.

Syria also found itself in a quagmire. It has been isolated in the Arab world because of its support of Iran in the Iran-Iraq war, and in the West because of its support of terrorism and its alliance with the Soviet bloc. However, it needed the economic aid provided by Saudi Arabia and the West to pay for its high defense expenditures and its costly presence in Lebanon, which has become a heavy burden.

Israel, which initiated the invasion of June 1982 hoping to settle the Lebanese civil war and secure peace with its northern neighbor, failed on all counts. Neither the United States nor Israel enjoyed the power and influence necessary to impose a political settlement in Lebanon. Even Syria, the most important external power there, is still fighting an uphill battle to maintain its control. Syria's long military campaign in Lebanon has taken its toll. On May 13, 1987, a group of air force officers tried to overthrow Assad's regime. Seventy Syrian pilots were reported executed.[1] The coup attempt indicated political unrest in Syria, most likely affected by its long campaign in Lebanon. The PLO, which between 1970 and 1982 successfully created "a state within a state" in Lebanon has become a shadow of its former power, and has practically disintegrated. Tunisia serves as its headquarters, but only 400 PLO members are living there compared with 7,000 who arrived there in 1982.

The upheavals in the Arab world of the early 1980s, the 1982 invasion of Lebanon, and the weakening of the PLO had a direct effect on the peace process. It undoubtedly encouraged local Palestinian groups on the West Bank to assume leadership and try to terminate the twenty-year-old status quo. This unexpected development resulted in an abundance of proposals and plans put forward by the United States, Israel, and the various Arab states. The proposals are mostly mutually exclusive, which complicated the negotiations and the U.S. role as a mediator.

In fact, the Lebanese crisis created a change in the power structure in the region. Israel suffered major setbacks, whereas Syria emerged as the major power and the ''patron state'' of Lebanon. It coerced Lebanon to nullify the May 17 agreement, thus proving that it controlled the peace agenda. The PLO could not stop the Syrian-supported Shi'ite attacks on the Palestinian refugee camps in Lebanon that began in 1985. Hence, the PLO position as the powerful representative of the Palestinian people has been challenged, a fact that strengthened King Hussein and local Palestinian groups.

King Hussein, however, knew that not all the local Palestinians accepted his leadership. Indeed, most Palestinians considered a federation with Jordan to be unsatisfactory. President Reagan, however, shared Israel's view and rejected the idea of an independent Palestinian state between Israel and Jordan. Washington also links the regional conflict to global conflicts and to the overall U.S.-Soviet competition for power. A Palestinian state could become a Soviet client, a fact that burdens the peace process and adds to its complexity.

As analysis of the prospects for peace, and the role of the United States as a mediator, must include all the actors involved. Their interests, power, and motivation are usually incompatible. Moreover, unlike the Israeli-Egyptian peace treaty, any future agreement must include a solution to the Palestinian problem. Israel's dilemma has been how to reconcile its security needs (territories) with peace (Palestinian state). Since Israel pulled out of Lebanon in 1985, the Labor party has argued that a settlement is inevitable. The Likud party, however, disagreed, and hoped to maintain the status quo. The violent riots in the West Bank and Gaza, which began in late 1987, proved the Labor party right.

Any peace initiative must address global and regional problems. First, the nature of Soviet participation must be defined. Second, the regional actors have to participate albeit their disagreements and strifes. The PLO and/or other Palestinian groups have to be part of the peace process, and the United States and Israel have to iron out their differences. The hawks in Israel reject any territorial concessions, whereas the doves are even willing to accept an independent Palestinian state. The majority in Israel and in Jordan, however, do not approve of the creation of a completely independent Palestinian state. The issue of an international peace conference under the chairmanship of the two superpowers, or under the auspices of the U.N. Security Council, is another issue that has to be resolved.

REAGAN'S SECOND PEACE INITIATIVE: AGENDA, ACTORS

The second Reagan peace plan was officially announced on February 1, 1988, both in Washington and in Jerusalem. During the first weeks of 1988 an intensive diplomatic campaign was taking place as American diplomats traveled to the Middle East and Middle Eastern officials visited Washington. They tried to understand and react to the new American initiative. Assistant Secretary of State Richard Murphy was in Jerusalem while Israel's Cabinet Secretary, Eli Rubinstein, and Nimrod Novik, a senior adviser to Foreign Minister Peres, visited Washington.

A few days earlier President Reagan met in Washington with President Hosni Mubarak of Egypt. The two leaders announced, albeit very vaguely, that they discussed a peace plan to settle the Palestinian problem. Mubarak asked for a more active American role, whereas Reagan asked for Mubarak's help in reducing the violence in the West Bank and Gaza. The two leaders seemed to agree on the issue of an international peace conference, but not on much else.

Almost simultaneously other meetings were taking place in Paris, Amman, Egypt, Morocco, Riyadh, and Rome.[2] An Egyptian-Jordanian statement, issued on February 16, surprisingly rejected the Camp David Accords as the basic framework for the negotiations. It called for a "complete solution of the Arab-Israeli problem that would carry the stamp of both superpowers."[3] Mubarak and Hussein demanded a breakaway from the Camp David Accords, not only in structure but also in substance. Unlike the autonomy plan, which was an interim arrangement, the Arab countries demanded a total solution. The process would begin with an international peace conference, supervised by the five permanent members of the Security Council and attended by the PLO, Arab representatives, and Israel.

The American plan, however, differed from the Arab plan. Washington developed a three-part plan. First, an international conference; second, direct negotiations leading to an interim agreement for the territories, lasting no longer than six months—elections in the West Bank could be held as early as October 1988; and, finally, the opening of talks designed to find a permanent solution, no later then December 1988. Autonomy for the Palestinians could go into effect as early as February 1989.

The Arab states and the United States were in agreement on the need to accelerate the peace process, regardless of the Camp David timetable. In Israel, however, Prime Minister Shamir declared his adherence to the principles and procedures established at Camp David. Peres, on the other hand, welcomed the U.S. plan for an accelerated Palestinian autonomy. A secret committee of Palestinians that has organized the demonstrations on the West Bank, and the PLO have also rejected the American plan. The first problem was U.N. Resolution 242, which meant, in principle, an exchange of territories for peace. Israel has been most reluctant to withdraw from any territories, although it had, in 1970, accepted U.N. Resolution 242. Most Israelis, and especially the Likud people, considered peace under such conditions extremely dangerous, unsound, and thus too threatening to Israel's security.

The Palestinians and the PLO rejected the plan because it did not offer them self-government and full sovereignty. Jordan and Egypt were unclear on the issue of an autonomous Palestinian state. Jordan probably shared the U.S. and Israeli opinion that a Palestinian state should be affiliated with Jordan in some form of a federal government. The PLO, which suffered a devastating defeat in 1982, had to join the radical Arab states; hence, Arafat was reluctant to make any public statements acknowledging Israel's right to exist within secure borders. This in turn gave Israel the excuse to claim that it would not negotiate with the PLO.

Whereas the PLO has been struggling to restore its power position, the question of what role it could play in the peace process has become crucial. Other related questions concerned how much power and influence the PLO enjoyed in the Arab world. On the one hand, Arafat needed the political and economic support of Jordan, Egypt, and Saudi Arabia. Hence, in 1985 he signed an agreement with Hussein accepting a formula of power sharing in the peace process. This was a complete reversal of the 1974 Rabat summit, when Hussein lost his negotiating power to Arafat. Second, Arafat had to consider the possibility that Syria or Jordan, or even both, would decide to follow the Sadat model, negotiate with Israel bilaterally, and exclude the PLO from the process. Several times the king had indicated that he might follow the bilateral option.

The agreement reached between Arafat and King Hussein in February 1985, announcing a joint Jordanian-PLO peace initiative, was a direct result of this dilemma. The agreement provided the PLO with an important benefit: the king allowed some PLO military units to return to Jordan, albeit in a restricted manner.[4] Arafat's concessions to Hussein included a recognition of all U.N. resolutions, without mentioning in name Resolution 242, which asserted Israel's right to exist within secure boundaries. Indeed, the idea of an international peace conference was part of this agreement. Arafat had no choice but to agree that the Jordanian delegation would include PLO representatives and he made the concession of not having a separate PLO delegation. This gave the leadership position to Hussein. In exchange, Hussein agreed to declare that the PLO was the legitimate representative of the Palestinian people. The February 1985 agreement, which was initiated by King Hussein and President Mubarak, stated that the Palestinian state would be based on a federation with Jordan. This was another major PLO concession to Hussein.

Following the Hussein-Mubarak-Arafat initiative, the United States began a tacit campaign to bring Israel and Jordan to the bargaining table. Not surprisingly, the 1985 agreement was short-lived. Arafat probably could not thwart his internal and external opposition and had to abrogate his 1985 commitment to Hussein. This act upset England's Prime Minister Margaret Thatcher, who formally invited the parties to London to pursue negotiations under British mediation. It also greatly angered the king.

Israel was skeptical of the agreement from its inception. It argued that Arafat would never concede his dream of an independent Palestinian state, however minuscule and perhaps unsound economically. The question of a Palestinian state becoming a Soviet client was another bothering issue.[5]

On February 19, 1986 Hussein announced, in a televised policy address, that he refused to negotiate further with Yasser Arafat and the PLO until such time as their word becomes their bond.[6] Moreover, in July 1986 Hussein ordered the closing of the PLO offices in Jordan. This was considered the greatest blow to the PLO since it was ousted from Lebanon in 1982. Indeed, in 1986 the peace process and the role of the United States as a major mediator, looked less clear and more complex.

In 1987 the role of the PLO in the renewed peace process looked even more unclear. The stigma of a terrorist organization was haunting it. It lost its cohesion and its infrastructure. Its missions to the United Nations and Washington were going to be shut down. Local leadership in the West Bank and the Gaza Strip challenged its authority and created a negotiation alternative, more supportive of Israel. The April 1987 Algiers Conference of the Palestine National Council made the issue even more compelling. The council decided that the PLO's executive committee would be expanded from fifteen to twenty seats to include Communist and extremist factions, which had never had a seat. The council also formally denounced the Hussein-Arafat agreement of February 1985.[7] Although Arafat was re-elected the PLO's chairman, the outcome of the summit proved that his loss of power has been substantial.

Arafat's announcement of 1987 that the PLO would participate in an international peace conference with Israel implied a recognition of the Jewish state. But his insistence on an independent Palestinian state based on a complete Israeli withdrawal without any concessions to security arrangements made his statement meaningless in terms of the peace process.

Following the 1986 developments, U.S. Assistant Secretary of State Richard Murphy was dispatched to the region. He held talks with Israel, the Arab states, and later with Soviet officials in Sweden in June of 1986.[8] Other negotiations and meetings included a ten-day visit to the Middle East by Vice President Bush in the summer of 1986, and a July 1986 meeting in Morocco between Israel's Prime Minister Peres and King Hussein. Meanwhile, the Soviet Union made a move that alerted the United States. In its drive to play a greater role in Middle Eastern politics, the Soviet Union held talks with Israeli officials in August 1986, in Finland, for the first time in nineteen years! The intensive political activity of Israel, Jordan, Egypt, Morocco, the U.S.S.R., and the United States was accelerated in 1988 following the violence that erupted in the West Bank and Gaza. The belief in Washington that this intensive activity would lead to a negotiated settlement led the administration to send Secretary Shultz to the region on February 1988.

The success of the 1988 American peace initiative depended on the parties' willingness to make concessions. The new round of talks proved that the parties were still very much at odds. Although Hussein said that he would negotiate with Israel, his first priority was to maintain his rule over Jordan. An independent Palestinian state might develop demands over the East Bank, already inhabited by a Palestinian majority. A united Jordanian-West Bank-Palestinian state is a real threat to Hussein. On the other hand, he viewed with anxiety the expansion of the settlements and Israel's drive to create facts on the West Bank. Torn between the PLO and its threat to "Palestinize" Jordan, and Israel's threat to "Israelize" the West Bank, Hussein probably believed that a peace conference could help him settle these two problems. Another option was a bilateral Israeli-Jordanian agreement, which might have served Hussein's interests better. However, the irreconcilable divisions within Israel on the issue of peace, and its frustration over the continued violence in the West Bank and Gaza resulted in even greater domestic conflicts that could not be resolved before the Israeli elections of November 1988.

The disarray in the Arab world was not less disturbing. The almost decade-old Iran-Iraq war was creating shock waves throughout the Arab world. Syria was experiencing major political and economic difficulties.[9] The Jordanian monarchy has become very anxious about the Palestinian unrest, which could spill over to the East Bank. Egypt was coping with the growing influence of Islamic fundamentalism that was challenging Mubarak's secular regime. The Gulf states were threatened by the continued war. Moreover, the Soviet Union was trying to exploit the situation and to gain inroads into the traditional conservative Gulf states. Soviet weapons were offered to Hussein after his request for American F-16 and Hawk missiles was denied. In April 1987 the U.S.S.R. agreed to provide protection to Kuwaiti oil tankers. Finally, Gorbachev surprised Israel and the United States when he showed willingness to renew diplomatic relations with Israel. On May 17, 1987, Minister of Foreign Affairs Peres met in Washington with the Soviet Ambassador; in April in Moscow, Gorbachev said at a dinner honoring President Assad of Syria that "the absence of such relations cannot be considered normal." Gorbachev continued to say that Israel has a right to a secure existence and that "military force in the region has become completely discredited."[10] Gorbachev must have created ripples not only in Damascus, but in Washington, too.

The United States, alarmed by these developments, dispatched Richard Murphy in May 1987 to the Arab countries and the Gulf states, to buttress the traditional U.S. alliance with these countries. The main issue on the agenda was the security of the Gulf and the international peace conference.[11] It seemed that Washington underestimated Israel's objection to the peace conference and assumed that Arab consent was the key to its success.

Another dilemma was the participation of the Soviet Union, that is, how to include them formally but exclude them from the meaningful negotiations. Secretary Shultz said on May 17 that they were a destructive force in the peace efforts. "They encourage the PLO to turn ever more radical and rejectionist. They align themselves with the worst terrorists and tyrants in the region. They refuse to re-establish diplomatic recognition to Israel."[12] On the other hand, Shultz told Peres, in a letter sent on May 10, 1987, that an international peace conference was a first and necessary step for direct Israeli-Jordanian negotiations.[13] By February 1988, Israel, however, could not reach a consensus on this crucial issue. The Labor party, lacking a clear majority, was hoping that Washington would use its leverage and pressure the Likud party to be more flexible on the issue of an international peace conference. For example, during Peres' visit to Washington, in April 1987, he asked Secretary Shultz to be more assertive with Shamir. Abba Eban, former Israeli Minister of Foreign Affairs, and other Labor leaders stated that an international conference was needed to start the peace process moving again. Moreover, the Labor party accepted Soviet participation and was willing to negotiate with Palestinians—not the PLO—should they participate in a joint Jordanian-Palestinian delegation.[14] This attitude was acceptable to Jordan and Egypt. However, Prime Minister Shamir and the Likud party were hard to convince.

Indeed, Shultz was aware of the fact that he could hardly use military aid to Israel as leverage while pursuing a policy of strong support of and cooperation with the Arab states in the Gulf. Some estimated the cost of the American naval armada in the Gulf to be as high as $40 billion per year.[15] The U.S. presence was expected to keep the Soviets out of the Gulf and to mend fences with the Arab countries after the ill-fated arms-for-Iran affair. Direct pressure on Israel would probably have been counterproductive, and was therefore not used.

However, during his February 1988 shuttle to the Middle East, Shultz seemed determined to convince Israel to agree to an international peace conference. His "carrot" was that the conference would have a continuing role but could not impose a settlement. The second concession was that the PLO would not be independently represented and would be part of a Jordanian-Palestinian delegation. Shultz's proposal was informally accepted, with reservations, by Jordan, Syria, and the PLO. It also received the blessing of the U.N. Security Council.

Shultz's initiative received unexpected support from a group of thirty U.S. Senators, who sent him a letter on March 4, 1988, criticizing Shamir's hard line. The letter, signed by many of Israel's staunchest supporters, argued that Shamir's rejection of the principle "land for peace" had been obstructing the peace efforts.

Another surprising development has been a Jordanian-Syrian rapprochement indicating that Syria wanted to be part of the peace process. In the past, that is, during the 1974 Israeli-Egyptian negotiations, Syria insisted on participating in the peace process, a policy that led to an international peace conference and, ultimately, to the Israeli-Syrian disengagement agreement. During his visit to Syria, Shultz held long talks with Assad, which created hopes that a negotiation framework was feasible. Syria's role in the negotiations is crucial, since after the 1982 invasion Syria became the center of Palestinian activism. About 500,000 Palestinians live in Syria, including over 100,000 militants. At least six major Palestinian guerrilla organizations maintain headquarters there.[16] Syria's participation in the peace process is therefore crucial.

THE STEP-BY-STEP ALTERNATIVE

The 1988 American peace plan that was presented to Israel and the Arab states during Secretary Shultz's visit to the region in the last week of February was defined by Shultz as a "comprehensive peace plan." It included proposals to settle the issue of the West Bank and Gaza, as well as a negotiation framework among Israel, Jordan, and Syria. The focus of the plan was, however, a settlement of the Palestinian issue. It suggested an accelerated autonomy followed by negotiations between Israel and a Jordanian-Palestinian delegation on the final status of the territories, no later than 1989. The negotiations would take place under an international umbrella that would legitimize direct talks between Israel and the Arabs. As expected, Israel, Syria, and Jordan all had negative reactions to various clauses of the proposal.[17] Prime Minister Shamir objected to both the structure and substance of the plan. He insisted on the Camp David formula and opposed the role that Syria and the Soviet Union would play in the negotiations. King Hussein, who was in Europe during the Shultz visit, insisted on including Syria and the U.S.S.R. in the negotiations. The Jordanian-Syrian rapprochement surprised both Israel and the United States. It could either help or obstruct the negotiations.

The Shultz initiative did not exclude, and indeed could instigate, a bilateral negotiation framework among Israel, Jordan, and Syria. It could lead to separate Israeli-Jordanian, Israeli-Syrian agreements, thus following the Kissinger model of 1974–75 disengagement agreements. Thus it is important to examine these options and evaluate their prospects for success. The Palestinian issue is likely to be the determining factor. The new Palestinian leadership in the West Bank and Gaza shattered the twenty-year-old status quo and changed the role of the PLO. It introduced a new factor that might make the negotiations even more difficult. The Shultz plan, which proposed a Palestinian-Jordanian federation, was probably unacceptable to the young, radical Palestinians. The picture, however, looked different from a Syrian perspective. Unlike Jordan, Syria could decouple itself from the Palestinian issue and follow the disengagement model or the Sadat model. Hence, it is necessary to separate the Israeli-Jordanian and the Israeli-Syrian theaters and analyze them independently. The two theaters differ in their agenda for peace; thus policies applied successfully to one may fail when applied to the other.

THE ISRAELI-JORDANIAN THEATER

Since the early days of the Israeli-Arab conflict, Jordan has been considered the natural partner to peace. However, the history of the conflict showed that this option might be very disappointing. Indeed, Jordan has been an "optical illusion." Although it was considered the most moderate of all the Arab states (with the exclusion of Egypt) and the most willing to accept the existence of Israel at its border, it has been reluctant to open bilateral peace negotiations with Israel. Syria, on the other hand, which has always been the most radical Arab state (with the exception of Libya) and has consistently rejected any proposal to recognize the state of Israel in any form, was less limited in its policy choices and had signed a bilateral agreement with Israel in 1974.

Indeed, Hussein has been a captive of his geopolitical situation. Over 70

percent of his citizens are Palestinians, yet he has been denied the right to speak for or represent them. Moreover, Jordan was part of the Palestine mandate and became a separate political entity only in 1922 by a British government decree. Over one-third of Jordan's population has relatives and family in the West Bank. Hence, the ties between Jordan and the Palestinians are hardly separable and many even consider Jordan to be a Palestinian state. "For Jordan, the shape of a settlement between Jordanians and Palestinians is almost more important than the shape of a settlement between Jordan and Israel."[18]

The question of who should represent the Palestinians bothers Jordan at least as much as it bothers Israel. The young, radical West Bank Palestinians, many of whom have been inspired by Islamic fundamentalism, are, perhaps, a greater threat to Hussein than they are to Israel. Hussein would like to reinstate his pre–1967 leadership over the West Bank; however, this might not be possible in 1988. The new situation in the territories also created a problem for the PLO. Arafat cannot act without the cooperation of his traditional enemy, Assad, or the local leadership that called itself an "extension of the PLO."

Indeed, the future of the West Bank is linked to the future of the East Bank. The two banks should not be completely separated. However, the pre–1967 Jordanian rule would probably be rejected by most West Bank residents. On the other hand, an independent Palestinian state might not be economically and politically viable. Hence, a federal system could satisfy both Hussein's and Arafat's demands. However, the local Palestinians might fight it as fiercely as they fight the Israeli rule. Israel would not accept an independent Palestinian state led by either radical Islamic fundamentalists or the secular PLO. (The PLO's charter vows to replace Israel with an Arab-Palestinian state.) Although in recent years the PLO softened its position on this issue, it never formally amended its charter. Moreover, it argues that under its rule, all the Palestinians would be encouraged to return to their homeland, although the majority of them were not born in Palestine. This, however, would not be accepted by Israel.

The Shultz plan suggested that Jordan play a major role, whereas the PLO would be represented in a joint Jordanian-Palestinian delegation. Arafat could accept it only if it were approved by the other Arab states, especially Syria.

Both Hussein and Israel have a shared interest in curtailing radical activities in the West Bank. In spite of strong PLO opposition, Hussein had developed a strategy of a five-year development plan for the West Bank and Gaza, with a budget of $150 to $240 million a year. However, he could neither finance nor raise the needed funds, and the oil-producing Arab countries, which under the terms of the Baghdad agreement of 1978 were supposed to contribute $150 million to a joint Jordanian-Palestinian fund for this purpose, did not fulfill their commitment. A token contribution came from the United States when Vice President Bush, during his visit to the region in 1986, promised Hussein $4 million in aid for the West Bank. Hence, Hussein's efforts to undermine the PLO and other radical influences in the West Bank were unsuccessful. Thus

Hussein insisted that his negotiations with Israel would be held under an umbrella of an international conference and be approved by Syria.

Although Hussein has not given up his 1972 plan in which he proposed to be the legitimate ruler of a Palestinian state,[19] it became clear that any negotiation framework must include both Hussein and representatives of the PLO and the local residents of the West Bank and Gaza. The Shultz plan addressed this problem, but it is unclear whether the radical Palestinians, who have already rejected it, would soften their position. Arafat, on the other hand, expressed his willingness to recognize Hussein's role in the negotiations. He went as far as going on record and saying that he was somewhat favorable of the ''Jordanian option.''[20] This, however, has yet to bear positive results. In fact, Arafat's peace overtures of 1983–85 were met with strong opposition within the PLO. The Palestinian National Council has become even more extremist and the moderate opposition was oppressed.[21]

The 1988 U.S. peace initiative actually began two years earlier when Israel's Prime Minister Peres and Egyptian President Mubarak, on separate visits to Bonn in early 1986, tried to elicit a stronger interest in peace. In May 1986 Prime Minister Thatcher, on a visit to Jerusalem, endorsed the Jordanian-Palestinian federation, and President François Mitterand, in July of 1986, joined with Soviet leader Mikhail Gorbachev in endorsing a Middle East peace conference. It seemed that any negotiation framework must begin with an international peace conference. This, however, does not promise the success of the Jordanian option.

Objection to the Jordanian option and to any Palestinian-Jordanian federation has been visible since the 1985 aborted Hussein-Arafat agreement. Hussein has been unable to develop a broad political support among the Arab states and the Palestinians; hence, his ability to play a pivotal factor in the peace negotiations is questionable. The fact that Syria insisted on becoming a major participant in the negotiations might obstruct the Jordanian option. Hussein hopes that an international conference that would include the five permanent members of the Security Council would provide him with a strong defense against any possible Syrian charges, as was the case with Egypt when it moved toward a separate peace with Israel.

On the other hand, the situation of ''no peace no war'' bothers Hussein, who shares the longest border with Israel. His ability to rule his country, control his multiethnic population, and manage his unfriendly Arab neighbors depends on the complex balance of forces that affects his rule. Peace with Israel might be a mitigating factor in this extremely delicate situation. Indeed, since Hussein could not reinstate his rule over the West Bank and considers an independent Palestinian state threatening to his rule, he is strongly interested in creating a Jordanian-Palestinian federation that would live in peace with Israel. This would receive the blessing of the United States, but questions such as secure borders for Israel, the future of the settlements, and the strong radical Palestinian opposition threaten the feasibility of this option.

Hussein would probably tacitly object to the creation of an independent Palestinian state at his border, which would encourage the influx of millions of Palestinians into the West Bank. He probably would equally oppose to completely incorporate the West Bank into his monarchy and turn it into a Palestinian state. A federation that would include both banks of the Jordan River would be the preferred option for all, including the United States, which fears that a strong Palestinian state might become the "Nicaragua" of the Middle East.

It is questionable, however, if this option could materialize anytime soon, given the recent uprising in the West Bank and the radicalization of the local Palestinian population in the West Bank and Gaza. Without their approval Hussein could not sign any bilateral agreement. The United States, albeit in strong support of the federation option, can neither bring the Palestinians to moderate their positions nor influence Israel to consider substantial territorial compromises on the West Bank. Even the Labor party would reject any concessions that were not outlined in the Allon Plan, which was rejected even by the moderate Palestinians.[22] The Shultz initiative vaguely addressed this issue by mentioning Resolution 242 and suggesting an acceleration of the Camp David autonomy plan. This, however, leaves the difficult questions unanswered. It is, therefore, highly unlikely that an international peace conference could create a meaningful change needed to end the deadlock.

Finally, the question of Jerusalem, which was not directly addressed by the 1988 American peace initiative, would probably become the bone of contention in any Israeli-Jordanian negotiations. It is unrealistic to expect any government in Israel to give up its united capital. Hence, even if an international conference would be convened, it would probably not solve the Israeli-Jordanian-Palestinian question in the near future.

THE ISRAELI-SYRIAN THEATER

Syria's participation in any peace process involves difficult questions. Assad, Syria's ruler since 1971, has maintained a consistent uncompromising position and his tyrannical minority rule was governed by an obsession with internal and external security. A member of the Alawi minority (12 percent of the population), he rules over a Sunni majority and spends about 50 percent of Syria's total budget on the military. He trusts only his family and close friends. His brother, Rifat Assad, is the commander of the Defense Companies, whose task is to protect Damascus from internal enemies.[23] Assad has only few friends in the Arab world because of his close ties with Libya, Iran, and the U.S.S.R. He is also involved in military cooperation with the Kurdish minority in Iraq. He is a pragmatist but dreams about "greater Syria" and his role as the leader of the pan-Arabist Middle East. Moreover, Assad believes that "Syria can be secure only when it has a voice in setting the affairs of its neighbors."[24]

Syria's participation in the peace process is crucial. Kissinger remarked that "no successful war against Israel is possible without Egypt and no peace is possible without Syria.'' It is clear that Hussein would not enter any negotiations without Syria's blessing and participation. Indeed, Assad insisted on taking part in the new peace process. His policy is to keep as many options open to him as possible. He established an unprecedented record in providing Syria with a durable regime. His tactic of putting his eggs in as many baskets as possible has been partly responsible for his success. He does not rule out negotiations with Israel, although he uses the harshest anti-Israeli rhetoric of any Arab leader. He supports the Palestinian cause but tries to destroy the PLO. He stays within the Soviet sphere of influence but signals to the West that he is willing to listen to other proposals. He does not rule out a military clash with Israel, but made extreme efforts to avoid an all-out war during 1982–84. He supports international terrorism but tries to control the Israeli-Syrian border against terrorist activity from the Golan Heights. His disagreements with the Arab world have not led him to break his ties with them. Assad keeps his channels of communications open to the moderate Arab states, although he supported Iran in the Iran-Iraq war. Indeed, he received vast economic aid from Saudi Arabia, which helps his ailing economy. Although he strongly opposed the Camp David Accords and has maintained that the Israeli-Arab conflict could only be settled when Israel withdraws from all the territories, he probably would agree to a similar arrangement in exchange for all of the Golan Heights.

It has always been difficult to predict Assad's actions. His participation in the 1988 peace process is, however, a fact. He invited Secretary Shultz to Damascus and announced that he would negotiate an agreement with Israel in the forum of an international peace conference. Moreover, Assad met with Senator Arlen Specter, a known supporter of Israel, on January 19, 1988, and told him that he "was serious about talking with Israel."[25] This implied that he would be willing to exchange land for peace. In another surprising move, Assad mended fences with his traditional foe, King Hussein. In 1987 the two leaders began coordinating their strategies, especially with regard to the peace process. Hussein, fearful of a displeased Syria at his border, fully cooperates with Assad. In fact, Syria has very good reasons to join the peace negotiations. First, Assad would never give up his leading role in the Israeli-Arab conflict. Moreover, he would not like to see Egyptian President Mubarak become the dominant Arab leader as Sadat was before him. Second, as the champion of the Palestinian cause, he wishes to speak for them and reduce the role of Arafat and the PLO.

One of Assad's major problems is Syria's crippled economy, which might threaten his rule. Basic commodities are absent from the markets for months. Syria's population is about 12 million, its per capita income is $702 and its gross domestic product has been 15.3 billion in 1986. Exports are almost non-existent and cash reserves fell to $40 million in 1987. Syria's military expenditures are about $4 billion annually, and its arms imports from the U.S.S.R. amount to $1.5 billion per year.[26] Hence, Assad is dependent on the $2 billion per year aid from Saudi Arabia and Kuwait.

Syria's continued involvement in Lebanon bore some political benefits, but the cost has been very high. It maintains a permanent military force of 400,000 men, a sixth of Syria's total work force! About 7,000 soldiers have been deployed in Beirut in 1988; over 30,000 are stationed in the Bequ'a valley. Indeed, Syria's political, economic, and military interests were hardly advanced by the prolonged status quo. Given Assad's vulnerability to a domestic upheaval, it is conceivable that he decided that a peace conference would advance his interests. Moreover, Assad had experienced unexpected problems with the Soviet Union. First, Gorbachev suggested, during Assad's visit to Moscow in April 1987, that he recognized Israel's right to exist. Second, Moscow's diplomatic campaign to renew its relations with Israel alarmed Assad. However, it is unclear whether Syria would be willing to follow the Egyptian model and decouple itself from the Palestinian issue, or whether it will become a captive of the Israeli-Jordanian-Palestinian forum that may not lead to a settlement.

The United States seems to overlook the fact that Syria might be more concerned with the boundaries of "greater Syria" than with the boundaries of the West Bank. Second, the dangerous status quo in the Golan Heights might lead to a resumption of the hostilities with Israel, a situation not favored by Assad at this point. Indeed, during 1987 Syria made an effort to improve the political climate with Israel. For example, it has reduced the number of armed forces deployed along its border with Israel. It also deactivated several regular army units, putting them in the reserves.[27] In a shift from its anti-Egyptian policy, Assad attended, in February 1987, an Arab summit held in Kuwait that was also attended by Egypt's President Hosni Mubarak. It was the first time that Egyptian and Syrian leaders had met since Sadat's visit to Jerusalem in 1977. Finally, after a visit to Syria in March 1987, former U.S. President Jimmy Carter stated that he was convinced that Assad wanted peace and that he would join an international peace conference.[28] These developments implied that Syrian and Israeli interests might converge.

However, Syria's radical ideology could not be overlooked. Its strong anti-Israeli policy might be rooted in deep anti-Semitic and anti-Zionist feelings, which go back more than a hundred years to the early days of Jewish immigration to Palestine. This was strengthened by the Ba'ath ideology that firmly rejects any non-Arab entities in the Middle East. However, the ideological and Realpolitik approaches are not necessarily mutually exclusive. In fact, Assad has been using the Israeli-Arab conflict as a tool to strengthen his power position in Syria and the Arab world. The Israeli-Syrian conflict also served as a justification to the unproportionately large defense budget needed mainly to protect Assad against internal opposition.

Whereas Assad maintained the harshest rhetoric against Israel's occupation of the West Bank, he nonetheless signed a disengagement agreement with Israel, decoupling himself from the question of the Palestinians. He also, at one time or another, sided with or against the PLO and helped destroy PLO bases in Lebanon. Indeed, Assad fears the influence of the PLO on the Sunni population in Syria. The uprising in Hamma, of February 1982, was a strong reminder of his vulnerability. His loyalty to the Palestinians and the PLO is, therefore, questionable.

However, a Syrian-Israeli-American dialogue would be difficult, given Syria's hostility toward Israel and the West. Moreover, Syria was linked to several terrorist acts in London, Paris, Rome, and Berlin, as well as the bombing of the marine barracks in Lebanon.[29] Some American leaders, among them former President Carter, believe that Assad has changed his foreign policy. After meeting with Assad in March 1987 Carter said that Assad was ready to enter into direct negotiations with Israel, if Israel would commit itself to a withdrawal from the Golan Heights in exchange for peace. However, it is highly unlikely that any Israeli government would be able to make any commitment before the 1988 elections.

An important mitigating factor has been Assad's hostile relationships with the PLO, a feeling he shares with Israel. Assad also opposed the PLO's "state within a state" created in Lebanon during the seventies because he considers Lebanon to be a Syrian sphere of influence. The possibility that the PLO would gain control over Lebanon, the West Bank, and Gaza, and perhaps Jordan, is Assad's nightmare. Hence, Assad has consistently provided shelter and support to Arafat's enemies in the Arab world. He also supported the anti-PLO campaign of 1983–84. It is clear that Syria wishes to contain the PLO and would welcome a Jordanian-Palestinian delegation to the international peace conference.

Hence, the Syrian-PLO rift could contribute to a Syrian-Israeli dialogue. Unlike the Israel-Jordanian theater, the PLO's participation in the negotiations is not crucial, and the 1974 disengagement agreement is a case in point. Assad preferred Kissinger's mediation to that of an international forum, and he made sure that Brezhnev remained out of the picture. Moreover, Assad exhibited a strong will not to violate the agreement during the Lebanese crisis and to maintain peace in the Golan Heights. Another example of a tacit Syrian-Israeli cooperation concerned the civil war in Lebanon during 1976–78, when both Israel and Syria supported the Christians against the PLO. Assad's actions were in complete defiance of the Soviet policy. The U.S.S.R. has been a long-time supporter of the PLO and strongly objected to Assad's anti-PLO campaign. Indeed, a Palestinian state, especially one ruled by the PLO, would have been a jewel in the Soviet crown. The Soviets threatened many times to "punish" Assad for his campaign against Arafat, but to no avail. Like the United States in its relations with Israel, Soviet leverage over its Syrian client has been very limited. Assad has been pursuing an independent policy in spite of his growing dependence on Soviet aid. Assad also ignored the fact that his anti-PLO campaign was strongly criticized by most of the Arab leaders, who also condemned his support of Iran.

Hence, unlike Jordan, Syria has not been a captive of Arab public opinion and was never denied the right to negotiate with Israel. Assad rightly believes that he is free to pursue those policies that would best serve his interests. Consequently, it is possible to assume that Syria would define a settlement with Israel—which would return the Golan Heights to Syria—a national interest. Reinstating Syrian rule over this lost land is a matter of personal esteem for Assad, as well as a matter of national and security interest for Syria. The Israeli forces are now stationed twenty-five miles from Damascus, posing a genuine strategic threat to Syria. Moreover, Syria would be able to reduce its military expenditures and allocate more resources to its ailing economy. Finally, an agreement with Israel would help restore Syrian relations with the United States and West Europe, a condition much favored by Assad. During the summer of 1986 Assad was negotiating with France, West Germany, and Holland a substantial aid package. The deal was called off after U.S. intervention and following Syria's involvement in terrorist acts in West Europe.[30]

Assad was very disappointed and tried to move away from the image of a "terrorist state." During his meeting with former President Carter, he clearly expressed his desire to renew Syria's ties with the West. He probably realized that his association with international terrorism has become too costly and has gained Syria a negative image in world opinion. It is clear that Assad wishes to reduce his dependence on the Soviet Union. Restoring his relations with the United States and the West is the only way to achieve it.

An Israeli-Syrian agreement would also strengthen Syria's power position vis-à-vis its traditional rival, Iraq. Because of the prolonged war between Iran and Iraq, the Iraqi Army is the most experienced, best-trained, and best-equipped of the Arab forces. This poses a threat to Israel, but Syria, who shares a long border with Iraq, is not less threatened. A settlement with Israel would allow Assad to allocate more resources to secure this troublesome border.

One cannot preclude another possible incentive for Assad. Since his early years in power, he hoped to assume a major leadership position in the Arab world. A settlement with Israel could establish him as Sadat's successor, and the most important Arab leader of the 1980s. Hence, the political options offered by a Syrian-Israeli settlement could be more promising than the options offered by an Israeli-Jordanian settlement.

Consequently, King Hussein has been coordinating his actions with Assad, realizing that Jordan and Syria might have more common interests than previously suggested. While preparing his response to the Shultz peace plan, Hussein contacted Assad, seeking his support to his proposal based on an international peace conference, with the inclusion of the PLO in a joint Jordanian-Palestinian delegation. Hussein asked that the United Nations guarantee the implementation of all the provisions reached in the negotiations.[31]

Syria could, however, find itself in conflict with much of the Arab world if it decides to sign a bilateral agreement with Israel, even one short of a peace treaty. It would violate all the Arab summit resolutions demanding that a solution to the Palestinian problem be reached *before* any agreement with Israel is signed. Thus Assad is faced with a dilemma. A continuation of the status quo is extremely dangerous because it might rekindle the Israeli-Syrian hostile relationships. Moreover, the existence of Israeli guns so close to Damascus is a source of anxiety

and unrest in Syria. Assad's image and personal esteem would be greatly enhanced by a return of the Golan Heights to Syria. On the other hand, an Israeli
withdrawal requires major political concessions, which Assad might not be ready
to make, especially not before the Palestinian question is resolved. Indeed, Assad
has maintained a low profile throughout the Shultz peace campaign of early 1988
and has played the role of a passive observer, waiting to see how events would
develop.

A key factor in Assad's willingness to negotiate has been Israel's interest in
an agreement, that is, its consent to exchange the Golan Heights for peace. This
issue has been bitterly debated in Israel since 1967. Interestingly, it was the
Labor party who insisted that this territory remain in Israeli hands, and it encouraged settlements in the Golan Heights as early as 1968. The fact that most
Israelis believe that control of the Golan Heights is vital to Israel's security
creates a major difficulty in establishing a negotiation framework between Israel
and Syria.

However, the Golan Heights might prove to be as questionable a strategic
asset as the Suez Canal proved to be in 1973. Defense of this territory could be
extremely costly and unnecessary in the era of medium and short-range missiles
available to Israel. Hence, unlike the Jordanian theater, progress toward a bilateral Syrian-Israeli agreement is possible. If Assad would take the risk and fly
to Jerusalem, and if Israel would take the risk and return the Golan Heights,
peace between these two long-time enemies could be attained.

It seems that the United States does not thoroughly explore the possibility of
a Syrian-Israeli agreement. Indeed, the United States has traditionally believed
that an Israeli-Jordanian agreement is a prerequisite for any progress toward
peace. This, however, might not be the case, given the complexity of the Palestinian question involved in any Israeli-Jordanian agreement. In 1988 Shultz
ignored once more the fact that Jordan's ability to maneuver is much more
limited than that of Syria. Hussein's decisions are constrained by the strong
geopolitical and personal ties between the East and the West banks. Unlike
Assad, he cannot circumvent the Palestinian question. Assad could follow the
Sadat Model, but Hussein can't. This basic fact seems to elude American foreign
policymakers, who for the past twenty years have focused peace efforts on Jordan.
Syria, on the other hand, although included and approached by Washington,
was never considered a reliable party. Indeed, Washington has been a captive
of the misperception that because of the Syrian-Soviet connection, Syria is not
seriously interested in a settlement. The Syrian-terrorist connection reinforced
this misperception. These facts, albeit true, could be irrelevant to Syria's willingness to reach an agreement with Israel. Moreover, the new leadership in
Moscow and its surprising openness to Israel should lead Washington to a reori-
entation of its Middle East policy. Should Washington apply a new approach to
the peace process, most of the frustrations and embarrassments could be avoided.
Indeed, Hussein's demand for an international peace conference proves that his
hands are tied. Unlike Sadat and Assad, the two Arab leaders ever to sign
agreements with Israel, Hussein is a captive of the Palestinian problem. The

Shultz initiative, like all the previous American peace initiatives, repeated the mistake of focusing the process on the most unlikely party, Jordan. It seems that Washington does not ask the right questions, and therefore, does not reach the right answers. Based on past experience and looking at the present situation, it seems more promising to move in the direction of a bilateral Syrian-Israeli agreement.

The idea of an international peace conference is the heart of the Shultz initiative and it seems to serve mainly Hussein's interests. Israel maintains its traditional demand for direct negotiations, whereas the Shultz plan tries to provide both: an international umbrella to answer Hussein's needs and direct negotiations to be carried out simultaneously, between a Jordanian-Palestinian delegation, to satisfy Israel demands. It seems, however, that the procedural question created a substantive question, both interwoven and difficult to solve. The participation of the five permanent members of the Security Council has been rejected by Israel, as well as the proposed agenda that established a new formula for "peace for territories." Shamir's three-day visit to Washington in the middle of March did not change these facts. Israeli Prime Minister Yitzhak Shamir left Washington on March 17 unyielding and raising objections to almost every item of the Shultz peace proposal. Washington tried its traditional tactic of inducement, promising Israel that military aid would not be linked to the peace process. Indeed, President Reagan promised Shamir, *before his arrival*, to speed up deliveries to Israel of seventy-five F–16 jet-fighters. Reagan also agreed to grant Israel a new memorandum of understanding that would institutionalize the close strategic cooperation that has developed between the two countries in the past five years. Hence, the Shultz plan followed the footsteps of its many unsuccessful predecessors, albeit under much more grave circumstances. The uprising in the West Bank challenged the traditional concepts of what is required and what is possible in order to settle the Israeli-Arab conflict. The 1988 American initiative did not have these features.

NOTES

1. The aborted coup was announced on WEVD radio (Hebrew), May 13, 1987.
2. On January 31 King Hussein met with the pope and members of the Italian government; *New York Times*, February 2, 1988.
3. Ibid., February 17, 1988.
4. After its evacuation from Lebanon, the PLO needed alternative bases at Israel's border. Bases in Jordan included military headquarters. In exchange Arafat signed the February 11, 1985 agreement, which was ratified by the PLO executive committee, February 18, and became public on February 23.
5. The U.S.S.R. and the PLO have maintained close relationships for over two decades. Farouk Khadumi acknowledged in an interview for *The Third World* (April 1986) that the U.S.S.R. supported the PLO both militarily and politically. The PLO reciprocated by supporting anti-Western guerrilla activities in Latin America. The PLO

has offices in Cuba, Nicaragua, Mexico, Peru, Brazil, and Bolivia. It opened a prestigious office in Moscow in 1976, and its leaders visit the U.S.S.R. often. For example, during 1985–86, PLO leaders held over 100 meetings with East European leaders in their capitals. Information from *Focus on the Middle East* (Hebrew), Israel Department of Information, Jerusalem (August 1986).

6. *Foreign Broadcast Information Services*, February 20, 1985.

7. *New York Times*, April 26, 1987.

8. *Washington Post*, June 26, 1986.

9. On May 4, 1987, Syria and Iran had renewed their agreement, which provided Syria with one million tons of free oil. The agreement, signed in Teheran, promised Syria an additional two million tons of light Iranian crude at about $2 per barrel lower than the market price. Syria's debt to Iran was estimated in 1988 to be between $1 to $2 billion in unpaid oil bills dating back to 1984. The situation changed in March 1988 with the discovery of large quantities of oil in Syria. Experts estimate that Syria might be able to provide all its own oil needs and export as much as 125,000 barrels a day for oil and refined crude products, reaping revenues up to $455 million in 1988; *New York Times*, May 5, 1987; March 16, 1988.

10. *New York Times*, May 24, 1987.

11. *New York Times*, May 5, 1987.

12. Secretary Shultz's statement before the Senate Foreign Relations Committee, January 27, 1987.

13. The message from Shultz to Foreign Minister Peres, which was welcomed by the Labor party, created severe tensions in the already divided Israeli Cabinet. *Israeli Broadcasting Service*, May 12, 1987.

14. *New York Times*, May 24, 1987.

15. Former secretary of the navy, John Lehman estimated the cost of the Gulf commitment, including forces, training, operations, bases, and support to be as high as $40 billion per year. ABC-TV "Nightline," May 19, 1987.

16. Information from various Israel Defense Forces publications and interviews, 1986–88.

17. *New York Times*, February 29, 1988.

18. Harold Saunders, *The Other Walls* (Washington, DC: American Enterprise Institute, 1985), p. 77.

19. See discussion in Saunders, chapter 5, pp. 70–83.

20. James L. Ray, *The Future of American-Israeli Relations* (Lexington: University Press of Kentucky, 1985), pp. 73–75.

21. The PLO leadership would not tolerate moderate Arab leaders. The assassinations of Sartawi and El Masri, among others, prove this point. For more details, see Susan Hattis Rolef (ed.), *Violence as Reality* (Jerusalem: Carta Press, 1983).

22. Yigal Allon, former Israeli leader, suggested that Israel withdraw from all of the West Bank except for a security zone, namely, the hills along the Jordan River.

23. It was the Syrian Defense Companies that crushed the Moslem Brotherhood uprising in Hamma in February 1982. An estimated 10,000 were killed and the city was erased. In January 1982 they reportedly executed 100 air force officers who tried to stage a coup; *Time* magazine, December 19, 1983; also "The Syrian Ruling Clique," IDF publication, Tel Aviv (January 1984).

24. Saunders, *The Other Walls*, p. 84.

25. *US News and World Report*, March 14, 1988.

26. Information from the Syrian consulate, New York; also *US News and World Report*, March 14, 1988.

27. *Washington Post*, March 15, 1987; also WEVD radio (Hebrew), March 11, 1987.

28. *Yediot Ahronot* (Hebrew), March 27, 1987.

29. Syria was accused of being behind the attempt to blow up an EL Al plane in London in October 1986. It was also linked to terrorist attacks in Rome and Paris. General Mohammed el-Khuli, head of Syria's air force intelligence, was said to be the key figure; *New York Times*, October 29 and November 19, 1986.

30. Following the severe economic repercussions, Syria tried to decouple itself from international terrorism.

31. *New York Times*, March 15, 1988.

7

Epilogue

In 1988 peace between Israel and its Arab neighbors seemed as elusive as four decades earlier. Since the Six-Day War, all U.S. peace plans have been based on the principle of "territories for peace" first established by the U.N. Security Council in its Resolution 242. Although it requires that Israel withdraw from most of the territories, it was accepted by Israel and by most of the Arab states. The resolution was rejected, however, by the PLO and the many other Palestinian guerrilla organizations, because it did not mention a Palestinian state. Not only has the principle of "land for peace" not been universally accepted, other problems, no less important, have been preventing a settlement.

The peace efforts in the 1980s, namely, the Shultz peace initiative, have encountered the same problems that "killed" the previous American peace initiatives. First, it does not answer the question of who should participate in the negotiations and in what capacity. This is more than a procedural question; it involves Israeli recognition of the PLO, and PLO recognition of Israel. Moreover, it opens the debate of who are the claimants for the territories: Israel, Jordan, the PLO, or the local Palestinians?

Second, the Jordanian demand for an international peace conference created major problems. Israel demands direct talks and rightfully argues that the U.S.S.R. and China, who refuse to have any diplomatic relations with Israel, are biased and openly hostile. It also questions the integrity of the Arab countries, who have been refusing to talk with Israel for over forty years. Indeed, it is difficult to determine how serious the Arab states themselves were taking the idea of an international conference; with so many participants and so many conflicting interests, it could hardly promise any results.

Third, the Shultz timetable seemed completely unrealistic. The proposal suggested that the international peace conference open in April 1988, and a Palestinian autonomy would follow six months later. The final status of the territories would be concluded in talks between Israel and a joint Jordanian-Palestinian delegation no later than December 1991. In fact, Hussein himself was probably not interested in accelerated Palestinian self-rule. It could result in a radical Palestinian state, hostile to his own, and with aspirations to take over the East Bank, which was part of Palestine under the Ottoman rule. Indeed, the king's relationships with Arafat have been volatile and unstable. He harshly criticized Arafat on many occasions during 1985–88, but on the other hand he invited him to Amman to discuss the Shultz plan and told him that he will not move without PLO approval.

Fourth, the Palestinians exhibited ambivalent feelings toward the PLO and would probably prefer to represent themselves in any peace negotiations. The PLO, therefore, is faced with a dilemma. As an organization dedicated to the cause of a Palestinian state, the realization of their dream might bring an end to their existence. The uprising in the West Bank, instigated by radical groups not necessarily affiliated with the PLO, gave rise to local leadership that advocates an independent policy. Although they use the PLO symbols and banners, the new leadership is very militant and claims not to subscribe to Resolution 242, which promises Israel the right to exist within secure borders, and which Arafat claims to have accepted.

Under these circumstances, the Shultz initiative could hardly be considered promising. It has not addressed the question of Hussein's legitimacy as a Palestinian leader; it has not attracted the support of the local Palestinian leadership who refused to meet with him. It antagonized Israel by insisting on an international peace conference, and it antagonized Arafat by suggesting that the PLO be represented in a Jordanian-Palestinian delegation. Indeed, it seems that the Shultz peace initiative, like its predecessors, has been accepted only by Washington.

It is, however, clear that the status quo could not continue for long. Understanding this, Israel, although deeply divided between hawks and doves, has reluctantly agreed to negotiate a Palestinian autonomy on the basis of the Camp David Accords. The Palestinians—West Bank residents and groups belonging to the PLO umbrella—have rejected this principle. Consequently, the parties involved can't agree on the framework, context, or substance of the talks. It is clear that the negotiations could not begin until Israel, Jordan, the Palestinians, and the PLO come to an agreement on the basic principles, procedures, and objectives of the talks.

Syria has not been a major factor in the Shultz plan. Although the Secretary has visited Damascus several times and held talks with Assad, the focus of the initiative has been King Hussein. This might be a major misperception. The Lebanese crisis showed that Syria could not be ignored or underestimated. Although not directly involved in West Bank politics, it has a de facto veto over any proposal. Syria's power position is growing and the recent discovery of oil in large quantities could eliminate its economic problems. Syria has doubled its population in less than a generation—from six million in the 1960s to over eleven million in the 1980s—and could become the major power in the region. Washington seems to ignore these crucial facts.

The current situation in the West Bank and Gaza, however, is unacceptable to all. Israel will not be able to continue its occupation indefinitely, the Palestinians will have to accept Israel's right to exist within secure borders, and the PLO will eventually have to accept the leadership of the local Palestinians. Syria and Israel will have to work out an agreement that will promise peace for Israel and territories for Syria.

Since these conditions have been only partially addressed in the Shultz peace plan, it is not likely to work. Another major issue lacking from the Shultz initiative is American leverage to pressure Israel to be more flexible, which has been raised in Congress (for example, the letter of the thirty Senators of March 3), as well as by the general public, Jewish groups, and supporters of the Palestinians. They have argued that the United States should suspend its military and economic aid, amounting to $3 billion annually, until Israel becomes more receptive to the U.S. peace initiatives. Others have argued, however, that the lack of progress should be blamed on Arab intransigence and the Palestinians desire to destroy Israel. Indeed, in the uprising in the West Bank and Gaza that began in December 1987, the Palestinians did not raise the banner of peace. Instead, they exhibited a strong desire to see Israel destroyed.

It is clear that the status quo has been shattered forever. Both sides have decided to use force to assert their claim to the disputed land. The key question, when and how will the Palestinians and the Israelis stop fighting and start talking, could be answered only after both sides honestly define their objectives and show a willingness to compromise. As long as each side denounces the other's rights, peace will remain unattainable.

U.S. efforts to break the impasse depend on its leverage to influence both sides to be more forbearing of the other's grievances. Israel's security anxieties are rooted in forty years of Arab hostility, whereas the Palestinians fear that their legitimate rights would continue to be ignored. It is, however, questionable whether the United States would try to use its leverage to promote the peace process. In early 1988 Reagan announced that no suspension of aid would be used. The assumption was that achieving peace was a strong enough incentive for Israel. In fact, Reagan submitted to Congress a foreign assistance request for fiscal year 1989, totaling $18 billion. It included an aid package for Israel—military and economic—of about $3 billion. This makes Israel the number one recipient of American aid. Since no strings have been attached to the package, the United States will not be able to use it as leverage. On the other hand, the United States has no leverage with the Arab states either. For example, Washington could not influence Saudi Arabia to cancel its arms deal of March 1988 to buy ballistic missiles from China. Hence, to assume that the suspension of aid would advance the peace process is unrealistic.

The foregoing illustrates a major lesson in international relations, specifically in patron-client relationships. Whether military and economic aid provided by a patron state to its client state will also provide significant leverage in influencing the foreign policy of the client state is highly questionable. Global and regional circumstances usually constrain the patron state leverage power. The Soviet Union as well as the United States have had to learn this lesson through their respective experiences.

Nevertheless, influence can be exercised through the development of sound, creative ideas, attractive to the involved parties, and promoted through skillful and sensitive diplomacy. Unfortunately, the Shultz initiative, though advocated with great skills, lacked the fundamental soundness and ingredients that would have made it acceptable to the parties concerned. So the settlement of the Israeli-Arab conflict remains as elusive in the 1980s as it was in the seventies and the sixties. Israel's vital need for American military and economic aid has not been, and is not likely to become, an important factor in the continued U.S. search for peace.

Selected Bibliography

UNITED STATES GOVERNMENT PUBLICATIONS

U.S. Agency for International Development. *U.S. Overseas Loans and Grants and Assistance from International Organizations Obligations and Loan Authorizations*, annual editions.

U.S. Arms Control and Disarmament Agency. *World Military Expenditures and Arms Transfers*, annual editions.

U.S. Defense Security Assistance Agency. *Foreign Military Sales and Military Assistance Facts*, annual editions.

U.S. Department of Defense, Secretary of Defense. *Statement on the Defense Budget and Defense Programs* (variously subtitled), annual editions.

U.S. Department of State Bulletin, 1968–88.

U.S. General Accounting Office. Various reports by the Comptroller General on U.S. Assistance to Israel.

U.S. President. *Public Papers of the Presidents of the U.S.* Washington, DC: Office of the Federal Register, National Archives and Records Services.

CONGRESSIONAL DOCUMENTS

Congressional Quarterly; Congressional Reports; Committees and Subcommittees Reports; Hearings: 96th to 99th Cong.; The Search for Peace in the Middle East: Documents and Statements, 1967–79. Committee print, 1980.

ISRAEL GOVERNMENT PUBLICATIONS

Israeli Consulate, New York City, briefing papers.

Israeli Defense Forces Spokesman, Tel Aviv, background information and briefing papers.

Israeli Embassy, Washington, DC, briefing papers.

Ministry of Defense Publications; Prime Minister's Office; Intelligence Bureau. Daily
    media reports, 1968–88.

ANTHOLOGIES AND YEARBOOKS

The Arms Trade Registers, various editions.
Institute for Palestinian Studies and Kuwait University. A quarterly on Palestinian affairs,
    selected issues.
International Institute for Strategic Studies (London). *The Military Balance*, annual edi-
    tions.
Jaffee Center for Strategic Studies, Tel Aviv University. *The Military Balance*, annual
    editions.
Record of the Arab World, monthly, quarterly, and yearly editions. Beirut: Research and
    Publishing House.
Stockholm International Peace Research Institute, Stockholm. *World Armament and Dis-
    armament Yearbook*, annual editions.

BOOKS AND ARTICLES

Ajami, Ajami Fuad. *The Arab Predicament*. Cambridge: Cambridge University Press,
    1981.
Allon, Yigal. "Israel: The Case for Defensible Borders." *Foreign Affairs* (October 1976),
    pp. 38–53.
Aronson, Shlomo. *Conflicts and Bargaining in the Middle East*. Baltimore: Johns Hopkins
    University Press, 1978.
Avi-Ran, Reuven. *Syrian Involvement in Lebanon (1975–1985)* (Hebrew). Tel Aviv:
    Ministry of Defense Publications, 1986.
Baldwin, David A. "Inter-Nation Influence Revisited." *Journal of Conflict Resolution*,
    No. 15 (1971), pp. 471–485.
Ball, George W. "How to Save Israel in Spite of Herself." *Foreign Affairs* (April 1977),
    pp. 453–471.
Benvenisti, Meron. *The West Bank Data Project: A Survey of Israel's Policies*. Wash-
    ington, DC: American Enterprise Institute, 1984.
Brecher, Michael. *Decisions in Crisis: Israel, 1967 and 1973*. Los Angeles: University
    of California Press, 1980.
———. *The Foreign Policy System of Israel: Setting, Images, Process*. New York:
    Oxford University Press, 1972.
Brookings Report. *Toward Peace in the Middle East*. Report of a Study Group. Wash-
    ington, DC: Brookings Institute, 1975.
Brzezinski, Zbigniew. *Power and Principle*. New York: Farrar, Straus, and Giroux,
    1983.
Carter, Jimmy. *Keeping Faith*. Toronto: Bantam Books, 1982.
Dayan, Moshe. *Breakthrough—A Personal Account of the Egypt-Israel Peace Negotia-
    tions*. London: Weidenfeld and Nicolson, 1981.
———. *Moshe Dayan: Avnei Derech* (My Life). Tel Aviv: Yediot Ahronot, 1982.
Eban, Abba. *Abba Eban: An Autobiography*. New York: Random House, 1977.
Elazar, Daniel J. *Judea, Samaria and Gaza: Views on the Present and Future*. Wash-
    ington, DC: American Enterprise Institute, 1982.

Eveland, Wilbour C. *Ropes of Sand: America's Failure in the Middle East*. New York: W. W. Norton, 1980.

Fabian, Larry L. "The Middle East: War Dangers and Receding Peace Prospects." *Foreign Affairs* (January 1984).

Feuerwerger, Marvin C. *Congress and Israel*. Westport, CT: Greenwood Press, 1979.

Finger, Seymour M. (ed.). *The New World Balance and Peace in the Middle East: Reality or Mirage?* Teaneck, NJ: Fairleigh Dickinson University Press, 1975.

Ford, Gerald. *A Time to Heal*. New York: Harper & Row, 1979.

Golan, Galia. *The Soviet Union and the Palestinian Liberation Organization*. New York: Praeger, 1980.

———. *Yom Kippur and After: The Soviet Union and the Middle East Crisis*. London: Cambridge University Press, 1977.

Golan, Matti. *The Secret Conversation of Henry Kissinger*. New York: Quadrangle Books, 1976.

Gross, Peter. *Israel in the Mind of America*. New York: Knopf, 1983.

Gross Stein, Janice. "Leadership in Peacemaking: Fate, Will, and Fortuna in the Middle East." *International Journal* Toronto (Autumn 1982).

Grossman, David. *The Yellow Wind*. New York: Farrar, Straus, and Giroux, 1988.

Haber, Eitan, Zeev Schiff, and Ehud Yaari. *The Year of the Dove* (Hebrew). Jerusalem: Zmors, Bitan, Modan Press, 1979.

Haig, Alexander. *Caveat*. New York: Macmillan, 1984.

Harkavi, Yehoshafat. *Palestinians and Israel*. Jerusalem: Keter Press, 1974.

Heikal, Mohamed H. *The Cairo Documents: The Inside Story of Nasser and His Relations with World Leaders, Rebels and Statesmen*. New York: Doubleday, 1973.

Herzog, Haim. *The Arab-Israeli Wars*. New York: Random House, 1982.

Hishmeh, George. "The Military Balance of Power in the Middle East: An American View." *Journal of Palestinian Studies* (Spring 1972).

Insight Team of the *Sunday Times*. *The Yom Kippur War*. London: Andre Deutsch, 1974.

Jabber, Paul. *Not by War Alone: Security and Arms Control in the Middle East*. Berkeley: University of California Press, 1981.

Kalb, Marvin, and Bernard Kalb. *Kissinger*. Boston: Little, Brown, 1974.

Kaplan, Stephen, and Barry M. Blechman (eds.). *Force Without War: U.S. Forces as a Political Instrument*. Washington, DC: Brookings Institute, 1978.

Khalidi, Ahmed. "The War of Attrition." *Journal of Palestinian Studies* (Autumn 1973).

Kissinger, Henry. *White House Years*. New York: Harper & Row, 1978.

———. *Years of Upheaval*. Boston: Little, Brown, 1982.

Klare, Michael T. *American Arms Supermarket*. Austin: University of Texas Press, 1984.

Labrie, Roger, John Hutchins, and Edwin W. A. Peura. *U.S. Arms Sales Policy*. Washington, DC: American Enterprise Institute, 1982.

Luttwak, Edward, and Dan Horowitz. *The Israeli Army*. New York: Harper & Row, 1975.

MacBride, Sean. *Israel in Lebanon*. London: Ithaca Press, 1983.

McPeak, Merril A. "Israel: Borders and Security." *Foreign Affairs* (April 1976).

Marantz, Paul, and Janice Gross Stein (eds.). *Peace Making in the Middle East*. Totowa, NJ: Barnes & Noble Press, 1985.

Margalit, Dan. *Sheder Me'Habait Halavan*. Tel Aviv: Otpaz, 1971.

Meir, Golda. *My Life*. New York: Putnam, 1975.

Naor, Arye. *Cabinet at War* (Hebrew). Tel Aviv: Lahav Press, 1986.

Nir, Amiram. *The Soviet-Syrian Friendship and Cooperation Treaty: Unfulfilled Expectations*. Tel Aviv: JCSS, 1983.

Nixon, Richard. *The Memoirs of Richard Nixon*. New York: Grosset and Dunlap, 1978.

Novik, Nimrod. *The United States and Israel*. Boulder, CO: Westview Press, 1980.

O'Leary, Michael. *The Politics of American Foreign Aid*. New York: Atherton Press, 1982.

Peretz, Martin. "Occupational Hazards." *The New Republic*, March 10, 1988.

Perlmutter, Amos. "Reagan's Middle East Policy: A Year One Assessment." *Orbis* (Spring 1984).

Pierre, Andrew J. "Arms Sales the New Displomacy." *Foreign Affairs* (Winter 1982).

———. "Beyond the 'Plane Package': Arms and Politics in the Middle East." *International Security* (Summer 1978).

———. *The Global Politics of Arms Sales*. Princeton, NJ: Princeton University Press, 1982.

Pollock, David. *The Politics of Pressure*. Westport, CT: Greenwood Press, 1982.

Quandt, William. *Camp David*. Washington, DC: Brookings Institute, 1986.

———. *Decade of Decisions*. Berkeley: University of California Press, 1977.

Ra'anan, Uri, Robert Pflatzgraff, Jr., and Jeoffrey Kemp (eds.). *Arms Transfers to the Third World*. Boulder, CO: Westview Press, 1978.

Rabin, Yitzhak. *The Rabin Memoirs*. Boston: Little, Brown, 1979.

Ramazani, R. K. *Beyond the Arab-Israeli Settlement: New Directions for U.S. Policy in the Middle East*. Cambridge: Institute for Foreign Policy Analysis, 1977.

Raphael, Gideon. *Destination Peace: Three Decades of Israeli Foreign Policy*. New York: Stein and Day, 1981.

Ray, James Lee. *The Future of American-Israeli Relations*. Lexington: University Press of Kentucky, 1985.

Rosen, Steven, and Mara Moustafin. "Does Washington Have the Means to Impose a Settlement on Israel?" *Commentary* (October 1977).

Sadat, Anwar. *In Search for Identity*. New York: Harper & Row, 1977.

Safran, Nadav. "American-Israeli Relations: An Overview." *Middle East Review* (Winter 1977–78).

———. *Israel, the Embattled Ally*. Cambridge, MA: Harvard University Press, 1978.

Said, Edward. *The Question of Palestine*. New York: Times Books, 1980.

Saunders, Harold H. *The Other Walls*. Washington, DC: American Enterprise Institute, 1985.

Schiff, Zeev, and Ehud Yaari. *Milhemet Sholal* (Hebrew). Tel Aviv: Schoken Books, 1984.

Shazly, Saad. *The Arab Military Option*. San Francisco: American Middle East Research, 1986.

Sheehan, Edward. *The Arabs, the Israelis, and Kissinger*. Pleasantville, NY: Readers Digest Press, 1976.

Sorely, Lewis. *Arms Transfers under Nixon*. Lexington: University Press of Kentucky, 1983.

Spiegel, Steven. *The Other Arab-Israeli Conflict*. Chicago: University of Chicago Press, 1985.

Steinberg, Belma S., and Paul Marantz (eds.). *Superpowers Involvement in the Middle East*. Boulder, CO: Westview Press, 1985.

Tillman, Seth. *The United States in the Middle East: Interests and Obstacles*. Bloomington: Indiana University Press, 1982.

Touval, Saadia. *The Peace Brokers*. Princeton, NJ: Princeton University Press, 1981.

Weizman, Ezer. *The Battle for Peace*. New York: Bantam Books, 1981.

Wells, Samuel F., and Mark Bruzonsky (eds.). *Security in the Middle East*. Boulder, CO: Westview Press, 1986.

Wheelock, Thomas. "Arms for Israel: The Limits of Leverage." *International Security* (Fall 1978).

Whynes, David K. *The Economics of Third World Military Expenditures*. Austin: University of Texas Press, 1979.

Williams, Louis (ed.). *Military Aspects of the Arab-Israeli Conflict*. Tel Aviv: University Publishing Projects, 1975.

Index

196

estinian cause, 108; trans-Siberian pipeline, 138. *See also* Camp David Accords; Disengagement agreements; Reagan, Ronald; Sinai

Vance, Cyrus: Camp David, 110–11, 116–17; peace negotiations, 98, 100, 103, 106; peace planning group, 109; Policy Review Committee, 95

Valdivostok, 80

Waldheim, Kurt, 66

Warnke, Paul, 25

War of Attrition, 32, 34–35, 41, 43, 48

Watergate, 56, 71, 75, 77

Weinberger, Casper, 144, 148

Weizman, Ezer, 100, 109–10, 114–17, 119

West Bank, and Gaza, 5, 39, 68, 77, 88, 94, 96–97, 99, 101, 107, 117; economic aid, 170; Israel's position, 110–11, 113–14, 117; Israeli settlements, 128, 140, 149, 153, 155, 167; Sadat's position, 117–18; uprising ("intifada"), 161–62, 169, 170, 172, 182–83

Yariv, Aharon, 63

Yom Kippur War, 57–58, 63; and cease fire, 67

Yost, Charles, 29, 39, 118

Zahla, city of, 129–30

About the Author

NITZA NACHMIAS is on the faculty of the City College of New York. Her articles on international relations have appeared in U.S. and Israeli journals.